Freedom and the End of Reason

FREEDOM
AND THE
END OF REASON

On the Moral Foundation of Kant's Critical Philosophy

Richard L. Velkley

The University of Chicago Press

Chicago & London

The University of Chicago Press, Chicago 60637
The University of Chicago Press, Ltd., London

LIBRARY OF CONGRESS CATALOGING IN PUBLICATION DATA

Velkley, Richard L.
    Freedom and the end of reason : on the moral foundation of Kant's
critical philosophy / Richard L. Velkley.
        p.   cm.
    Includes index.
    ISBN 0-226-85260-1
    1. Kant, Immanuel, 1724–1804.   2. Reason—History—18th century.
3. Teleology—History—18th century.   4. Ethics, Modern—18th
century.   5. Liberty—History—18th century.   6. Rousseau, Jean
Jacques, 1712–1778—Influence.   I. Title.
B2798.V37   1989
193—dc19   88-8029
                                                                              CIP

RICHARD L. VELKLEY is assistant professor of
philosophy at Stonehill College, Massachusetts.

To my mother and the memory of my father

This new doctrine [of Kantian idealism]
is not an object for curiosity, nor a passing
fashion, nor is it a system in the ordinary sense,
like so many which are useless and devoid of meaning.
Rather it is the genius of "living in harmony with
virtue," subordinated to a rule of
the greatest certainty and rigor, embracing and
organizing the totality of human intellectual
and moral faculties.

FRIEDRICH SCHLEGEL

The philosopher is not a misologist, but
rather a lawgiver of human reason, and
the preeminent laws are those limiting
the pretensions of reason for the
sake of humanity's end.

IMMANUEL KANT

Contents

Preface

Interpretations of Kant's project of a "criticism of reason" tend to focus on one question: What is the primary intent of Kant's account of the conditions and limits of the human cognitive powers? Generations of thinking about Kant have resolved this question into the consideration of four major historical alternatives. Is Kant's "critique" an "all-destroying" consummation of the skeptical and scientific Enlightenment's discrediting of speculative metaphysics? Or is it a vindication of the natural human interest in metaphysics, and therewith of the metaphysical tradition from Plato to Leibniz? Is it a rejection of "scientific realism" identifying "things in themselves" with the object of modern scientific knowledge, whereby Kant initiates the "metaphysics of freedom" seeking to limit or transform science for the sake of a new moral idealism? Or is Kant's "criticism" directed at Hume's skepticism, laying the foundations of a "transcendental" defense of the "objectivity" of science and ordinary experience?

While the answer must be that the Kantian critique is somehow all of these, it is not primarily any one of them. Rather, it is possible to uncover a level of this "criticism of reason" that embraces these alternatives while pointing beyond them to another dimension. That dimension of the problem of reason is a teleological one; it consists of Kant's wrestling with the question of the telos of reason itself. Teleology here does not chiefly refer to the reflection on the final causal ordering of the natural whole. The stress in Kant's questioning is on the perplexities of human purposiveness and self-determination. Central among these perplexities is the question of the place of philosophic reason in human life—the relation of such reason to the human good, social and individual. Kant's foremost instructor and inspirer in this reflection is Jean-Jacques Rousseau. By making evident to Kant reason's tendency to "dialectic" and to "crisis," and thus by exposing the necessity for a new consideration of the end of reason, Rousseau provides a fundamental (and generally neglected) level of reason's self-criticism.

This essay is a historical inquiry that seeks to lay bare that hidden level of the Kantian critique. It takes the form of a study of the origins of Kant's mature philosophy, from the perspective of the "precritical" writings of the 1760s. It investigates the sources of Kant's conception and redefinition of reason and preeminently examines Rousseau's presence in that redefinition. There has hitherto been no analysis of Kant's writings from the standpoint of the Rousseauian elements in the "critical" account of reason. My hope is that such an inquiry will contribute to an understanding of Kant's fundamental philosophical motives, of modern approaches to reason, and of the recurrent "crises" in modern reason.

The major concerns of this essay revolve around three theses: first, that the "transcendental turn" which forms what is most distinctive in the Kantian account of reason is conditioned by a prior "Rousseauian turn" in Kant's thought; second, that the latter turn introduces an essential shift in Kant's determination of the end of reason based on new understandings of freedom and of reason as a whole; and third, that the Kantian "revolution" in the end of reason is a response to a crisis in reason emerging in the eighteenth century on the basis of the modern foundations established a century earlier, relating centrally to the "Enlightenment" view of human reason and the human good.

Alexis de Tocqueville, the last century's leading critic of the extreme "rationalism" of the theorists and political leaders of the French Revolution, offers us a starting point for the reflection on the crisis of reason in Kant's time. The various political programs that led to the revolution had one point in common—the belief that "the complex of traditional customs governing the social order of the day" should be replaced "by simple, elementary rules deriving from the exercise of human reason and natural law."[1] This idea, which "had haunted men's imaginations off and on for three millennia," only at this time succeeded in making itself accepted as a basic principle. Tocqueville notes the new status of "theory" within practical life: philosophy had become the dominating force in the world, at least in human self-understanding. Whereas the remaking of political life in the image of philosophic reason was in the past a purely theoretical possibility entertained by certain thinkers, now general and abstract theories of the nature of society were the daily topic of passionate conversation for all classes.

This was not altered by subsequent developments. Much of the nineteenth century politically and philosophically was an effort to rectify the errors of the revolution and its theorists, without abandoning modern progressive ideals. Nonetheless the past two centuries of European history, and of world history as affected by it, could be described in these words of Edmund Husserl: "The genuine spiritual struggles of European humanity as such take the form of struggles between the philosophies." What is at issue in these struggles is "the faith in man's freedom, that is, his capacity to secure rational meaning for his individual and common human existence."[2]

The central struggles of political life became struggles between philosophies at the close of the eighteenth century, largely because philosophy took upon itself a new task—of providing "meaning" and "faith in freedom," a faith of a new sort, for all human beings. Whereas the first seeds of this new task were sown at the beginnings of modern philosophy, it did not burst forth fully ripe until a crisis in reason in the mid-eighteenth century led to a rethinking of what reason is. The reckless reformism of the Jacobins was not where the rethinking took place. For the philosophers of the age, there was "a growing feeling of failure" concerning the soundness of the foundations of modern reason, as Husserl notes. The outcome of their rethinking was an unqualified affirmation of the leadership of philosophy in human affairs, which took the shape of a new "idealism." Kant's philosophy is the first, and perhaps the greatest, expression of this new approach, insofar as his rethinking incorporates the whole of metaphysics and a "critique of reason." Yet the father of Kant's revolution is Rousseau. These two theorists of freedom sought to reconcile the fundamental modern effort to emancipate the human species from "dogmatism," with fulfillment of the human needs for the sacred, the noble, and the beautiful. They thought that lacking such a reconciliation, modern rationalism must collapse in chaos. Of the two, Kant is the thinker who grounds the reconciliation in a systematic account of reason and its telos. But Rousseau provides Kant with certain decisive elements of his account of reason, especially through a new concept of freedom.

The Kantian corpus, including the *Nachlass*, reveals five areas of problems in reason leading to the new determination of this power. (1) Reason is responsible for justifying what one could call "the moral view of the universe"; Kant has this notion as early as 1754. (2) The modern effort to emancipate and enlighten humanity needs sanctioning from ideas of the sacred, the noble, and the beautiful, and philosophic reason must provide these ideas; Kant holds such views by 1762, before the decisive influence of Rousseau. (3) Modern reason is not only incomplete, but it also reveals a self-undermining tendency, resulting in skepticism about the goodness and competence of reason; the set of insights and arguments revolving around this point gets its first formulation at the time of Kant's greatest engagement with Rousseau's writings, in 1764–65. (4) More generally, reason reveals a "dialectical" character in all its uses, and the dialectic's resolution, in an account of a unifying telos of reason, is urgent for the salvaging of modern emancipation and its chief instrument, modern scientific philosophy; modern moral idealism in its "critical" version emerges out of such reflections, after 1765. (5) Also, reason must be able to satisfy its inherent urges toward the unconditioned wholes, or ideas of totality, that are the objects of its metaphysical interest; this interest acquires a new legitimacy and urgency for Kant after 1765, as it becomes evident to him that the moral needs of reason are linked to the fate of metaphysics, while the latter partakes of a destructive dialectic.

By means of one "system," reason must justify ordinary moral consciousness, satisfy the metaphysical interest, and rescue modern emancipatory science from self-consigned oblivion. The origins of this system are traced below, back to the involved constellation of questions and problems that formed Kant's philosophical consciousness well before 1781. But as we trace this account of the end of reason back to an earlier Kant, we also point forward to the characteristic "idealism" of the later modern age. For we are uncovering the sources of the problematic claim, made by that idealism, of philosophy's comprehensive responsibility for human welfare.

Acknowledgments

The research and writing for this book have been generously supported by grants from the National Endowment for the Humanities, the American Council of Learned Societies, the Earhart, Bradley, and Olin foundations, the University of Toronto, and Stonehill College. The final stages of composition were made vastly easier and more enjoyable by the research fellowship I held in 1986–87 in the political science department and St. Michael's College, the University of Toronto. I had many fine discussions there on Kant and other topics with members of the political science and philosophy departments. For the encouragement, insight, and advice they have extended to me in the past several years, I am much indebted to Richard Kennington, Dieter Henrich, Joseph Cropsey, Hans-Georg Gadamer, José Benardete, Kenneth Schmitz, Nathan Tarcov, Michael Davis, Thomas Pangle, Clifford Orwin, and Martin Sitte. The Stonehill administration and staff have on numerous occasions provided invaluable assistance. I thank the many friends with whom I have broached the themes of this book, and especially my wife, Dolores Iorizzo Velkley. Finally, I pay special tribute to the humanity, scholarship, and brilliance of my late friend, James C. Leake, who had a very important role in the formation of this work.

Abbreviations

L   *Logik: Ein Handbuch zu Vorlesungen.* Ed. G. B. Jäsche.

Lo   *Immanuel Kant's Logic.* Trans. with intro. R. S. Hartman and W. Schwartz. Indianapolis and New York: Bobbs-Merrill, 1974.

MA   *Mutmasslicher Anfang der Menschengeschichte.*

MS   *Die Metaphysik der Sitten.*

N   *Nachricht von der Einrichtung seiner Vorlesungen in dem Winterhalbenjahre von 1765–66.*

OH   *On History: Immanuel Kant.* Ed. L. W. Beck and trans. R. E. Anchor, L. W. Beck, and E. L. Fackenheim. Indianapolis and New York: Bobbs-Merrill, 1963.

P   *Prolegomena zu einer jeden künftigen Metaphysik, die als Wissenschaft wird auftreten konnen.*

Pr   *Prolegomena to Any Future Metaphysics.* Trans. L. W. Beck. Indianapolis and New York: Bobbs-Merrill, 1950.

R   *Reflexionen.*

Re   *Die Religion innerhalb der Grenzen der blossen Vernunft.*

Rw   *Religion within the Limits of Reason Alone.* Trans. T. M. Greene and H. H. Hudson. New York: Harper and Row, 1960.

SPW   *Kant: Selected Pre-Critical Writings and Correspondence with Beck.* Trans. G. B. Kerferd and D. E. Walford. Manchester: University of Manchester Press, 1968.

T   *Träume eines Geistersehers, erläutert durch Träume der Metaphysik.*

UD   *Untersuchung über die Deutlichkeit der Grundsätze der natürlichen Theologie und der Moral.* Known as the *Prize-Essay* of 1764.

UG   *Über den Gemeinspruch: Das mag in der Theorie richtig sein, taugt aber nicht für die Praxis.*

UP   *Über Pädagogik.* Ed. T. F. Rink.

VpR   *Vorlesungen über die philosophische Religionslehre.* Ed. K.H.L. Pölitz.

W   *Was heisst sich im Denken orientieren?*

WORKS OF ROUSSEAU

CS   *Du contract social ou principes du droit politique.*

DO   *Discours sur l'origine et les fondements de l'inégalité parmi les hommes.*

DS   *Discours sur les sciences et les arts.*

Em   *Émile, ou de l'éducation*. Ed. F. Richard and P. Richard. Paris: Garnier, 1964.

OC   *Oeuvres complètes de Jean-Jacques Rousseau*. 4 vols. Ed. B. Gagnebin and M. Raymond. Paris: Gallimard, 1959–69. Bibliothèque de la Pléiade.

RP   *Les Rêveries du promeneur solitaire*. Ed. J. Voisine. Paris: Garnier Flammarion, 1964.

SECONDARY WORKS (Frequently Cited)

Books and Articles

BsE   D. Henrich. "Der Begriff der sittlichen Einsicht und Kant's Lehre vom Faktum der Vernunft." In D. Henrich, W. Schulz, K.-H. Volkmann-Schluck, eds., *Die Gegenwart der Griechen im neueren Denken*, 77–115. Festschrift for H.-G. Gadamer. Tübingen: J. C. B. Mohr, 1960.

DC   T. Seebohm. "On the Deduction of Categories." In *Categories: A Colloquium*, 21–40. University Park, Pa.: Pennsylvania State University, Department of Philosophy, 1978.

DGS   W. Dilthey. *Gesammelte Schriften*. 18 vols. Stuttgart: B. G. Teubner and Göttingen: Vandenhoeck and Ruprecht, 1914–77.

DKV   K. Ward. *The Development of Kant's View of Ethics*. Oxford: Basil Blackwell, 1972.

EGP   L. W. Beck. *Early German Philosophy: Kant and His Predecessors*. Cambridge: Harvard University Press, 1969.

EKT   H. J. de Vleeschauwer. *The Evolution of Kantian Thought: The History of a Doctrine*. Trans. A. R. C. Duncan. London: Nelson, 1962.

GCH   G. G. Iggers. *The German Conception of History: The National Tradition of Historical Thought from Herder to the Present*. Middletown, Conn.: Wesleyan University Press, 1968.

HK   D. Henrich. "Hutcheson und Kant." *Kant-Studien* 49 (1957–58): 49–69.

IO   D. Henrich. *Identität und Objektivität: Eine Untersuchung über Kants transzendentale Deduktion*. Heidelberg: Heidelberger Akademie der Wissenschaften, 1976.

JGP   N. Rotenstreich. *Jews and German Philosophy: The Polemics of Emancipation*. New York: Schocken, 1984.

KM   M. Wundt. *Kant als Metaphysiker*. Stuttgart: Enke, 1924.

KPE   P. A. Schilpp. *Kant's Pre-Critical Ethics*. Evanston, Ill.: North-
        western University Press, 1938.

KPH   Y. Yovel. *Kant and the Philosophy of History*. Princeton, N. J.:
        Princeton University Press, 1980.

KTD   K. Ameriks. "Kant's Transcendental Deduction as Regressive
        Argument." *Kant-Studien* 69 (1978): 273–87.

LZA   L. Borinski and W. Walter, eds. *Logik im Zeitalter der Aufklä-
        rung: Studien zur Vernunftlehre von Hermann Samuel Reimarus*.
        Göttingen: Joachim-Jungius-Gesellschaft der Wissenschaften,
        1980.

MFL   M. Heidegger. *The Metaphysical Foundations of Logic*. Trans. M.
        Heim. Bloomington: Indiana University Press, 1984.

PA   H.-J. Engfer. *Philosophie als Analysis: Studien zur Entwicklung
        philosophischer Analysiskonzeptionen unter dem Einfluss mathe-
        matischer Methodenmodelle im 17. und frühen 18. Jahrhundert*.
        Stuttgart-Bad Canstatt: Frommann-Holzboog, 1982.

PhG   K. Düsing. "Das Problem des höchsten Gutes in Kants prak-
        tischer Philosophie." *Kant-Studien* 62 (1971): 5–42.

PIK   *The Philosophy of Immanuel Kant: Studies in Philosophy and the
        History of Philosophy*. Vol. 12. Ed. R. Kennington. Washington,
        D.C.: Catholic University of America Press, 1985.

PRE   E. Cassirer. *The Platonic Renaissance in England*. Trans. J. P. Pet-
        tegrove. Edinburgh: Nelson, 1953.

RK   K. Reich. *Rousseau und Kant*. Tübingen: J. C. B. Mohr (Paul
        Siebeck), 1936.

SCS   M. Kuehn. *Scottish Common Sense in Germany, 1768–1800: A
        Contribution to the History of Critical Philosophy*. Kingston and
        Montreal: McGill-Queen's University Press, 1987.

SKpE   H. Heimsoeth, D. Henrich, and G. Tonelli, eds. *Studien zu
        Kants philosophischer Entwicklung*. Hildesheim: Olms, 1967.

SPIK   H. Heimsoeth. *Studien zur Philosophie Immanuel Kants: Meta-
        physische Ursprünge und ontologische Grundlagen. Kant-Studien
        Ergänzungshefte* 71. Cologne, 1956.

SV   D. Henrich. *Selbstverhältnisse: Gedanken und Auslegungen zu
        den Grundlagen der klassischen deutschen Philosophie*. Stuttgart:
        Phillip Reclam, 1982.

U   G. Tonelli. "Die Umwälzung von 1769 bei Kant." *Kant-Studien*
        54 (1963): 369–75.

UEK   J. Schmucker. *Die Ursprünge der Ethik Kants in seinen vorkritischen Schriften und Reflexionen.* Meisenheim: Anton Hain, 1961.

UKE   D. Henrich. "Über Kants Entwicklungsgeschichte." *Philosophische Rundschau* 13 (1965): 252–63.

UKfE D. Henrich. "Über Kants früheste Ethik: Versuch einer Rekonstruktion." *Kant-Studien* 54 (1963): 404–31.

VKrV M. Gueroult. "Vom Kanon der reinen Vernunft zur kritik der praktischen Vernunft." *Kant-Studien* 54 (1963): 432–444.

Journals

JHI   *Journal of the History of Ideas*
JHP   *Journal of the History of Philosophy*
KS   *Kant-Studien*
RM   *Review of Metaphysics*

Introduction

The Problem of the End of Reason
in Kant's Philosophy

The Kantian intellectual revolution consists of a systematic argument linking three elements: (1) an idealist account of knowledge, (2) a moral doctrine that grounds human dignity upon self-legislative freedom, and (3) a teleology that ascribes a moral end to all employments of reason. This book is the result of an effort to understand that revolution. It does not reconstruct all the phases of Kant's argument, which as a whole constitutes the three *Critiques*. Rather, it exposes certain primary reflections, to some extent presented in Kant's published writings and to some extent presupposed by them, that establish the necessary relations between the revolution's three basic elements. In particular, this study attempts to show, in large measure with the help of the neglected ethical reflections of the 1760s, that the third of these elements—the moral and practical end of reason—is the necessary starting point for understanding the underlying logic of Kant's argument.

The Kantian accounts of epistemological and moral idealism are not fully comprehensible except against the background of reason's characterization as a free power of determining itself and of prescribing ends to itself, independent of nature. Kant arrives at his understanding of reason through an effort to resolve a crisis in the modern period concerning the end, status, and meaning of reason. This crisis marks his true beginning as "critical" philosopher; his doctrine of the "end of reason" is his proposed solution. Kant's epistemological and moral idealisms are in their fully articulated versions subordinate parts of that doctrine and completely intelligible only when regarded as such. Taken as a whole, the critical philosophy is a response to a problem Kant sees as intrinsic to reason, although first fully exposed in modern times—the teleological problem of reason's goodness. The primacy of this problem and its solution, with their unmistakable moral and practical bearing, is the true meaning of "the primacy of

1

the practical" in Kant's philosophy. The moral foundation of Kant's critical philosophy can be uncovered in the manner in which this "primacy" determines the content and direction of all inquiries belonging to the "criticism" of reason.

The unpublished ethical reflections of the 1760s are crucial for understanding Kant's critical philosophy, since they disclose a "Rousseauian turn" that precedes and conditions the better-known "transcendental turn" in Kant's thinking. The first of these turns is the outcome of Kant's profound encounter with Rousseau's writings, which compels Kant to face the question of reason's goodness. Through Rousseau, Kant comes to realize that modern Enlightenment accounts of the relation of philosophy and science to the human good have failed to establish that reason is a beneficent force in human life. Kant's striving to meet Rousseau's arguments, which are the first great philosophical criticism of Enlightenment, constitutes a new justification or "theodicy" of reason. Kant's new justification assigns to the theoretical and moral employments of reason diverse but complementary roles within an overarching moral project—one that claims to fulfill human reason's essential demands. Thus the interpretation offered here departs from those traditional readings of Kant that regard the theoretical and practical parts of his philosophy as wholly independent realms of discourse. It makes extensive use of largely unexplored "precritical" sources in Kant's corpus, since these are especially helpful in revealing an original architectonic unity of theoretical and practical concerns at the very basis of the mature critical philosophy. Thus the following essay examines what these sources tell us about the "revolution of the 1760s," and it also considers the enduring presence of this revolution in Kant's philosophy during the period of the great *Critiques*.

Central to the criticism of modern Enlightenment, for both Rousseau and Kant, are the difficulties raised by the Enlightenment accounts of the instrumentality of reason, according to which the ends of reason are given to it by passions or sentiments. Both thinkers, in diverse but related ways, object that such accounts inadequately determine reason's telos (or the telos of man as rational). The result of the expansion of reason in modern progressive projects of transforming society through science has been, in their view, the unanticipated deformation of the social, moral, and psychophysiological life of man, because such projects have been undertaken recklessly, with no clear conception of their goal. Previous thinkers, they believe, have not grasped the limits to the application of reason as instrument in projects of bettering and mastering the human condition. The first point to grasp, according to both Rousseau and Kant, is that the guidance of reason in mastery cannot be handed over to passion, untutored or undisciplined by some form of legislative reason. For human reason, when employed as the uncritical servant of the passions, has the capacity to emancipate human life from a natural order of simplicity and self-sufficiency and to create the artificial realm of "culture." That emancipation produces more harm than good, and the realm of culture is characterized by servitude and debilitating luxury, as long as the expansion of reason is not guided by an adequate concept of its telos.

The comparison of Rousseau's writings with Kant's ethical reflections of the 1760s discloses a significant difference of emphasis in their respective critiques of instrumental reason. For Rousseau the whole problem is, viewed from many different vantage points, the problem of human happiness. Kant also speaks of the threats to happiness or instinctual satisfaction posed by modern enlightenment. Yet he is at least initially more concerned with the failure of the instrumental account of reason to explain and support the experiences of nobility or dignity that, in his view, human reason necessarily associates with its free and self-governing powers. The degrading and demoralizing effect of modern definitions of reason threatens to issue in widespread hatred of reason, or "misology," and thus the overthrow of the only possible source of human dignity. Already Kant's writings of the 1760s assert that modern metaphysical determinations of reason have to be reformed or criticized, as part of a larger project of determining the proper teleology of reason, and thus of setting "Enlightenment" upon a proper foundation. The rescue of metaphysical reason from the self-inflicted fate of "misology" is at the core of Kant's project of a "critique of reason," including his response to Hume's skepticism. Although Rousseau is not led by his own reflections in the direction of such a critique, Rousseau's exposure of internal tensions in reason provides premises indispensable to the Kantian approach. We shall see that Rousseau does not hold along with Kant that a true justification or theodicy of reason is possible.

The Kantian justification of reason and Rousseau's role in its conception have implications that go beyond a scholarly discussion of the origins of Kant's mature thought. The Kantian justification entails a radical separation of autonomous reason from human nature; the separation in turn is one of the most immediate and conspicuous sources for the replacement in later thought of human nature by various forms of historical and cultural reason. Rousseau pushes Kant in the direction of that separation, without fully embracing it himself. Thus the dramatic encounter in the 1760s between Kant and the writings of Rousseau is the moment of nascence for the transcendental and historicist approaches in later thought and the attendant disappearance of human nature as the ground for knowledge of the human good. With some poetic excess, one can say that a "dialogue" between Kant and Rousseau on the goodness and nature of reason is simply the decisive first scene in a continuing dialogue about the role of reason in human affairs, in which the later principals include Fichte, Hegel, the Romantics, Marx and Nietzsche, Husserl and Heidegger. The whole philosophical development of the later modern period on the European continent, it could be said, has its primary roots in that dialogue of the 1760s. In every major thinker of that later modern tradition, the central issue is the same as the issue first addressed in the mid-eighteenth century—the soundness of the modern understanding of the relation of reason to society and the human good, and the effort at a reform or self-criticism of that understanding, whose outcome is to be a new and higher "beginning" in modern man's relation to his own "modernity."

The Primacy of the Practical
End of Reason

A study of the end of reason in Kant's writings between 1764 and 1781 sheds light on the role of the practical within the whole of Kant's philosophy, for it discloses how Kant, in the twenty years leading up to the *Critique of Pure Reason*, undertakes to redefine reason from the standpoint of a moral account of its end. Such a line of argument will naturally bring to mind the famous Kantian doctrine of "the primacy of the practical." Ordinarily, however, that primacy is understood by the scholarship in a fashion that is both historically and systematically too narrow. Thus Kant's arguments for the primacy of practical reason within the whole of reason are usually taken to refer solely to the following attempted demonstration: that consequent upon establishing the limitations of theoretical inquiry in the realm of noumena or unconditioned being, practical reason (based on the moral law) has a "right" to an extension into that realm which has been denied to reason from a theoretical standpoint. Thus the objective reality of the postulations of God, freedom, and immortality that are necessary to the fulfillment of the moral requirements of reason can be asserted from a practical standpoint. This holds even though the same "ideas" or postulations are problematic or merely thinkable according to theoretical reflection.[1]

Kant's account of primacy may seem to mean only this: that where theory must be ignorant or indecisive, morality can provide content and affirm what must be the case. Within a certain sharply defined realm left "vacant" by theory, the "ought" holds sway, and overrides the merely possible "is" that theoretical speculation might propose. But such a view of the intent of "primacy" exposes Kant to the criticism that his doctrine is a trivial and contrived appendage to his more central theoretical interests. Or worse, as may appear suggested by the famous description of the chief benefit of the criticism of reason (that it "denies knowledge in order to make room for faith" of a moral sort), the doctrine of primacy is simply a retroactive and disingenuous effort to lend respectability to what must otherwise seem to most readers of Kant to be a bleak and "all-destroying" dismantling of traditional supports of the moral order.[2]

It will be argued here that the defense of the requirements of moral reason is not a later addition to Kant's concerns, and it is neither theoretically superfluous nor secondary to those concerns. Rather, such a defense is constitutive of his whole conception of theoretical inquiry after 1765. Furthermore, it will be argued that the defense as constitutive of theoretical inquiry is not simply a demonstration of the practical reality or validity of postulations. It is a decisive element in a new account of reason as a whole. In the genuinely Kantian understanding of primacy, nothing less is at stake than the meaning, status, and content of reason. The scope of the redefinition of reason involved in this primacy can best be understood in terms of Kant's efforts to secure a new characterization of the ultimate end, or purpose, of reason as a whole. Only this approach does justice, historically and systematically, to the role of the practical in Kant's philosophy.

Evidence that Kant arrives at a moral or practical determination of the end of reason by the close of the 1760s is abundant and forms a substantial basis for the present discussion. Thus Kant writes around 1769: "The practical sciences determine the worth of the theoretical. What has no such [practical] employment is indeed useless. The practical sciences are the first according to intention because ends must precede means. But in execution the theoretical sciences must be first."[3] By this date, it should be noted, "practical science" is already centrally a pure moral philosophy. And also by this time, theoretical inquiry is conceived as "propaedeutic," to determine the powers and the limits of reason and to be followed by a metaphysics elaborated in accordance with its strictures. Since such a metaphysics will be above all a metaphysics of morals, the role of theoretical inquiry is to provide, above all else, the preparatory foundation for such a metaphysical morality. The theoretical propaedeutic is first in "execution" although second in "intention," for its task and systematic function in the whole account of reason are assigned to it by the ultimate moral end of reason. As the *Nachlass* and the writings of 1764–80 unquestionably establish, this "critical" view of the relation of theoretical propaedeutic to moral telos is the theme of a continuously developing reflection that culminates in the *Critique of Pure Reason* of 1781. In other words, the philosophical problem of the "end of reason" (of the nature and systematic function of the telos of reason and of the "means" of executing its requirements) is a central component, and indeed the very heart, of the emergence of critical philosophy.

Given its concern, the present study does not undertake extensive analysis and exegesis of the most familiar Kantian moral texts. This is not another attempt to expound the foundations of Kant's moral philosophy in terms of its most conspicuous categories. This study is, however, very much concerned with the "status" of the ethical in Kant's philosophy as a whole. It proposes the thesis that Kant's determination of certain essential features of the foundations of ethics is inseparable from his determination of the foundations of philosophy as such, and that both determinations occur within the context of reflection on the end of reason. The present discussion is also not a history of the development of Kant's ethics, although it explores carefully certain episodes in that development. Certain writings before 1781, usually called "precritical" although they contain important elements of critical doctrine, must be called upon if one is to have a full view of the determining role of morality within the architectonic of reason.

Rousseau's Insight

The most decisive moment in the prehistory of "criticism" is Kant's intense engagement with Rousseau's writings in the early and middle 1760s. Especially important to the philosophical historian is the record of that engagement in the reflections, dating 1764–65, that go by the name *Remarks to the Observations on the Feeling of the Beautiful and Sublime* (hereafter called simply the *Remarks*).[4] One finds there the famous autobiographical statement that Rousseau brought Kant around to the true conception of the function of theoretical inquiry in human life: inquiry's sole dignity lies in its contribution to the defense of the rights of humanity.[5] It is argued here that of all external influences on Kant, Rousseau is the one having the largest effect on the mature account of the end of reason and of the internal articulation of reason into practical and theoretical employments. In so arguing, the present discussion revises the usual scholarly estimate of Rousseau's importance for Kant, while it revises at the same time prevailing estimates of "the primacy of the practical." Rousseau's place in the Kantian endeavor is normally conceived in terms of the contribution of Rousseauian formulations about self-legislative freedom, in the *Social Contract*, to the related Kantian formulation about the supreme moral law, the categorical imperative.[6] The textual support and philosophical defense for a much larger and profounder scope of Rousseauian influence on Kant are presented later in this study. A few of the main issues are indicated now.

One can say that Rousseau decisively prepared the ground for these central features of Kant's thinking: (1) an account of reason as a whole, in which a spontaneous power to project "ideals" and to determine ideal ends freely in such projection, is essential to reason; (2) the view that the specifically moral form of that spontaneous power is what determines the final end of reason, to whose actualization all uses of reason must contribute and in relation to which they have "worth"; (3) an account of the relations of reason, theoretical inquiry, and science to practical and moral life; this account offers an analysis of recalcitrant problems in all human efforts to advance the species rationally and morally, while it also stresses the possibility of "ideal" resolutions of such problems.

Of these three features, the third is the most fundamental and provides the context for understanding the first two. The third is Kant's reception and transformation of Rousseau's basic analysis of human existence in terms of the relations between reason and passion, science and sociality, virtue and happiness. For Kant, Rousseau's most important insight is this: the human capacity to project and pursue "ideal" goals (or ideal objects of desire) that are not limited or determined by instinct, inclination, or in general by nature is the source of the gravest human perplexities and evils, as well as of their possible overcoming in a future that surpasses all previous peaks of humanity. Kant discovers in Rousseau an account of how "culture" arises out of and in opposition to nature, thereby producing the central problems of human life, as well as its true excellences. One must begin, as Kant does, with Rousseau's description of these human phenomena, the abysses and the peaks of human life, for these are the starting point for the analysis that proceeds to their causes in human reason and its formative or deformative powers. In Kant's language, reason as the key to the creation of culture discloses peculiar self-conflicting or "dialectical" characteristics. Kant finds in Rousseau both certain basic features of that dialectic and suggestions of how human powers can resolve the dialectic that they originate.

In what follows I argue that the Rousseauian analysis of human reason is an indispensable basis for understanding Kant's account of the freedom and spontaneity of reason, evidenced in its ideal-projecting powers and its dialectical tendencies. Those features of reason are, in turn, foundational for the accurate grasp of (1) the Kantian moral doctrine in its most immediate and narrow sense, as an account of a pure moral will legislating an end for itself according to a universalizing formula; (2) the manner in which Kant subordinates all theory to an ultimate end proposed by such a self-legislating will; (3) the Kantian view of the internal structure of that end, as the unification of the rational-moral perfection of man with an appropriate consummation of his nature and inclinations.

Since Rousseau contributes so much to this articulation of the various phases of the structure of reason in Kant, one can point to a Rousseauian core in the critical architectonic of reason. Hence there is a pressing need to examine the precritical essays within the context of the *Nachlass* in order to acquire a just appreciation of that architectonic and its guiding end. These earlier writings are not only invaluable for their clarification of Rousseau's enormous importance in the Kantian problematic. They also frequently exceed statements of the "critical," post-1780 writings for vividness, concreteness, and philosophical suggestiveness on the topics under discussion.[7] Of course the interpretation of the earlier materials cannot replace the interpretation of the later mature works. The latter must be the primary context for the ascertaining of Kant's account of the end of reason. Yet the former can enrich the understanding of the major publications by offering insight into considerations, some of which are even first premises, that condition the later arguments, although these considerations are sometimes not fully presented, or are only outlined, in the mature writings.

The Highest Good and the End of Reason

The end of reason in Kant is most readily and frequently approached as a part of the moral philosophy, especially that part of it treating "the highest good," as the idea of the totality of ends of a human rational striving. In an account of the end of reason, there is much to be said for starting with Kant's discussions of that idea, for Kant has underlined its importance. Indeed Kant sees himself, as we shall see, as a thinker who is reviving an ancient concept neglected by modern thinkers, and he stresses his fundamental agreement with the ancient (post-Socratic) definition of the philosopher as the seeker of scientific knowledge of the highest good.[8] Kant notes his agreement with that definition in numerous statements about the nature of philosophy.

Thus the explication of the idea of the highest good shows that it contains the "ultimate end of human reason," which must be the focal point of philosophic deliberation about the architectonic functions of the various forms of cognition.

Hence it is not an error to approach the end of reason in Kant by way of the explicit treatments of the highest good. Yet it is a gross distortion to restrict the meaning of the highest good to moral philosophy, as defined by the major themes of the explicitly moral writings. We cannot without peril ignore two facts that argue against such a restriction: (1) the critique of theoretical reason is intended to be propaedeutical to moral philosophy; (2) the same critique has a primary telos in moral concerns, and the idea of the highest good expresses the completed totality of ends that is identical with that telos.[9] It is thus impossible to confine reflection on the end of reason to those writings concerned with the foundations of practical philosophy and the "metaphysics of morals." A full account of the end of reason must include an explanation of why that end compels philosophy to have the peculiar structure of a propaedeutical critique of theoretical cognition, followed by the elaboration of a moral doctrine. It is true that some of the most detailed and systematic statements on the highest good are found in the moral writings. Yet there are many other statements about it—in writings on history, politics, religion, aesthetics, teleology, and the theoretical writings themselves—which are at least as revelatory of the largest architectonic considerations raised by the notion of the highest good as the ultimate end of reason.[10] Very few writings of Kant after 1781 fail to say something of interest about the end of reason or the highest good.

A difficulty frequently noted in the literature stands in the way of serious consideration of the theme of the highest good or the end of reason in Kant, in spite of Kant's loquacity on these topics. This is the initial difficulty of finding a place for a doctrine of the highest end within a morality of autonomy, which seemingly abjures all consideration of ends in the self-legislation of the will according to universalizing maxims that disregard the self-love of the legislator. It is nonetheless hard to miss the recurrent discussions in Kant of how the legislative moral will qua moral, and not qua self-interested, must have regard for ends of a purely moral nature. The rational will cannot determine itself without having regard for some end. The rational will is essentially purposive; in Kant's view this means something altogether different from doctrines that the will is directed by its nature toward consequences, in a utilitarian sense.[11]

Problems remain in Kant's doctrine of moral ends. Not the least of these is Kant's view that from a purely moral standpoint the moral self-legislative will must be interested in the happiness and natural condition of other rational wills. How happiness and nature can have moral significance, and form an essential component of the highest end of reason, is a question still unresolved in the scholarship.[12] For the moment, we must leave this issue by noting that the question of whether there are theoretical difficulties in Kant's account of the end of reason must be kept separate from the question of whether that account is as central to Kant's thinking as he claims. The uncovering of theoretical difficulties in a philosophic doctrine cannot be equated with the discovery that the formulator of the doctrine lacks good reasons for holding it. He may be aware of such difficulties, yet nevertheless he may know of considerations in favor of the position that prevails, in the balance, over those difficulties. It behooves us to learn what those reasons are and why they are regarded by the philosopher as compelling. This is not to deny that we must always be interested in the criticism of a thinker and that indeed criticism is inseparable from genuine understanding.

There exist many valuable discussions of various aspects of Kant's account of the highest end or highest good. These largely consider the subject from a single technical standpoint. They mostly attempt to evaluate Kant's doctrine of the highest good as a supplement to the foundations of moral reason in the categorical imperative. Accordingly, the usual approach is to attempt to elaborate a purely formal concept of the "totality of ends" which will be consistent with the "formal" morality of the categorical imperative. I have already indicated that I cannot regard the doctrine of ends as merely supplementary to the categorical imperative. The doctrine of the end of reason is conceived by Kant as an answer to the question of how the *whole* of human reason can be understood as guided by and fulfilled within a single telos. Because that question has a leading role in the Kantian inquiries that eventually result in "critical" morality and transcendental philosophy, it is necessary to say that the "formalistic" tendencies of Kant's thinking have their sources in a "substantive" reflection on reason's end.[13]

In the interpretation of Kant, as in that of other major "liberal" philosophers, we must resist the tendency to regard the "formalist" aspects of liberal thought as both the starting point and the end point of the thinker in question. A strong proclivity of philosophic discussion in ethics and politics today is to take a certain formal liberalism (abstracting from most questions about ends, the good, and ethos or way of life) as the only rational framework within which morality can be discussed. We forget that such a "framework" was established by great thinkers who aimed at creating a new way of life and that "liberalism" is a way of life that originated in opposition to other substantive ways of life. A morality which teaches that we must abstract from certain kinds of ends is itself proposing a new end. In this essay I hope to show how Kant's central concern with an adequate definition of the end of reason is the best starting point for grasping the intent of the most fundamental components of his very distinctive version of "liberal" philosophy.

The statements of Kant on the end of reason that predate the *Critique of Practical Reason*, where the mature form of the doctrine appears full-fledged for the first time, must be taken seriously. The adequate grounding of morality in the moral law as the "fact of reason" does not appear before 1788; accordingly the relation between the highest good and that ground does not take its definitive form until that date. But all the same, Kant after 1764–65 is constantly reflecting on how the ultimate end of reason, with its moral character, determines all uses of reason.[14] The manner in which happiness is a component of the highest good in the "Canon of Pure Reason" in the first *Critique* may not represent Kant's last thoughts on the subject. But as I show below, his thoughts there are not as distant from his later formulations as some scholars suppose. And furthermore, certain aspects of that presentation and other earlier presentations throw light on how the highest good provides an end for theoretical inquiry, whereas the second *Critique* is rather laconic on this subject. Yet if one does not have regard for the function of the highest good as the end of theoretical inquiry, the doctrine in its full bearing is not intelligible.[15]

A Prospectus of the Argument

It is useful to indicate the main course of the analysis of the end of reason proposed in this study. Chapter 1 introduces some of the themes of Kant's "revolution in the end of reason," prior to the historical study in chapters 2–5 that proceeds for the most part chronologically. The "themes" in chapter 1 constitute some of the components of the revolution, and they are taken, with one exception, from Kant's "critical" writings. The exception is Rousseau's protest against modern enlightenment, which is in decisive respects absorbed and transformed by Kant. The Kantian revolution is unthinkable without Rousseau's protest, and hence it is a necessary theme for an interpreter of that revolution, even if Kant in his "critical" writings does not openly assert the full scope of his debt to Rousseau. By starting with the final expression of Kant's principles and by reading earlier materials as pointing toward that conclusion, I know I risk overstressing the continuities in Kant's thought. But if hermeneutical distortion is implicit in this approach, it may be a valuable corrective to other approaches that have neglected the important continuities I have noted. The merit of the present approach will be seen (1) if one learns from it that the particular continuities it underlines are not peripheral matters but basic to the intent of Kant's philosophy and (2) if what one learns about these matters from the earlier sources lends greater coherence and significance to the maturest statements of Kant's doctrines.

Chapter 1 provides a general introduction to the reflection that the well-known transcendental revolution of Kant in moral and theoretical principles is inseparable from a new formulation of the end of reason. Further, it shows that the revolution taken as a whole is a reform of modern philosophical foundations, which centrally involves a revision of the practical ends that governed the laying of those foundations in the principal philosophical doctrines of the pre-Kantian modern period. On the whole, the major thinkers from Bacon and Descartes to Hume propose "instrumental" views of reason, even in the realm of the "purest" theorizing. That instrumentality is subordinated to a project of emancipation, of rendering the human species relatively more autonomous of superhuman powers and authorities. This project would assert a new "right" of human self-awareness, especially in a more individualistic or "egoistic" form, to determine ends for itself without regard for the putative restrictions or laws of a superhuman order. Undoubtedly Kant agrees with this project very substantially. But Kant requires a revision of some of the first premises of the emancipatory project as conceived by his predecessors.

Rousseau's critique enters here. Rousseau brings to Kant's attention that an instrumental conception of the role of reason in such a project is ultimately self-defeating. Whereas the modern employment of reason as instrument to liberate man would, by its own account, result in greater human independence and self-sufficiency, it brings about the opposite: deeper enslavement of humanity to its own artifacts. This critique uncovers an unnoticed inconsistency or self-subversion in the modern principles of reason. Kant expands on Rousseauian insights to argue that all human reason has an inherent tendency to self-subversion, by way of destroying the possibility of the freedom that must be presupposed by the employment of any form of reason. The Kantian "transcendental" limitation of theoretical reason is the propaedeutic that will definitively end that self-subversion and secure the free employment of rationality in a project of maximizing independence.

The crisis in reason that Rousseau and Kant confront can be defined by the following three questions: (1) Is the modern account of reason able to justify itself through a rational and scientific discourse on its own purposes and thus establish its own goodness? (2) Is the relation of modern scientific reason to the practical world of custom, morality, and belief a healthy and salutary one? (3) Can modern philosophy maintain its position as the dominant force in human affairs and continue to promote the emancipation and enlightenment of humanity? Rousseau convinces Kant that the answers to all three questions must be negative, unless modern rationality can in decisive respects be altered.

Hence Kant's philosophy can be described as a "transcendental practice" that offers new foundational principles to render a modern "Enlightenment" project internally consistent and to overcome its tendency to crisis and self-destruction. A key to this rectification is the philosophic authorization of the freedom implicit in the moral certainties of common reason to be the ultimate legislator of the ends of reason and to override the dictates of passion. For only the common moral reason (which by its nature, in Kant's view, aims at consistency and unity) can be the highest principle for the direction of reason, nullifying the internal "dialectic" of reason as instrumental to given natural ends. Speculative thought itself is vitiated by its failure to be master over its own natural "dialectical" tendencies. It must turn to free rationality, implicit in its own operations, as the sole ground for unity and consistency in its principles. At the same time, speculative reason should arrive at the insight that the true satisfaction of its "demands" for cognition of the whole according to ideas of totality will be found in the noncognitive employment of reason in moral self-legislation. For only a moral whole—the highest good as moral world—is a whole that human reason can strive to realize self-consistently and without self-subversion.

Chapters 2–5 detail the argumentation that produces the Kantian doctrine summarized above. Chapters 2 and 3 elaborate the problems arising from the instrumental view of reason, and from the account of passionate mastery of nature for the sake of freeing humanity from the evils of the natural order, as Rousseau and the early Kant of 1764–65 see these problems. The difficulties are subsumed under the heading of the "teleological problem" in the modern "individualistic" emancipation of the passions. If reason has no other end than to serve the passions aiming at freedom and mastery, what prevents reason, as a modifiable and expanding power, from unfolding in ways that exacerbate the passions and that increase human servitude to socially generated and factitious desires? By suggesting that the whole modern emancipatory effort may be self-defeating, Rousseau initiates the later modern criticism of the modern world as the realm of "alienation" in which man is subjugated by his own creations.

Kant is acutely aware of these implications of Rousseau's writings, as the *Remarks*, analyzed in chapter 3, plainly exposes. Rousseau also makes evident to Kant that the various "moral sense" or "moral sentiment" responses to passionate individualism do not address the profound teleological issue, for they ignore the dangers inherent in the radical dynamism of modern emancipatory reason. In the *Remarks* Kant develops his own version of the Rousseauian analysis of the teleological problem. Starting from Rousseau's "dynamical" characterization of reason, Kant proposes an account of reason as spontaneous, historical, and self-legislative. Reason realizes itself (first by way of a destructive dialectic) through the unfolding of its latent capacities for self-legislation and self-limitation. It is not too much to say that the *Remarks* accordingly contains the first elements of Kant's "critical" solution to the teleological problem of reason. For more clearly than any other "precritical" writing, it adumbrates the Kantian "Copernican revolution" in the approach to reason. Furthermore, it discloses a profound level in the motivation for that revolution, which is more directly available from the *Remarks* than from any of Kant's other writings.

Chapter 4 addresses the elaboration between 1765 and 1780 of the Kantian solution as a new kind of moral idealism. The spontaneity of reason is the source of a rationally constructed order of the soul, effected through the self-legislation of a moral ideal. The principle of this moral ideal is not natural inclination or passion, but the rational construct ("ideal") of a universal and "systematic" harmony of free self-legislating beings. These achieve maximum freedom, in the form of independence from the "arbitrary" wills of other humans and the "arbitrary" powers of nature, through a self-imposed legal limitation of the scope of the inclinations and passions. But as man is a natural being whose sentient and appetitive nature cannot be discounted, the moral ideal at which all self-legislation is directed must be the ideal of a world in which all rational beings combine the maximum of self-legislated freedom with an appropriate satisfaction of natural desires. This ideal, called both the "moral world" and the "highest good," is also understood by Kant as the *arche* of a "system" of reason that unites and consummates all the interests of rational beings.

Thus well before the famous disquisitions of the *Critique of Judgment*, the unity of freedom and nature is the ideal goal or telos of man as rational and is the ideal that comes prior "in intention" to the theoretical inquiries that must be executed to support its realization. Furthermore, it is the ideal that Kant formulates in response to the "crisis" of the wayward and self-subverting rationality of the modern "culture" of passionate mastery. The new ideal achieves a just and harmonious relation between the "spontaneous" and "receptive" aspects of human rational nature, which are in disproportion and disharmony in the present (and also in all past) "culture." Thus, again, the background to the "critical" inquiries, including the place of dialectical "antinomies" and Hume's skeptical paradoxes in the critique of speculative reason, is an analysis of the condition of human reason that is decisively Rousseauian. This chapter contains, accordingly, a discussion of how Kant's formulation (during the years 1769–78) of ineluctable antinomic tendencies in reason's efforts to cognize ideal "wholes" is shaped by the account of reason's ultimate moral telos. Kant conceives the resolution of the theoretical dialectic as the essential task of a propaedeutical critique of cognition that prepares the ground for a moral system of reason.

Chapter 5 discusses how Kant, in the final passages of the *Critique of Pure Reason* and in other writings and reflections of the vastly productive "critical" epoch of 1781–1800, sets forth the outlines of the new "systematic" conception of reason in which the "ideal" operates as the organizing end and *arche*. In the light of this ideal, all of reason comes under the legislation of the critical philosopher so as to secure the grounds for humanity's unobstructed progress toward a final practical goal—the achievement in history of a definitive "culture" that embodies the ideal. Such culture would combine the maximum of human autonomy (emancipation from nature's arbitrariness) with satisfaction of the unavoidable exigencies of desire in human nature. Kant also at this time brings into focus the central difficulties blocking human advance to this goal. The various writings on religion, aesthetics, teleology, history, and politics are all concerned with looking at the sources of "evil" that obstruct the way and with disclosing hopeful prospects for the removal of these evils.

In all of this, one can say that critical philosophy is pointing toward the ideal realization of a self-consistent human rationality, wherein reason's inherent emancipatory strivings can be fulfilled with a minimum of "dialectical" self-subversion. The epilogue briefly notes how tensions natural to human rationality are a necessary condition for the transcendental mode of argument in Kant and how later thinkers who owe much to Kant nonetheless ignore or merely presuppose without argument his genuine starting points. But this "forgetting" is itself something that the Kantian "ideal" resolution of human problems has promoted. The book concludes accordingly on a somewhat ironic note: Kantian philosophy, which offers an exemplary analysis of such problems and which has established the terms for many later accounts of reason, has also contributed to the near disappearance of the problem of the end of reason from recent philosophy.

1

The Revolution
in the End of Reason:
Some Principal Themes

The Revision of Modern Foundations

The transformation of philosophy in the eighteenth century that is closely associated with Kant's proclamation of his intellectual "revolution" is a decisive reformulation of philosophical "foundations," both in metaphysics and the account of knowledge and in moral or practical philosophy. Historians of philosophy usually agree that the notions of theoretical and moral-political foundations in the major philosophers from Bacon and Descartes to Leibniz and Hume share certain basic features, and that as a group these notions of foundations are strikingly different from the foundational notions that first appear in Kant. Thus nearly all philosophy after Kant gives evidence of being influenced by his revision of modern methods and procedures.[1] Yet this revolution is not often understood as one that brings about a basic revision of the end of reason. It is sometimes noted that the fundamental theoretical changes that emerge in Kant are connected somehow to a different approach in the aim or the end of the philosopher and, therewith, of "reason" in its philosophic and paradigmatic sense. But a careful and truly philosophic account of this connection has been lacking.

One should expect that Kant's thought would give evidence of a revolution in end as well as in theoretical method, or that the revolution in foundations would crucially include one in end. For Kant has expressly stated that a doctrine of the end of reason governs the employment of reason in the various realms of philosophy, guiding and orienting the nature and direction of inquiry in these realms. Thus Kant has written that "philosophy is the science of relating all cognition and every use of reason to the ultimate end of human reason, to which, as the supreme end, all others are subordinated and in which they must be joined into unity." Also, "Philosophy is the idea of a perfect wisdom that shows us the ultimate ends of human reason."[2]

If Kant expressly states that his foundational inquiries are subordinated to the ultimate end of reason, one would suppose that the critical doctrine of the end would be especially helpful, if not indispensable, to uncovering the revolutionary character of those inquiries. Indeed, the doctrine of the end should be the locus of the revolution itself. According to Kant, the philosopher is to be defined as a legislator, not as a mere theoretician. His legislation establishes the architectonic order of reason wherein the various investigations of philosophy and science are to take their places and in which they are to be viewed as collectively furthering the ultimate end that the philosopher defines. In other words, the philosopher legislates the systematic unity of reason as governed by a single organizing principle, or telos.[3] The revolution taking place in the foundational inquiries of theoretical and moral philosophy has a principal architect—the philosopher as legislator. That is to say that the "local" revolutions in theoretical and moral foundations are reflecting a larger, more comprehensive revolution planned and initiated by the legislative activity of the critical philosopher.[4]

The most familiar of all Kantian revolutions is the revision of the foundations of theoretical philosophy that occurs in the transcendental grounding of all metaphysical inquiry by means of a "critique" of reason's powers. One of the main theses of this study is that the transcendental revolution is not wholly prior in the order of philosophical argument to the defense of moral reason and the erection of a new doctrine of moral autonomy. The argument is often made that the Kantian critique of speculative metaphysics is undertaken wholly without regard to the moral and the human dimension. The critique, it is said, resolutely completes a characteristically modern destruction of the cosmic supports for theoretical contemplation, moral nobility, and beauty; after such a "disillusionment of the world," Kant finds himself morally shipwrecked. The world having become deprived of "value," Kant looks about and finds that only a new doctrine of moral autonomy, wholly divorced from theoretical cognition, provides a certain way of recovering the lost ideals.[5]

Certainly it is true that Kant brings to a consequent conclusion the primary thrust of modern philosophy as critique of speculative metaphysics. But that critique, as initiated by Bacon, Descartes, and Locke, does not aim solely at a scientific "disillusionment" of the world. Rather, it is in the service of a new practical goal of the emancipation of humanity—the assertion of human freedom from superhuman constraints. The destruction of traditional metaphysically supported theology is absolutely central to that aim, and thus also is the creation of a new science of nature that is "neutral" to final causes in the cognizable order of nature. All the same, the modern critique of speculation is not neutral to all human purposes or human finality. The rejection of metaphysical first causes is to make room for the supremacy of human final causes. The order of cosmic final causes is replaced by the legislated order or by the ideal construct supported only by human volition—the establishment of a new universal *nomos* that promotes the maximum of human freedom from the evils and unwelcome constraints of the natural order.[6]

Kant's own critique is quite clearly a continuation of this emancipatory project. His proclamation of allegiance to "Enlightenment" as the liberation of man from self-imposed tutelage to authorities other than his own reason has its counterpart in a theoretical dictum. Reason must assert itself as the source of the conditions of knowledge, and abandon the "leading-strings" of nature, in determining the cognizable order.[7] The necessary corollary of such maxims is the turning away from all metaphysics of first causes or absolute wholes (speculative "dogmatism") that would assign ultimate responsibility for the human order to something beyond the legislative jurisdiction of human reason. Thus it can hardly be maintained that the critique of speculative reason is undertaken with no regard for the practical good. Kant informs us of the philosophical lineage of his conception of the practical aim of theoretical inquiry by placing a Baconian motto at the head of the *Critique of Pure Reason*: the object of philosophy is to lay the foundations of human utility and welfare.[8]

Kant thus does not reject the emancipatory end of modern philosophy or Enlightenment but reformulates it. At least initially, it is better to say that Kant seeks to enhance the modern project's chances of success rather than to say that he seeks to restore some lost premodern "values." His criticism of previous versions of the emancipatory end concerns the internal weaknesses of those versions, which put success of the project in jeopardy. It is not that unwittingly Kant has, through his critique of metaphysics, brought about the total success of a project whose human and moral consequences he now deplores and must seek to rectify. On the contrary, his critique *starts* from the insight that the modern efforts to achieve the emancipatory goal are collapsing upon themselves and must collapse upon themselves. The causes for this collapse are basic flaws in the conception of both the final end of these efforts and of the theoretical methods and procedures employed to realize the end. The two areas of basic flaws are furthermore very deeply related.[9]

Again, Kant's revision of the end and methods of modern philosophy occurs within a broad agreement he has with his modern predecessors in both areas. Several of the features of Kant's critical "epistemology" are quite clearly of a modern, post-Cartesian sort: (1) the procedure of doubting the "realist" starting point in ordinary experience, as above all revealed by the senses, and of turning to the "immanent" sphere of consciousness for the uncovering of universal, necessary, indubitable and unrevisable truths; (2) the substitution of an "artificial" or "methodical" order of cognition to arrive at a total construction of the knowable world, for the unreliable natural procedures of our reason; (3) the securing of foundations for all genuine knowledge on such certitudes and methods, without appeal to first causes or the hidden natures of things in themselves; (4) the distrust of the natural telos of the human mind towards ultimate or unconditioned wholes or toward the contemplative goal of absolute rest in a final and perfect cognition.[10] Kant's writings on metaphysics of the early 1760s, before the decisive Rousseauian and transcendental "turns," clearly evince these aspects of the modern account of cognition. And it is evident that Kant agrees with his modern predecessors that ancient and medieval trust in the natural anticipations of "wholes" by the human mind is incompatible with both genuine theoretical science and the practical goal of emancipation.[11]

Yet certain costs had to be paid for the achievement of the very efficient instrument of modern "method," and the problems that give rise to critical philosophy lie in the region of these costs. First, the rejection of the quest for knowledge of ultimate wholes or first causes may advance the aims of an emancipatory science, but leave unexplained, not to mention unsatisfied, the metaphysical urges or longings of the human mind that are irrepressible. Second, the modern construction of knowledge introduces a divorce between new scientific accounts of nature and of human experience and "ordinary experience" of the world as good and bad, noble and base, beautiful and ugly; it is uncertain that this divorce can actually help to secure the emancipatory aim it is meant to serve. For that aim, after all, is presented as desirable, and even as prescriptive. And if that is so, the aim must be described in terms of the good, or the noble, or the beautiful. But according to the epistemology serving the aim, such terms have dubious cognitive status. Thus in pursuing the project of scientific emancipation we must after all trust certain natural promptings that compel us to pursue that aim, but which have no rational status—passions or sentiments that promote self-preservation or the love of mastery or the love of freedom. According to modern philosophy, reason is and must be only a servant of the passions.[12]

Kant objects that in several crucial respects modern philosophy has suffered from lack of self-knowledge. Its own principles cannot account for themselves on both teleological and methodological levels. While it summarily dismisses the urge for metaphysical wholeness, it cannot account for what it dismisses. In fact all metaphysical thought must employ certain concepts of wholeness. Thus even while he is opposing metaphysical ultimates, the modern philosopher is presupposing notions of ultimates in his own discourse. He fails, however, to justify their use and thereby proceeds "dogmatically." Furthermore, while modern philosophy would make the telos of emancipation the sole end that justifies science, its science is unable to justify that end. Kant thus comes to the insight that modern rationalism must eventually undermine itself. Because it is unable to pursue its emancipatory aim consistently and with security, the foundations need reform. The modern account of reason, being unable to demonstrate its own goodness, may be unable to answer those who speak for the forces of reaction or for the legitimacy of the human mind's subordination to an authoritative whole.

Yet there is a school within the modern metaphysical tradition that presents a somewhat different picture of reason. The historical background to Kant includes the attempts of Leibniz and Wolff to incorporate the mind's quest for totality within the framework of modern philosophy, and their attempts entail an acknowledgment of a spontaneity or dynamical aspect of human reason (and in Leibniz's case, of nature as a whole). On the basis of modern principles, Leibniz reintroduced concepts of substance and the whole, not as fully actualized forms, but as the products or ideal limits of spontaneous and dynamical processes. Kant sees in the work of this great synthetic mind a role for the metaphysical demands of reason, but also the danger of a lapse into "dogmatism." The achievement of a cognitive totality (of the totally determined individual substance all of whose attributes are known adequately) is the Leibnizian ideal of theoretical understanding which is, in Kant's view, valid only for a divine understanding.[13]

Again Kant suspects an internal difficulty within Leibniz's formulation of a modern metaphysical position—a contradiction between the goal of emancipation or self-rule, appropriate to a "finite" being, and the postulation of an object of total cognition. But the Leibnizian endeavor is in many ways the model for Kant's—to account for the metaphysical striving of reason within the framework of the modern emancipatory project.[14] In Kant's view, to grant a certain irreducibility to such striving is also to give a certain place to rational autonomy: reason is not merely an inert instrument that responds to the dictates of passion or sentiment. In some way, reason prescribes its own object; it spontaneously originates the goal of wholeness. If one can grant that reason is the origin of its own goal, then one can begin to justify rationally the final goal of philosophy or science.

The Critique of Instrumental Reason

The critique of theoretical cognition must be understood within the context of such concerns. As I argue in more detail below, the function of Kant's metaphysical and epistemological inquiries is not well described by the most frequent characterizations in the scholarship. The "critique" is not primarily an effort to place Newtonian science on a more secure foundation, nor is it primarily an effort to secure the "objectivity" of science or ordinary cognition against the skeptical threat of Humean arguments. One must go back to the issue of the teleology of reason to determine sufficiently the aim of Kant's "transcendental" arguments.

In the critique of theoretical cognition as it relates to the epistemological thought of his modern predecessors, Kant's starting points are (1) reason is driven by its own nature to seek a total determination of the whole of the knowable, including the first causes of the whole; (2) philosophy in the past, while attempting to base a secure science of philosophy on the most immediate and evident sources of certainty, is driven at the same time to arrive at a determination of the whole by these means; and (3) the result is a "dialectic" in which reason comes into conflict with itself.[15] The cognitive determinations of the whole are inconsistent with the movement toward self-grounding autonomy that is evident in modern philosophy's turn to consciousness and freedom.[16]

Stated in other terms, Kant believes that the modern employment of the "immanent" certainties that are well suited for grounding a universal and necessary science (one that owes nothing to the contingencies of the "real" as "given") has been "uncritical." In various ways, modern rationality has confounded itself through insufficient regard for the role that reason, as spontaneous and self-legislative, must play in determining the end and the scope of valid employment for the instruments of modern methodology. Most characteristically, modern philosophy turns either to intuitive certainties immediately given to consciousness (mathematical or merely "empirical" and perceptual) or to logic for the determination of the knowable. In both cases, reason proceeds as though these obviously attractive sources of evidence could be employed as an organon to extend human knowledge even in the realm of ultimate ends or to attain its highest object, metaphysical totality. The modern philosophers developed a whole array of procedures whereby reason discovers "analytically" the ultimate elements of knowledge in simple and intuitive certainties and then advances with them "synthetically" towards the construction or reconstruction of the knowable whole.[17] Kant's transcendental critique is centrally a criticism of the view that such procedures give reason a true organon in the knowledge of most concern to reason—the knowledge of ends.[18]

All of Kant's critical philosophy, as an account of reason, is a critique of instrumental reason, either from a moral or a theoretical standpoint. From the latter standpoint, the critique is an investigation of the limits of past approaches to metaphysical inquiry and a determination of the possible context, defined by human reason itself, for all such inquiry. In Kant's view, the reliance of earlier philosophers on the ultimate elements of knowledge—intuitive or logical and conceptual—has not enabled them to determine the context of possible metaphysical inquiry. They have assumed that the final objects or goals of such inquiry—the ideas of the whole—are accessible to human determination and thus that they are in some sense real and "given."[19] Kant regards that assumption as natural to our human reason and predisposing it to dialectical error. And in his view this assumption must infect modern philosophical thinking as much as ancient, until modern philosophy becomes truly self-critical. What all earlier approaches in metaphysics lacked was a prior critique or "propaedeutic" to metaphysical inquiry which would determine the total context of possible knowledge. Such a total context is not available through the analysis of our knowledge into its most secure and evident elements. Indeed, the use of such elements presupposes the context of possible knowledge. But the latter can be defined only by way of a novel "transcendental" inquiry.[20]

Such an inquiry is of unusual difficulty and obscurity, for it attempts to define the conditions of the employment of the various forms of thought that we must use as instruments in any inquiry. Thus it crucially must investigate the question: How is logic possible?[21] In attempting to uncover something more "ultimate" than logic, we seem in some sense to transcend what defines for us an ultimate limit upon our thinking—its obedience to the "laws" of logic. The "transcendental deduction" of these most ultimate conditions of thought especially turns upon the issue of the possibility of logic, and indeed Kant's deduction is the core of a new kind of logic he calls "transcendental." In uncovering the conditions of ordinary logic we are exposing the context of the "discursive mind" for which alone, as far as we can tell, such logical forms as we have are useful and meaningful.[22]

At the same time, we uncover that there are certain basic notions of "objectivity" (the pure concepts or categories) implicit in all logical thought. These, too, by implication, are limited to the same discursive context. But it has been the tendency of all past philosophy to suppose that such pure concepts have a knowable application in some other context, that is, reality "in itself" as it may exist for any sort of mind—human or divine. This tendency is equivalent to the "naïve" use of logic as a means to extend our knowledge to things in themselves without a prior reflection upon the conditions of the application of this basic instrument of human thought. To regard this instrument as the ultimate determinant of the knowable is not a willful or foolish error but is evidence for an intrinsic "self-forgetting" that belongs to the use of any instrument of thought.

The basic intent of Kant's "Transcendental Deduction of the Categories" is to show that the categories (the notions of "objectivity" underlying all scientific knowledge and ordinary experience) both are necessary for defining the context of possible knowledge for minds such as ours ("discursive") and have no application beyond that context—they are limited to the very same realm they help make possible.[23] The argument has one aim: to uncover a well-defined and perspicuous function for the basic "pure concepts" that all metaphysics strives to understand and elaborate—substance, causality, unity, existence, possibility, necessity, and so forth. Kant's concern is not with securing objectivity for our concepts in general, for the purpose of overcoming skepticism about the validity of our ordinary perception or judgments about objects. The rationale for his peculiar inquiry is found in the metaphysical striving to determine the pure concepts and in what seems to Kant to be the evident failure of all such striving.[24] Transcendental inquiry starts from a telos given in reason—its striving for wholeness or complete satisfaction. The "deduction" of the valid use of the pure concepts is the principal part of the "propaedeutic" that will ground a new culture in which human reason will truly satisfy that striving, nondialectically. The propaedeutic makes clear that this striving cannot be satisfied theoretically. For in their valid theoretical use, the pure concepts do not define "unconditioned wholes" but merely supply conditions for the synthesis of intuitions and concepts in ordinary judgments made by discursive minds.

In a startling way, Kant claims to disclose an error that undermines all previous forms of philosophy, ancient and modern. Both the premodern assumption of a knowable natural whole that defines the fully satisfying object of the human mind and the effort of modern philosophy to employ methodical means for the aim of emancipating the mind from the given whole (while constructing a new whole congenial to the aims of mastery) partake of this error. It is not enough to characterize the error as "uncritical use of methods in metaphysical inquiry." More accurately and profoundly, the error, in Kant's estimation, is one of assuming that nature, in some form, determines the total context for the use of human reason. All earlier philosophy (and human reason naturally) assumes a teleological view of things wherein final purposes are already defined and given for man as rational. In modern philosophy this takes usually the more attenuated form of turning to passion, sentiment, or, broadly speaking, human nature for the defining context.[25] Kant would point out that reason must itself define the context for itself and that it has a far more comprehensive role, as the legislator of its own employment, than previously noted.

This insistence on a comprehensive (noninstrumental) role of reason is far from being an abandonment of the fundamental modern drive to emancipation or a return to a premodern view of reason as contemplative. It is a new affirmation of the modern effort at emancipation. All the same, it arises out of a reflection, over several decades, on how that effort has inherent difficulties that have produced a "crisis" in which reason discloses itself as the principal source of human quandaries. And in anticipation of later discussion, it can be said that it was chiefly Rousseau who brought this crisis to Kant's attention.

The emphasis in Kant on a dialectic of reason and on a natural waywardness or self-forgetting in human reason, may well remind us of the "aporetic" beginning in philosophy to which Plato and Aristotle make constant reference. Yet one can point to two major differences between the Kantian aporetic and the ancient one. In the first place, the Kantian aporetic is the account of perplexities arising from reason's pursuit of a dogmatic interest, and that interest is fundamentally respected rather than criticized by Kant. Put more precisely, metaphysics begins for Kant not in wonder (nor in an "erotic" quest) but in a dogmatic striving of reason for moral and religious certainties. In its critically disciplined form, which avoids the errors of speculative metaphysics, first philosophy provides the true foundations for religious and moral certainties. The nature of philosophizing is not for Kant an interest in advancing insight untrammeled by moral and practical presuppositions. Kant, in agreement with the dominant trend of modern philosophy, asserts that preconceived and foundational practical interests must place limits on and give the decisive goals to theoretical inquiry.[26] The common moral reason has demands for certainty whose legitimacy and urgency are not placed in question by Kant. On this he is altogether different from the ancient Socratics, whose open-ended dialectic cannot be tolerated by Kant, even though their dialectic is a nondogmatic search for knowledge of the human good and hence practical in nature. On the contrary, the primacy of the practical for Kant requires that metaphysics become a secure science, with unquestionable foundations, in order to secure the ground for moral reason. Metaphysics must become a closed and completed science, and thus the perplexities that animate its inquiries, as well as their solutions, must have a wholly perspicuous character.

This difference points directly to the second one. For the sake of such perspicuity and completeness in metaphysics, the dialectical perplexities at its beginning must be viewed as arising entirely from within reason rather than from the nature of things apart from the mind. Thus Kant asserts that it *must* be possible to arrive at definitive answers to these perplexities, for they "are imposed on reason by its own nature, and not by the nature of things which are distinct from it."[27] This assertion expresses again the practical demands at the origins of metaphysics. Those demands are, above all, that reason have the assurance that it can rule itself and determine ends for itself freely without the self-obstructions of dialectic. It can have that assurance only if the dialectic can be definitively resolved. In the interest of the closure of the dialectic, Kant postulates the origination of the metaphysical problems in reason as a human faculty, rather than in the nature of things themselves. The "Analytic" and "Dialectic" of the "Transcendental Logic" would make transparent the emergence of these problems from rational necessities and their resolution.

The Kantian demand for a closed and completed science of metaphysics, grounded in the immanent realm of the certainties of consciousness, surely is more in the spirit of Descartes than of Socrates. The aim of all modern foundations that seek such closure is a practical one—to create and secure a lasting nomos of human autonomy. The creation of such a new world entails the distrust of the natural telos of the mind toward truth, insofar as the pursuit of a natural love of inquiry offers no assurance of coming to stable and definitive results. The practical urgencies that guide modern philosophy necessitate the construction of an avowedly artificial world—one that supplants the disorderly "natural" proliferation of doctrines and beliefs generating discord, fanaticism, and conditions hostile to free self-determination.[28]

The Crisis in the Relation of Metaphysics
to Common Reason

While it is perhaps very un-Socratic to elevate any form of assumed practical goal above the unfettered pursuit of the truth, which is ultimately to liberate one from the "cave" of opinion, Kant nonetheless sees himself as a kind of Socratic.[29] Surely Socrates dwelt on the central importance and inescapable character of the moral and political problems, while all the same rejecting any solutions of them that prevailing practical life, or common opinion, proposed. Kant's Socratism, on the other hand, is a defense of the solutions proposed by common reason against the understanding of the practical necessities offered by a "corrupt" form of theory that claimed to speak for the common reason. That corrupt theory attributes to common reason, and to all reason, only an instrumental view of reason's concerns. Kant's Socratism does not liberate from the "cave," but claims to restore the "cave" to its pristine and wholesome foundations. This Socratism is a liberation of the cave from the corruptions of a misguided reason or false philosophy. As such it establishes a theme, and a tone, for much later philosophy as self-criticism of reason: philosophy becomes the defender of the "life-world" or common reason, whose bases are ultimately some form of the sacred. Such a project, however, assumes something very questionable from the standpoint of ancient Socratic wisdom—that philosophy and the sacred (or the "cave") are fundamentally in harmony and that philosophy can even ground the sacred for all of common life.

Thus Kant's thought, although it is a critique inspired by Rousseau of the earlier Enlightenment account of the relation of reason to common life, is in the end a more ambitious form of Enlightenment thinking than any that had appeared before. It undertakes a more drastic re-creation of the "cave" than any thinker had undertaken before—in the name of common reason itself. For the earlier Enlightenment had maintained the view that certain aspects of common life must remain basically intractable to rational legislation. The greater expectations that Kant attaches to the rational self-legislation present in common reason must be connected, as we shall see, with his rejection of the elements of an enduring "human nature" in earlier modern philosophy, which acted as a kind of limit on the reformative ambitions of philosophy.[30]

Aspects of modern philosophic and scientific doctrine and their application to society could indeed provoke Kant and many of his contemporaries to question whether the advance of reason in modern life had been all for the good of man as moral, social, and intellectual being. Kant, in a number of important passages, speaks of the relation of philosophy to society or of metaphysics to common reason, as having reached the point of crisis in his time. Kant writes that various forms of modern speculation are generating unsound and "pernicious" doctrines incompatible with a moral understanding of human life and the natural whole. Thus "materialism, fatalism, free-thinking, fanaticism and superstition, which can be injurious universally," form the list of diseases fostered by uncritical philosophical thought.[31] It notably contains the extreme wings with respect to the religious question. Both extremes undermine the free self-legislation of sound common reason; both extremes are "dogmatic" accounts of the whole in which freedom has no place. Dogmatism is the most natural tendency of the mind in speculations about the whole. Although the philosophic schools may entertain skeptical or "indifferentist" doctrines, these have no enduring hold on human reason, even for their creators.[32] They can help, however, to precipitate a "scandal among the masses," an adoption by the masses of extremist and fanatical positions in response to the dialectical uncertainties of speculative thought, once these pass beyond the lecture halls of the academy. Skepticism is the reflective and rare response to the confusing melee of doctrines; fanaticism is the unreflective and far more common one.[33] Whereas the former is at home in the Schools, the latter threatens to overthrow every form of public order, including the legal foundations of the state.[34]

In Kant's view the source of the present crisis that threatens to worsen is a disorder in philosophic reflection on first principles that is inseparable from a profound theoretical error about the relation of metaphysical reason to common moral reason. Only "a thorough investigation of the rights of speculative reason," that is, philosophical "criticism" of reason, can sever the growth of fanaticism at its root; the first obligation of philosophy is to "deprive metaphysics, once and for all, of its injurious influence by attacking its errors at their very source."[35] In other words, speculative thought has a vocation, beyond the acquisition of knowledge, to provide secure moral foundations for humanity.

The first phase of the current disorder is "decay of the human understanding," by which Kant seems to mean an incapacity, induced by erroneous habits of thought, to think clearly about the foundations of knowledge.[36] Yet such decay is perhaps the necessary prelude to the discovery of genuine criticism in speculative thought; Kant expresses the belief that a general self-dissolution of the sciences will precede their rebirth upon true foundations.[37] This account of a sequence of dissolution and renewal takes on the specific and technical form of a speculative dialectic in the shape of "antinomies." These prove to be the saving grace of philosophy, compelling it to take the theoretical approach consistent with reason's moral vocation. The precise articulation of the perplexities of speculation in a dialectical logic is the unexpected outcome of the crisis in reason, which can provide the principle for the overcoming of that crisis—assuming that philosophical criticism comes to the rescue soon enough, preempting a general collapse of reason and civility. Thus the discovery of the antinomies may be "the most fortunate perplexity" ever to befall reason.[38] The present age then has the historical significance of being the moment when reason, through the extremity of crisis, is enabled to uncover the principle of its own internal coherence and order. Past ignorance of that principle has prevented reason from achieving its ultimate goal—the secure foundations for human moral striving.

All the same, until the dialectic of reason is definitively resolved and humanity enlightened about the salutary outcome for its moral beliefs, the present age is especially fraught with dangers. Speculative thought has already so beclouded the ordinary man's sense of his own moral vocation that "the natural bases of man have become unrecognizable."[39] The latter remark occurs in the context of Kant's most extensive meditations on Rousseau's critique of the modern enlightenment. But from these meditations Kant draws the conclusion that philosophy, which has introduced new ills into human life and exposed its own weakness, must be able to cure those ills and convert its weakness into strength. In no previous age could philosophy or metaphysics have been so aware of its duty and its ability to secure the "true and lasting welfare of the human race."[40] Metaphysics is empowered by the modern crisis to attain a new level of insight into the unity of its theoretical bases and its practical vocation. Indeed, the very fact that "human nature" itself has become problematic is a crucial ingredient of the establishing of the new foundations.[41] The dissolution of the authority of all merely empirical concepts of the human good is a condition for the assumption by autonomous reason of full responsibility for the legislation both of reason's internal coherence and of the highest good as the ideal goal of moral striving.

The crisis created by metaphysical thought for common reason will come to an end happily only if the principle for the legislation of internal coherence in reason is as available to the common reason itself as it is to the critical philosopher. The erection of the new order upon the ashes of the older orders needs a universal base, for in Kant's view the destruction of the old orders is complete and irreversible. There is no possibility now of restricting metaphysical speculation to the confines of academies. Kant needs to demonstrate that the highest principles of concern to all "finite rational beings" can be found in the common reason and the maxims it actively employs. Yet this must be asserted with a qualification: these principles can be found there to the extent that common reason has not been corrupted by speculative doctrines. This entails that the general devastation of the old dogmatisms is compatible with preservation of sound moral principles in common reason. Kant cannot hope to find guidance out of the crisis from common reason, if this is not the case. On the other hand, there would be no crisis if common reason were not endangered by the dialectic of speculative thought. The delicate position Kant hopes to define here is that critical philosophy is required only to buttress the basically sound tendencies of common reason.[42] Such a heuristic relation of philosophy to common reason is a theme of much of the eighteenth century. The turn to "common sense," accompanied by a skeptical approach to metaphysics and a rejection of the ultimacy of scientific concepts for the account of ordinary experience, is found in a number of thinkers. It reflects awareness of a crisis in the relation of metaphysics to common reason that surely extends beyond Rousseau and Kant.[43]

Kant believes he finds in common reason, uncorrupted by speculation, a sound dogmatic foundation on which to determine the structure of reason, at least as regards its determining telos. Common reason is not guilty of "dogmatism" in the pejorative speculative sense, that is, the concern with determining the function and the end of reason on the basis of a prior account of nature as a whole. Again it only becomes inclined to unhealthy dogmatism when exposed to the sophistry of speculation.[44] Well before his decisive encounter with Rousseau, Kant appeals to sound moral reason over the claims of speculative science as a criterion in the central question of "theodicy." This is an interesting feature of one of the earliest fragments of Kant known to us—some notes on the problem of "optimism" composed for a prize question announced by the Berlin Academy. Against the arguments of Leibniz, which Kant complains reveal that our world is the "best of all possible worlds" only to the most sophisticated theoreticians, Kant asserts that common reason must possess an answer it can understand to the question most pressing to it: Is the virtuous or the vicious man happier in this world? The only adequate theodicy is one that answers the question unambiguously (as Leibniz's assuredly does not), and furthermore that answer must be on the plane of the common reason that raises the question. Some of the earliest philosophizing of Kant thus shows that from the beginning, Kant regarded the philosopher as having the primary task of confirming and even grounding the moral man's view of the world.[45]

Nonetheless it is also in relatively early writings that Kant exposes some of the difficulties standing in the way of such a confirmation of the moral view of the world. These go beyond the obvious fact that disease, death, earthquakes, accidents, and other natural evils afflict good and bad alike. The most serious difficulty arises from the human will itself and its apparently nonteleological character. The human rational will knows no object that, within the natural order, satisfies its restless striving. Thus it is doubtful that one can reasonably look for a happiness, at least as earthly happiness, that corresponds to the just claims of a moral will for confirmation of its worth. It seems that the natural whole as we know it is incapable of containing or supporting the moral order.[46]

From such considerations more than one conclusion might be drawn. One might argue: if the primary question for man must be the theodicy question, and theoretical reason is incapable of answering that question, then theoretical inquiry must be regarded as a secondary matter or even rejected as pernicious. Or one might argue: theoretical inquiry remains a worthy concern of man, but must not undertake what is impossible for it, that is, the justification of the moral view of the world. Both of these positions have very respectable defenders throughout the Western tradition, but Kant chooses neither one. Kant regards the simple rejection of theoretical reason as entailing, at least in the modern world, the wholesale rejection of reason and thus the destruction of the civilized order. He sees signs of such rejection emerging in his time and opposes them.[47] On the other hand, as a defender of the life of theoretical inquiry, Kant assigns to it, even more clearly and dramatically after studying Rousseau, the primary task of justifying the moral view of the world. Although no traditional or past form of theoretical reason can fulfill this task, Kant discovers eventually the "critical" form that can do so.

This form of inquiry succeeds, in Kant's view, in grounding a legitimate version of metaphysical thought and in securing the dictates of sound moral reason against sophistical speculation by means of an adequate delimitation of the spheres of speculative and moral reason.[48] All the same, moral reason, not "pure theory," provides the guiding principles for this delimiting. A new description of rationality, in which self-legislative freedom is the defining core, offers the key to the whole structure of reason—a structure directed toward actualizing the moral view of the world. But Kant's pre-Rousseauian views on common moral reason could not supply him with this account of reason. Rousseau provides Kant with insights into the nature of reason of a twofold character: (1) reason, in a profounder fashion than Kant previously thought, is the source of obstacles to justifying the moral view; (2) at the same time, reason is at its core "freedom," so a nontheoretical form of reason exists that can justify the moral understanding of the order of the world. Kant finds the elements of his response to the "counterenlightenment" from Rousseau—such that Rousseau himself would not easily recognize his own thought in Kant's theodicy of reason.[49]

Rousseau's Protest against Modern Enlightenment

Rousseau and Kant are the greatest early figures in a movement of thought that expresses a powerful protest, indeed often a feeling of revulsion, against the spirit and aim of modern philosophy and whose later flowering is Romantic thought and German speculative idealist philosophy. The thinkers in this by no means homogeneous "movement" are united by their tendency to see in earlier modernity a spirit of "low individualism," grounded in passion and self-interest—a spirit that fails to combine legitimate demands of the human soul for freedom and autonomy with its "higher needs" for "wholeness," "community," and profound dedication to the noble and the sacred.[50] The objection was that the founders of the modern rational reform of society had placed the foundations of both philosophic inquiry and civil life chiefly in the pursuit of private satisfactions of mostly bodily needs and that they had understood "freedom" principally as the freedom to pursue such satisfactions with minimal interference from state, religion, or even moral law. Again the problem is that the earlier modern view makes reason, or even the soul, chiefly an instrument of the body.

Surely the great minds instituting such reform found their highest personal satisfactions to be connected with inquiry, although their metaphysical principles may be unable to account adequately either for that satisfaction or for the dedication to humanitarian projects. In any case, they were content to regard whatever import philosophy may have for the life of the mind as the preserve of a few. For the masses of men it was the largely practical or even material benefits of their discoveries that justified the activity of the philosophers, and the philosophers themselves made such "utility" the ground for a certain rapprochement between the philosophers and society. The unified and cooperative project directed toward the mastery of nature for the relief of man's estate could provide the philosophers with a degree of respectability, security, and peace of mind, not to mention glory, such as they had never enjoyed in any society before. The character of society itself had to be transformed by this new project—otherworldly or quixotic strivings for salvation or immortality must give way to concern with the secular and tangible benefits of peace and bodily well-being. But surely it was not the ambition of the great reformers who truly originated "Enlightenment"—Bacon, Descartes, Hobbes, Locke, Spinoza and Leibniz—to universalize philosophy itself, or the higher freedom of mind it provides. Their expectations concerning the reformability of man and society were in a profound sense moderate.[51]

Indeed these early modern thinkers tended to suppose that just as the foundations of civil life were largely passionate and certainly never to become wholly "rational," so also civil life would always contain a residue of intractable devotions, attachments, and sentiments that would, for good or ill, focus on the sacred. The point of reform is to make the passions connected with the sacred less dangerous and less likely to be the dominating force in the institutions of society. Yet such thinkers only tolerate this residue; they do not regard it highly, much less share in the veneration. Philosophy per se is distant from such concerns and at least inwardly detached and critical. Philosophy and sacred attachment are such different things that one cannot reasonably hope for either (1) a complete supplanting of the sacred element in society by a philosophical spirit, or (2) a form of philosophizing that would re-create, on its own level, the experience of the sacred, and not threaten the sacred element of social life but ground it on a new principle.

If the more extreme philosophes of the eighteenth century tended to harbor hopes of the first variety, it is the movement coming in the wake of Rousseau that is animated by the second hope. As we shall see, Kant's account of the end of reason in terms of freedom is above all aiming to reconcile the modern emancipatory goal with a new grounding of the sacred and noble. This new telos, already evident in the writings of the 1760s, is directly related to the most novel features of the transcendental approach to philosophy: its use of a new kind of "deduction" to uncover the context of discursivity for all inquiry, and its rejection of past philosophy as uncritically and recklessly aiming to "extend" theoretical science. Not theoretical insight but the free self-determining will provides the highest organon of philosophy. The character and aim of philosophy undergo a most remarkable change, such that philosophy becomes less distinguishable in crucial ways from the defense of the noble and sacred. The latter, on the other hand, are no longer understood as principally rooted in the element in which earlier philosophy placed them—the human passions that are political, exclusive, and concerned with various forms of love of self and the extensions of oneself in family and society. For

Kant and his "idealist" successors, the noble and the sacred become philosophical.

Not all of these changes in the meaning of philosophy are visible in Rousseau's thought, but their sources are in his criticism of earlier modern philosophy. It is necessary to stress that Rousseau's attack on earlier modernity is based on modern principles. It thus provides the basic model for the later efforts to "elevate" the modern world—the recovery of the noble and the sacred must enhance, not inhibit, the modern drive toward individuality and freedom. Yet Rousseau, unlike most of his successors in this, is aware of profound and perhaps irresoluble tensions between modern freedom and the task of "recovery." Kant, by contrast, attempts to make the argument that only a securing of the noble will enable modern reason to resolve conflicts and pursue the goal of emancipation successfully. Again, this is why Kant is not really "torn" between what may seem at first to be conflicting aspects of his thought—the destruction of the older "dogmatic" bases of morality and theology, and his "critical" formulation of a "moral world," with its new approach to the "supersensible."

The year 1750 marks the first philosophical publication of Rousseau. It is the opening statement in that great series of works presenting the most searching inquiry hitherto undertaken into the moral and spiritual health of the society built on the modern principles.[52] Rousseau's works, on the surface appearing to be chiefly a "cultural criticism" of modern civilization, at a profounder level address the foundations of all civilization and therewith the status of reason itself. The central question is whether the rational advance of the human species toward greater freedom and autonomy from nature, God, and man is compatible with the moral well-being and happiness of the species. Understood correctly, Rousseau's argument is that the advance cannot be undone or reversed, and any changes in the condition of man must now be made on the basis of modern insights. The development of reason has irrevocably altered man's relation to the bases of moral and political life.

The element of custom and of primary attachments to the sacred, upon which all healthy moral and political life must rest, is inherently vulnerable to the progress of reason. Thus the periods of healthy customary foundation for moral-political life are relatively short and rare in the history of any society. But the modern development of reason has altered the character of the customary basis so radically as to render questionable the possibility of any future periods of sound moral and political life. Thus previously unknown dangers to man's psychic and moral well-being have arisen accordingly. More precisely, the development of reason has torn away a veil of illusion that until recently surrounded and protected the foundations of human social existence. Scientific reason has arrived at a certain peak of self-consciousness wherein man's true nature as primordially individualistic and self-interested has been exposed to the glaring light of day. This revolution in human self-understanding cannot be reversed. Yet Rousseau does not hesitate to assert that the exposure of this truth by science makes evident how problematic reason itself is. Certainly it causes one to wonder how sound is the assumption of modern Enlightenment, that there is a fundamental harmony between the advance of reason and the health of society. The combination of doubt of this assumption, together with affirmation of the truth of the modern accounts of the amoral or immoral origins of human moral-political life, could result in Rousseau's having a largely pessimistic view of the human future.

The modern development of reason is, on a practical level, inseparable from a pursuit of freedom and individual well-being on a scale never before seen. In Rousseau's time it is beginning to damage, perhaps irreparably, the texture of traditions, institutions, and ways of life that foster love of duty, dedication to the "whole," and self-restraint necessary for the inculcation of such virtues. The modern theoretical insight has buttressed and furthered this development of "individualism," if it has not simply created it. Yet Rousseau believes that the very extremity of the modern development, the apparent loss under modern conditions of certain higher forms of humanity and experience, may make possible the creation of a new kind of humanity. It would be able to re-create, on the basis of new principles, certain premodern virtues and experiences. On the practical level, the unfettered individualism of modern man contains certain seeds of its self-destruction; the passionate striving for freedom and self-fulfillment in fact leads to greater dependence of individuals on one another, for the growth of artificial needs entails the increase of dependence on one's fellow man to satisfy such needs. That is accompanied, of course, by greater spiritual enslavement to the needs themselves. A legitimate response to this situation of man's enslavement to his own creations is a demand for genuine freedom—a more extreme individualism in which the individual tries to reduce his servitude to the social order itself.

On the other hand, the higher theoretical consciousness of modern times might also bring about some remedy, if only its arguments are carried out more radically. Rousseau holds that earlier modern thinkers on the origins of morality and society did not in their reflections go back to the true state of nature, and they assumed that man's passionate nature was his original nature. Thereby the passionate individualism of modern life received a blessing from an erroneous view of a primordial human passionateness—natural fear of death, greed, violence, and love of glory and victory. But the modern account of the origins is only half true; the original human condition was indeed individualistic, but it lacked the malignant passions, and indeed all passion. Rousseau argues that from the consideration that social life is acquired, one concludes that the chief causes of social life, the passions, are also acquired and not natural. Original man lacks all interest in his fellow humans, which could give rise to fear, envy, and competition. The passions have at most a latent existence, for they eventually arise through the awakening of capacities that surely distinguish men from other animals—capacities for speech, self-awareness, imagination of the future, and for comparison of oneself with others. But even these capacities are problematically natural and do not themselves define a concept of "human nature."[53]

Therefore on both a practical and theoretical level, the modern development may point to an overcoming of the ills it has instituted. It may do so through a combination of theoretical insights that establish the possibility of a prepassionate form of individualism, and of practical exigencies that awaken longings for such a "higher" form of individualism. Indeed, it may be possible that genuine social virtue (not merely the self-serving agreeableness of the modern individualist) may be built on the love of freedom itself, if that love of freedom is kept distinct from the pursuit of unfettered acquisitiveness and, in general, from the satisfaction of "artificial" desires.[54]

Kant was deeply affected by the theses of Rousseau—that virtue and freedom may be reconcilable, that they may have a common ground in a nonpassionate source, and that it may be a peculiar "dynamism" and modifiability of human reason that create the ills of the social passions and that may overcome them as well. It was above all in *Emile* that Kant found certain elements of a new kind of virtue, based on the free self-legislation of a rational will that preserves autonomy through this legislation. For it is in this work that Rousseau gives a foundation to virtue by means of a profound educational device—the employment of the demand for freedom to combat the acquisition of harmful passions forging dependence on others, especially all passions relating to amour-propre. A salutary individualism can thus conquer, or forestall, a corrupting and enervating individualism of passionate self-interest. Virtue can be recovered on a thoroughly modern basis. Such a reconstruction of virtue entails a rejection of the ancient foundations of moral and political virtue in the intensifying of human dependence on the social whole through habit and custom, enforced by praise and blame. For the effectiveness of the latter presupposes the acquisition of amour-propre and therewith the principal root of the passions. Furthermore, the new foundation of virtue in a more radical demand for independence makes possible a kind of virtue that is compatible with experiences of solitude, intimacy, and free expression of "self" or individuality that are excluded or not promoted by the ancient foundations.

In spite of very great differences between Rousseau's account of virtue in *Emile*, and Kant's version, Kant is indebted to that account for its view of the modifiability of human nature, such that passionateness is neither the most fundamental nor the most unchanging feature of what is human, and for the role it ascribes to a certain "dynamism" of reason in that modifiability. In fact one could say that it is as much for its suggestion of a wholly new approach to reason as for its account of virtue that *Emile* has such importance for Kant.[55] One can summarize by saying that Kant finds in Rousseau the suggestion that humanity itself, through the development of reason, inflicts on itself all the forms of "alienation" tending to destroy both freedom and virtue. And that it is also reason, in a certain self-legislative form (as the source of autonomy), that can restore humanity to wholeness and soundness, uniting freedom and virtue.[56]

Essential to the entire Rousseauian conception of reason is (1) the departure from "nature," in its passionate early modern version, as the source of either freedom or virtue, and (2) the introduction of a new kind of rationality. The importance of these innovations for the transcendental self-limitation of reason lies in this: only a form of rationality whose essence is to seek independence from nature supplies a reliable principle for the unification and self-consistency of the human faculties. In the account of reason as instrumental or subservient to passionate human nature, reason has no reliable guidance from something that is itself internally coherent. Rousseau shows how reason as subordinate to such "nature" is exposed to self-contradiction and "dialectic." All the same, it is the modern "dialectical" development and its erosion of premodern virtue that make possible the discovery of the true character of reason.

Yet it must be said now that Rousseau does not break all ties with the earlier modern view of nature, and in this area there is still a large gulf between Rousseau and Kant. Some of the subtleties of this complex issue are discussed later. For the moment only a couple of major points are noted. In the first place, reason never loses its instrumental character in Rousseau's efforts to form the human soul according to new ideas of virtue. Indeed the educational project of *Emile* makes use of natural inclinations and even passions in creating a soul structure. Individual autonomy is preserved through an artificial and complicated structuring and redirecting of passions: amour-propre is employed in beneficial ways, such as the inculcation of taking pride in active benevolence; amour-propre can become the moving force of virtue, if it is not allowed to degenerate into the entanglements of vanity.[57] Whereas Kant offers similar proposals for the utility of vanity, competitiveness, and pride in the advancement of human talents and powers, there is yet this difference with Rousseau: the ultimate source of human pride or dignity is an unequivocally autonomous rational power, for which there is little or no place in Rousseau's account of reason. In the last analysis, Rousseau partially agrees with an instrumental view of reason. Freedom, rather than a characteristic of autonomous agency, is a condition of unobstructed achievement of the ends of passion and desire.

Rousseau departs from his earlier modern predecessors in proposing that the most primordial condition of desire is nonpassionate, and that the "ideal" of freedom corresponds to the unobstructed pursuit of prepassionate desire. This change is of momentous importance, for it ascribes a certain dynamic and originative function to reason as the source of the transformation of man from the prepassionate to the passionate condition; this drastically alters what the "instrumentality" of reason means. The rational pursuit of the ends of desire is not an unproblematic and fixed principle. On the contrary, the rational (as opposed to prerational) pursuit entails the creation of passions and the erosion of freedom. The problem of securing freedom for rational and social man is that of artificially instituting a telos for the acquired passions, since their "natural" development cannot be trusted, even to the limited degree that earlier modern "natural right" doctrines trust the natural direction of the passions.[58]

This difference between Rousseau and Kant is at the heart of their divergent estimations of the prospects of "enlightenment." The absence of rational autonomy in Rousseau is connected with his view of the impossibility of achieving genuine human emancipation on a large scale; the artificial devices of Emile's tutor are required for bringing the ordinary human being to something close to a condition of freedom within social life. The authority of "common reason" with its sure sense of duty is not present in Rousseau; the majority of mankind is enslaved to blinding passion, and in all likelihood it always will be. Reason's liberating power is limited; the philosopher is an exceptional being who only by a kind of miracle is less enslaved than others. It is not clear that his superiority is attributable to the strength of his reason. In any case, his condition of relative freedom of spirit is very rare and is not the goal of Rousseau's educational and political projects.[59]

The revolution that Rousseau thinks possible on his new principles might be characterized as new illusions for the majority of mankind (illusions of freedom based on new experiences of selfhood and individuality) and perhaps a genuine insight into nature, reserved for a few remarkable spirits. The new illusions are derived from the new insight to the extent that they are the sort of illusion possible after the destruction of the old orders, by the dissemination of modern enlightenment. In this respect, Rousseau shares a a belief with earlier thinkers that practical life has at all times a foundation in opinion or prejudice. By contrast, Kant looks forward to a complete emancipation of humanity from its self-inflicted bondage to prejudice.[60] It is the novelty of the prejudices, not the fact of relying on prejudice, that distinguishes Rousseau's doctrine from earlier thought.

Kant's ideal of a "moral world" is one of the asymptotic approach to a culture in which human emancipation is no longer an illusion but a reality, grounded in the efficacy of autonomous reason. It begins with Rousseau's account of the modifiability of reason and nature, but proceeds from there to give reason greater power to direct the transformation of both. Kant insists that to demonstrate the possibility of the moral world is the principal task of philosophy, for only thereby will the ideal of moral emancipation not be for us a mere illusion.[61] The "end of reason" is to satisfy the highest demand of reason—the demand for the reality of this ideal.

Kantian Philosophy
as Transcendental Practice

The preceding reflections point to a thesis, whose defense is the main task of the following chapters: Rousseau's critique of the possibility of subordinating reason to any notion of a determinate human nature is basic for Kant's whole conception of reason not only as moral, but as the architectonic principle for philosophy. The various stages of the argument emerge only if one looks closely at the writings between 1764 and 1780. Briefly the terminus ad quem, that is, the critical form of philosophy as "transcendental practice," can be reviewed.

At its most fundamental level, critical philosophy is a transcendental defense of a conception of reason as the supreme end-determining power. Crucial to that defense is the exposure of three errors committed by instrumental views of reason: (1) when such views subordinate reason to the project of achieving a sum of instinctual satisfaction called "happiness," they fail to note that the quest for such happiness is "chimerical" and that such happiness in principle is unattainable;[62] (2) all such views neglect what is most essential to human reason—its power to elevate human motives above inclination and passion, and therein to secure for human life the sole source of its "worth" and "dignity";[63] (3) they commit a profound theoretical error in failing to provide reason with an end-giving and end-legislating power, which alone can make possible a perspicuous unity and coherence of rational principles; thus they cannot do justice to the urgent "systematic" and "architectonic" tasks of reason.[64]

The most familiar features of this doctrine as a moral teaching— that only the free self-legislative will entitles finite rational beings to be considered "ends in themselves"[65] and to be the final end of all nature itself[66]—are simply the immediate foreground of a new ordering of reason as a whole. It is the case not only on the moral-practical plane of everyday deliberations, but also on the plane of philosophical deliberation, that reason seeks universality and necessity in its legislation of maxims. Reason must find the principle of such legislation in itself, since principles taken from external sources result only in contingently binding maxims. Nature apart from reason's lawgiving cannot give rise to the stringent universality of commands.[67] It also cannot give rise to the stringent coherence and unity of a system of reason as a whole.

In pursuit of fulfilling the fundamental telos of modern rationality to achieve human emancipation, Kant claims to find the principle for the ordering of reason that makes such pursuit "nondialectical," in "common reason." More precisely, he turns to a common reason that has within itself a demand for independence from natural determination; that demand alone can result in unity and coherence of principles. Reason as purely scientific or concerned only with the articulation of phenomena does not express that demand, although it must presuppose it. It is thus moral reason, present universally in human reason, that one consults for the highest legislative unity in reason. Accordingly Kant makes the astounding claim that "the idea of the legislation" of the philosopher is found in all men. This claim is connected with another one—that the interest in the metaphysical ideas is universal. For this latter claim means that the concern with metaphysical ideas is at bottom a striving of universal human reason for total emancipation, whose intent and significance are moral. Thus the full elaboration of what that striving is, and how it can be fulfilled, is nothing less than the whole philosophical system of reason. Common moral reason provides the telos and the guiding principle that compels reason to give up all subordination to nature. It thus makes possible the self-sufficient coherency of a rational system.[68]

The radicality of this account of reason, which breaks all or nearly all of the remaining ties of modern reason to an independent order of nature, receives the major impetus from Rousseau. But in order to rest everything rational on common reason understood as "freedom," Kant has to ascribe a unity and consistency to common reason that certainly is alien to Rousseau and, for that matter, to Socratic ancient philosophy. Common reason is the home of a coherent view of the noble and the sacred, on which the whole structure of reason can rest. What is more, Kant proposes a new role for ideas of the noble and the sacred as providing the most basic, or "transcendental," presupposition for all philosophy. Thus philosophy has to be above all else a defense of the noble and the sacred, for these make philosophy itself possible.[69]

Looked at a slightly different way, one could say that the principal concern of Kant's philosophy, and perhaps of all German idealist philosophy, is to reconcile the metaphysical "demand" for the "whole" with human freedom and autonomy, which reconciliation takes the form of a new doctrine of the end of reason. In at least Kant's case, this project assumes that moral freedom is (through the moral will) a "given" and, in some sense, a dogmatic starting point. The project takes the form of disclosing "transcendental" conditions for the coexistence of the facts of the demand for the whole and of human freedom. As moral freedom must have that foundational character, its internal soundness must be assured. Moral freedom becomes a touchstone against which one tests theoretical approaches for their soundness. Indeed a principal, if not the sole, preoccupation of the tradition emerging from Kant is to uphold the realm of human autonomy or of "practice" which expresses that autonomy against false forms of theory or "ideology." In this way the assumption is made, implicitly or explicitly, that the chief source of ills in human life is false forms of theory rather than incorrigible defects in human nature itself.

This new approach to the status of common moral reason and its concerns with the noble and the sacred, within the whole of philosophic reason, are connected with other major features of the German idealist tradition. Among these prominently are the recurrent treatments of "alienation" and "theodicy." The former emerges from the Kantian mode of arguing about evil that leads to the conclusion that the primary evils are humanly instituted and corrigible: man has enslaved himself to his own creations. This conclusion can be argued, however, only if there is a basic substrate or foundation of human goodness that has been corrupted by human doing; nature is not responsible for evils. Rousseau's presence in this line of thinking is easily discerned.[70]

At the same time, this account of evil as self-alienation is part of a "theodicy." For to show that human self-alienation is a necessary stage in a process leading to the conquest of evils (as an "ideal," if never fully actual condition) is to offer a certain justification for those evils. As we have seen, Kant regards the "decay" and "dialectic" of theoretical reason in his age as such a necessary condition for reason's self-rectification. But such thinking is more generally basic to his whole account of the system of reason and to the "ideal" of human rational development which it projects as the goal of history. The entire scheme rests on the view that reason's own dynamic "spontaneity" is at the origin of human ills and can also give grounds for hope of their overcoming. Reason's spontaneity brings about the "dialectical" opposition between freedom and ideas of the whole; that fundamental perplexity of modern reason is therefore not built incorrigibly into the nature of things themselves. Reason's alienating itself spontaneously and its discovering the source of internal coherence in this spontaneity are the content of the "theodicy of reason" in Kant. Furthermore, a fundamental source of this theodicy lies in Rousseau's denial of the fixity of nature and in his new approach to reason.

One can sum up by saying that Kant's discovery of a new order of reason bequeathed to the German idealist tradition these very basic themes: the primacy of reason as free and spontaneous (or "practical"), its self-alienating character, and its self-rectification according to a new "theodicy."[71] This view seems to make possible a new grounding of the sacred and the noble, and a new account of virtue whose essence is freedom. This alliance of modern freedom and a renewed sense of the sacred does, however, tend to take moral virtue out of its primary political context and to give it a new transpolitical or nonpolitical form. By claiming to be able to ground virtue and the sacred on philosophy alone, German thought produces the modern notion of "culture." Inevitably this notion has tended to undermine the older understanding of the political-moral virtues as grounded in incorrigibly prephilosophical attachments. One can say that the move from prephilosophic tradition to "culture" as the realm of moral freedom constitutes the essence of the German tradition of *Bildung*.[72]

The description of Kantian philosophy as transcendental practice refers, in the first place, to Kant's statements that the fundamental critique of the rational powers "levels the ground" of reason "to render it sufficiently secure for moral edifices."[73] But it intends more than this. For Kant's new form of "Socratism" goes beyond being a defense of the moral worldview held by common reason, through dismissing all "sophistical objections" to that view.[74] By arguing for the sufficiency of the deliverances of common reason and by drastically reducing the possibilities for theoretical knowledge, Kant would undercut the "ascent from the cave." Yet his turn to the primacy of practice is not intended to be antiphilosophic; it is meant to provide an alternative to the Platonic speculative striving on its own level. The new principle of the practical— the autonomy of reason—can alone ground the whole structure of reason and, in particular, satisfy the rational demand for the reality of ideas of totality. Ultimately Kant discloses that these metaphysical ideas are, for critically enlightened reason, only the outlines of endless projects wherein reason determines the moral and natural constitution of the human species according to an "ideal" of wholeness. Reason finds its final completion not in knowledge of a supersensible realm, but in the practical advance of humanity toward a consummate "culture."[75] Our concern now is to turn to the original sources and motives behind this conception of the structure and end of reason.

2
The Teleological Problem in Modern Individualism

Individualism and Moral Sense

Kant's critique of modern instrumental accounts of reason brings about, on a modern basis, a renewal of certain aspects of the classical autonomy of reason. We have yet to investigate this fact as well as Rousseau's contribution to this renewal.[1] But we should not suppose that these two thinkers were alone in their attempts to correct certain features of earlier modern thought. Indeed a cursory examination of the moral and political philosophies of the seventeenth and eighteenth centuries can quickly lead to the conclusion that the second of these centuries saw a number of attempts to ameliorate the seeming harshness or even inhumanity of modern thought. Some of these attempts are of much importance for Kant, prior to his epochal exposure to Rousseau's works. To understand the nature of the changes in modern thought sought by the "moral sense" writers, to whom the pre-Rousseauian Kant belongs as a moral thinker, some features of seventeenth-century doctrines must be recalled briefly.

The major philosophers of the seventeenth century are, by and large, the founders of a massive critique of classical and scholastic teleological thinking, in both natural and moral philosophy, and their efforts provide the foundations for new sciences of man frequently characterized by the following: (1) an account of reason as instrumental to the ends of passion, connected with a moral psychology stressing self-interest and a certain limitlessness or insatiability in the primary passions; (2) a denial of the possibility of prescribing final ends or goods which individuals or societies ought to pursue, connected with an account of the variability and indeterminacy of all accounts of happiness or the "highest good," and thus with a general dismissal of classical accounts of the final end of man as empty; (3) an effort to describe the conditions for the securing of external freedom to pursue the good however understood, which pursuit is endorsed as long as it is compatible with peace and respect for the limitations imposed on it by a freely created and "contractual" legal order.

44

This set of new principles is centrally directed against the classical view that the highest concern of political life, and of moral philosophy insofar as it can give some guidance to political life, is the formation of a virtuous character in the citizen. Such formation must solve the problem of how to habituate the sentient and appetitive parts of the soul so that the rational part can learn to exercise autonomous rule over the other parts—a rule to which it is by nature directed but which it does not simply possess by nature.[2] The modern approach is animated by the conviction of the desirability of reducing every human being's dependence on conceptions of ultimate ends or goods held by other human beings. For in the modern view, these conceptions, far from being natural and salutary, are largely conventional and often destructive. Let us not forget, though, that the modern emancipatory project is itself surely proposing an "end," or a new way of life, and that many difficulties in modern thought stem from a tension between the theoretical rejection of teleology and the implicit or explicit use of a new teleology.

This complex of notions, often going by the familiar denominations of "modern liberalism" or "individualism," is modified in certain respects by many eighteenth-century writers. Some authors ascribe more importance to natural "benevolent" or "sympathetic" strivings or sentiments, thus placing greater stress on various aspects of human sociality. Among such thinkers writing before Kant are a few who emphasize moral sentiments as providing the basis for unconditioned duties and who argue that social duties are not simply reducible to ulterior motives of self-interest. From another quarter, one hears a protest against the limitlessness and restlessness of modern acquisitive striving. If the dominant motive of humanity is preservation of existence, then existence must be good and desirable. But it is not good and desirable if characterized as a painful and futile quest for an ever-elusive satisfaction. In making this criticism, Rousseau looks back to Epicurean and other ancient accounts of equanimity as a counterpoise to modern enthrallment with the projects of practical mastery of nature and society. This, of course, is but one facet of Rousseau's complex attack on modernity. Both the moral sense doctrine and Rousseau's sympathy for ancient accounts of the complete and sufficient good are taken over by Kant. But they are radically transformed by other considerations which again come in large measure from Rousseau. The result, we shall see, is an account of moral imperatives that are based on rational self-legislation rather than sentiment and a new account of the highest good as the total satisfaction of the demands of an autonomous moral agent.

Yet in all such modifications of earlier positions, one fundamental assumption of modern thought remains intact. Insofar as man is considered an appetitive being who seeks to satisfy desire with the aid of reason, the content and the sum of goods that he seeks is indeterminate and neither to be described nor prescribed. The position is quite central to the rejection of classical teleology, and it applies equally to the moral sense theorists, Rousseau, and Kant. It applies to Rousseau, for he argues that equilibrium or contentment is thoroughly elusive to man as rational; it may be accessible, at least in pure form, only to prerational man. Kant tries to provide a rational foundation for the highest good and to unite in one concept modern antiteleology, a modern notion of a limitlessly striving reason, and the classical idea of a complete and sufficient good. The result is a new kind of teleology. An ultimate teleological ideal is an unavoidable concern of our reason, for the rational powers develop in a chaotic and conflicting way without the legislation of an organizing end. But this ideal originates solely in reason and not in the natural constitution of man or of the cosmos. Thus the revival of teleological thought in Kant is based on freedom and the spontaneity of reason, and preserves the modern assumption of the indeterminacy of the natural good.[3]

Even Kant's concerns with teleology in its aesthetic and organic embodiments derive from the principal ground of freedom. The "reflective judgment" that seeks out instances of unity in those realms, according to subjective ideas of purposiveness, is guided by reason's quest for unity between the laws of freedom and of nature. That quest is nothing other than the effort to realize the rationally legislated ideal of the highest good.[4] The concept of "happiness," which is a component of that ideal, has a necessary indeterminacy, and in this respect the new importance accorded to the summum bonum by Kant is consistent with the dominant thrust of modern liberalism. On the other hand, Rousseau's and Kant's distrust of the pursuit of happiness by instrumental reason and their demand for a supreme legislation organizing the pursuit of the good according to ideas of the "whole" good clearly bring them into a certain tension with liberalism.

For Kant, in sum, neither an individualistic antiteleology that falsely alleges to preserve freedom nor a metaphysical teleology that openly subverts freedom can adequately satisfy reason's highest demands. Kant's attempt to meet these demands with his doctrines of moral freedom and the highest good can be understood as a response to a crisis in modern individualism. It must be underlined that Kant fully assents to the most basic premises of that individualism: the goodness of the project of emancipating human strivings from a restrictive natural order, and the consequent endorsement of "diversity" in ideas of the good. For Kant and other modern thinkers (and for modern liberal institutions), the strength in these premises lies in a consideration that Kant repeatedly dwells on: for man as a being guided by self-reflection and reason rather than by instinct, there can be no simple identity between the good of the individual and that of the species.

At the same time, man as a being "transcending" strict determination by instinct is not self-sufficient and does not transcend dependence on the species. Indeed, reason as a power of extending passions and desires and of even creating wholly new ones tends to deepen human dependence on the species and to forge a servitude worse than any of subhuman animals to mere instinct.[5] That expansive or dynamic power of reason, insufficiently noted by earlier modern individualism, jeopardizes both emancipation and diversity. Unless reason imposes a legislative order on the inclinations, individualism must degenerate into the tyranny of luxury and "artifice" over the human will, whose proper destiny is to rule itself and not to be ruled. This, briefly, is the "teleological problem" in modern individualism, as seen by Kant: how is reason to supply an ordering telos to itself, and to the human inclinations, without reasserting dogmatic teleology and losing thereby the advantages of modern individualism? This problem arises for Kant before the transcendental turn in his thought, before the mature critique of speculative reason, and at the time of the Rousseauian *Remarks*.

At the heart of Kant's rejection of the moral sense approach after 1764–65 is his new awareness of this teleological problem. One can appreciate the full extent of the dramatic change in Kant's thinking in the mid-1760s only if one examines the earlier moral sense doctrine in his first published account of the principles of ethics. This account occurs within the framework of a treatise on the method of metaphysics and philosophy as a whole—the *Prize-Essay* composed for the question announced by the Berlin Academy for 1763.[6] The ethical portion of this treatise reveals an avowed affinity with Hutcheson's moral sense ethics. Kant writes that "Hutcheson and others have provided, under the name of moral feeling, a beginning to fine observations."[7] Although Kant begins to abandon the attempt to ground ethics in feeling just shortly after this essay, at the time of the encounter with Rousseau, Kant continues to have a high regard for Hutcheson's thought. This regard can be understood only if one does not make the error of supposing that Hutcheson's ethics is eventually rejected by Kant on the ground of being "eudaimonistic" or hedonistic. Indeed, Hutcheson is an important predecessor to Kant insofar as Hutcheson is principally endeavoring to avoid a reduction of the moral to the selfishly pleasant and to preserve the special character of moral experience. This quite evidently is the source of the attraction to Kant of Hutcheson's doctrine in the *Prize-Essay*.[8]

Hutcheson's theory and Kant's in the *Prize-Essay* share these features: (1) a search for primary "material principles" of moral obligation in the form of "immediate" approbations of moral goodness; these approbations are unanalyzable, unprovable from other principles, and irreducible to other principles;[9] (2) an effort to establish that such principles are heterogeneous from concepts of truth, that is, that practical knowledge is wholly different from theoretical knowledge. One can say that the search for such principles is fully in the spirit of the modern quest for a replacement of the ancient emphasis on habituation with its presupposition of a hierarchical soul structure.[10] "Moral sense" provides immediately and universally effective principles that require a minimum of social habituation, if any. This theory is thus a version of the appeal to common sense or common reason against the dogmatic authorities of metaphysics and theology; it is inseparable from the modern enterprise of creating a nomos of an enlightened and self-ruling humanity.

The moral sense approach is in accord with earlier modern philosophy in proposing that the springs of practical action and virtues are immediately available in every consciousness or ego, with minimal soul-formation. It differs from earlier modern versions of anti-teleological and anti-"dogmatic" morality not only in according to the immediate motives or inclinations a greater degree of sociability and humanity. It recognizes, somewhat inchoately, that the modern emancipatory project is in need of a sanctioning from the beautiful or the sacred, as perhaps all large-scale human projects are. Moral sense philosophy, while not yet addressing the neglected teleological problem in modernity, nonetheless rejects a simply "instrumental" view of higher faculties, and it perceives that practical life requires a justification that bare utility cannot provide.[11]

Yet even at the time of the *Essay* Kant experiences doubt concerning the grounding of moral principles in feeling. He concludes the treatise with this remark: "It has still to be discovered in the first place whether the faculty of knowing or of feeling (the first inner ground of the faculty of appetite) exclusively decides the primary principles of practical philosophy."[12] The Kant scholarship has already reconstructed important aspects of the reflection leading from the early moral sense doctrine of the *Essay* to the morality of self-legislative reason. The reconstruction briefly goes as follows. Feeling shows itself to Kant to lack sufficient stringency for giving rise to unconditionally obliging maxims. Only a form of reason able both to apprehend and to prescribe a universal maxim can propose unconditioned imperatives. The difficulty then is that reason by itself seems unsuited for providing moral incentives, although suited to cognize principles of obligation. The early moral theory of Kant has been praised for appreciating that reason as theoretical can only apprehend an obligation; it cannot give rise to moral approval and to the execution of obligation. On the other hand, Kant did not yet arrive at the idea of a form of reason that can both apprehend and give the motive for executing a moral maxim. The Kant of 1762–64, like Hutcheson, restricts reason to a logical faculty and thus places the ground of moral execution in feeling. He is aware (as the conclusion of the *Essay* suggests) that he must turn to reason to account for the universality of maxims and that feeling doubtfully supports motives with a universal object. To bridge the gulf between apprehended universality and its enforcement as duty, Kant needs a new notion of practical reason. Under the influence of Rousseau, he discovers it; the latter shows him the existence of a "third faculty," one of freedom, understood as self-legislative reason.[13]

In what follows my concern is to relate this reconstruction to Kant's reflections on the teleological problem in modern individualism, at the time of the *Remarks*. By so proceeding, a dimension is added to Kant's movement away from the moral sense tradition, toward his discovery of a new form of reason, that has been lacking in previous discussions.

Rousseau's Challenge to Moral Sense

It would be useful at this point to show that the large claims made here for the *Remarks'* importance receive support from a number of European studies of the history of Kant's thought, although the topic is hardly known in the English-language literature. The principal discoveries in this area were made on the basis of G. Lehmann's publication in 1942 of a whole portion of Kant's *Nachlass* that unmistakably records an intense encounter of Kant with Rousseau's writings in 1764–65.[14] These reflections, taking up nearly two hundred pages of the Academy edition's twentieth volume, are marginalia made by Kant in his copy of his aesthetic and moral treatise *Observations on the Feeling of the Beautiful and Sublime*. They normally go by the title of *Remarks* to that work, although Kant gave them no title. In fact the *Remarks* is not a systematic work of any sort. It is not certain but it is possible that it is preparatory notes for an improved version of the *Observations*, yet such a revision was never written. There is some correspondence, by no means frequent or consistent, between the subjects discussed in the main text of the *Observations* and those in the marginalia. The most thorough and circumspect student of the *Remarks* argues that it is better regarded as notes to Rousseau's writings than as corrections or addenda to the *Observations*.[15] The aesthetic treatise itself reveals a superficial acquaintance with Rousseau's thought. It would then be appropriate for Kant to place his deeper reflections on Rousseauian topics in the context of his earlier thoughts on them, even if he were not planning a revision of the treatise.

Both the content of the *Remarks* and the circumstances of its composition point to an origin in the reading of Rousseau's works. It is established beyond doubt that Kant was reading the major works in French as they were becoming available in the early and middle 1760s.[16] Furthermore, the *Remarks* can be assigned its date of composition more securely than any other part of Kant's *Nachlass*. The numerous references to *Emile* and the arguments, which everywhere develop in relation to ideas of Rousseau, reveal that the *Remarks* is a dialogue with Rousseau's chief works, above all *Emile*.[17] J. Schmucker calls the *Remarks* such a "dialogue" in which "not only the basic theses of Kant's new standpoint in ethics are clearly formulated, but one in which also the way Kant followed to arrive at these theses is traceable."[18] The *Remarks* offers the principal foundation for the judgment that a "second phase" of Kant's moral thinking is "not only introduced but decisively determined by Kant's study of the chief works of Rousseau."[19] The breadth and depth of the impact on Kant of *Emile* in particular can be compared to a revolution: "The reading of *Emile* called forth a revolution in Kant and had a powerful effect on him unlike that produced by any other book."[20]

In holding the view that a "second phase" of Kant's moral thinking begins with the *Remarks*, Schmucker is joined by Dieter Henrich. Indeed these two cognoscenti of the early Kant maintain that most of the basic notions of Kantian ethics are already established in the *Remarks*, such that the first two parts of the *Foundations of the Metaphysics of Morals* could have been written in 1765.[21] The key to this second phase is the discovery of freedom as a human power or faculty. In the *Remarks* but also in the contemporary notes of Herder on Kant's ethics lectures, there appears for the first time the attempt to derive moral feeling from freedom, and therewith the abandonment of the ultimacy and irreducibility of moral feeling, that is, of the central tenet of moral sense philosophy.[22] Henrich in particular brings out the point that Kant undertakes to base moral consciousness on the "self-agreement of the will" or, in other terms, on freedom as "rational self-activity," which activity carries out "the formal law of unity of the will with itself."[23] The self-agreement of the will, rather than the disinterested feeling of moral approbation, is the "immediate end" of the will, in the new conception. In fact the shift of emphasis in the foundation of morality from feeling to freedom entails a shift in the immediate object of approbation from others to ourselves, that is, to approval or admiration of our active rational powers, as able to achieve unity with themselves through legislation.[24]

Not yet in the *Remarks*, but later in the critical writings, Kant gives the name "categorical imperative" to the formal moral law. This law expresses the formula of perfection for a will that strives to achieve unity with itself and that derives a feeling of self-esteem from that striving. The *Remarks*, insofar as it contains this conception, also therefore delineates a new concept of "practical reason." For now it is the case that reason has more than just the capacity to apprehend an obligation of a universally valid nature, independent of the variable contingencies of inclination. Reason has also within itself a moving power or incentive to obey such a universal law, since the law valid for all wills is identical with the formula whereby the individual will achieves unity with itself, and thereby a maximum of freedom. The "interest" in a universal and rational principle is therefore "immediate," inherent in the individual's own willing, and does not have to be derived through the problematic route of a special moral feeling. In our discussion of the *Remarks* we shall see what crucial role Rousseau plays in this conception.[25]

Furthermore we shall see how this principle whereby the will maximizes its freedom and which it can adopt only on the assumption that the will is a "faculty" of freedom independent of feeling or passion for its end, is at the same time of first importance for speculative inquiry. For the new moral principle, "unity of the will with itself," emerges out of the background of the problems of the will's (or reason's) self-alienation, and of its striving for a unity with itself. And for Kant that problem exists as much for speculative inquiry as for practical life; in fact, it is the same problem in both areas. We have seen that Kant found that such unity (or telos) cannot be grounded on nature. Rousseau, who really makes Kant aware of the problem in its full extent, shows how the unity reason seeks must be grounded on freedom.

Scholars have made a number of important observations about the influence of Rousseau on the relation of theoretical and practical philosophy in Kant, and on Kant's conception of the end and concerns of philosophy as science. But it is a principal task in what follows to make a thorough and persuasive case for such influence and to show how it illuminates the basic intent of Kant's endeavors.[26] Since most readers of Kant are familiar only with the major publications of 1781 and after, some persuasion may be needed. For Kant mentions Rousseau rarely, and with little elaboration on his importance, in the later writings. Whereas most scholars look at the *Remarks* only for aphorisms of tantalizing biographical interest, one must disclose that it contains a complex argumentation about the meaning of philosophy. That Rousseau somehow compelled Kant to admit that the end of philosophy is "practice" and that he helped him to discover a new principle for practice in freedom, are facts generally regarded as having some rather limited biographical interest. Their full import can be grasped, however, only by examining the context of the statements of such indebtedness to Rousseau, and the argumentation found there that links them to the fundamental issue: the teleological problem inherent in the emancipated rationality of modern individualism.

The Teleological Problem in Rousseau

Before examining the *Remarks*, it is necessary to discuss further the teleological problem as it emerges with full consciousness and clarity in the thought of Rousseau. The problem must be related to the often-noted paradoxical character of his thought, which is inherent in Rousseau's protest against the modern movement of philosophy with its central burden of undertaking a new kind of enlightenment. The paradox, or seeming paradox, arises from Rousseau's sharing many of the basic premises of the modern movement while attempting, nonetheless, to arrive at altogether different conclusions from this movement. One of these different conclusions can be stated simply: Rousseau rejects the alleged necessity of the "mercenary" form of society that (on his account) earlier modern thinkers argued followed from the natural individualism of man. Rousseau hopes, on the basis of a version of individualism, to show that the renewal of some forms of classical virtue is possible, or of "citizen virtue" in the form of the individual's dedication to nation, state, or city. But he thinks that for this purpose, the grafting of benevolent or sympathetic feelings, as immediate and irreducible, onto the primary self-interested passions will not suffice.[27]

Citizen virtue in the classical republic, Rousseau's primary model, did not rest simply upon a good-natured and gentle benevolence but instead required a certain spirited sternness toward oneself and others, together with a certain intolerance of luxurious indulgence. Such spiritedness and strength of character cannot be produced merely by an appeal to philanthropic feelings.[28] Rousseau urges us to recall the exclusive spirit of the ancient virtuous societies he admires—a spirit that cannot thrive unless citizens are impressed with the importance of the distinction between friend and enemy. The virtue of the classical republic is inevitably, to a large extent, military virtue. Rousseau praises such virtue not as one who glorifies war, but as one who sees the preparedness to suffer hardships for the defense of "one's own" as a source of desirable strengths and even as a condition for many kinds of human elevation and greatness. The maintenance of political freedom requires a discipline and self-denial that are surely akin to the self-control and endurance that any freedom of the mind presupposes. Nevertheless the creation of such virtue entails a drastic transformation of man's natural individualism, such that the citizen is nearly like a different kind of being altogether when compared to the natural man.[29] Rousseau is confronted with the striking difficulty that one of the forms of existence he regards most highly, one that gives some dignity to being human, is doubtfully natural and possibly only a product of human conventions, laws, and institutions.

Rousseau's difficulty can be stated more precisely. In attempting to make a transition from natural individualism to social virtue, Rousseau does not avail himself of an account of the soul, wherein the rational part has a certain autonomy and authority over the appetitive part, through natural tendencies abetted by habituation. Since he agrees in large measure with earlier modern thinkers about the instrumental nature of reason, he cannot easily deny that a society based on self-interest is what necessarily follows from man's nature and that a form of such society corresponds to the idea of the "best regime." It would seem that Rousseau can hope to fashion a virtuous citizen out of the material of original man not by appealing to a higher part of human nature, but only through defiance of human nature. Rousseau must either ignore the given nature of man or he must follow the path of his modern predecessors and seek the basis of the good political order in immediately available natural motives—the postulated benevolent feelings, or some version of self-love. Ultimately Rousseau is compelled to derive citizen virtue from self-love or self-preservation, since he denies that benevolence or sympathy is universally effective, and since a total ignoring of "nature" would render the account of the best regime groundless.

Even so, Rousseau's solution does not remove the doubt as to whether the political and social realm is natural. Indeed, citizen virtue falls far behind the life of the solitary individual as an alternative to "bourgeois" or "mercenary" virtue, in the ranking of desirable ways of life. Since that is unavailable except to a few, a certain account of virtue that achieves a "middle ground" between the "whole" dedication of the citizen and the wholeness of the solitary thinker is the most appropriate goal to set before the ordinary man of modern times. Such is the goal proposed in *Emile*. For in the "ideal," Emile retains much of the natural man's freedom and the enjoyment of life connected with that freedom, which the classical citizen forfeits. At the same time, his individualism is not corrupted by social passions, and thus it is consistent with a certain spontaneous regard for the general welfare, that is, a certain imitation of true citizen virtue.

Rousseau reasons through the whole problem of grounding virtue on man's natural individualism with extraordinary cogency and subtlety, and his efforts to resolve this difficulty deeply impress and influence Kant. It is not the mere appearance of paradox that impresses Kant, for that could be dismissed as mere inconsequentiality of thought. Kant evidently believes that Rousseau solves, or comes close to solving, his basic difficulty, whereas there is ground for thinking that Rousseau does not suppose that he or anyone else can find a solution wholly satisfying to philosophic reason.[30] Kant's proposed solution should not be regarded, however, as the replacement of a true solution for a mere quandary. Much of what is most penetrating in Kant's reasoning derives from Rousseau; many of Rousseau's insights into grave obstacles to a solution are ignored or missed by Kant.

We can return to a point made earlier. Rousseau introduces a modification of the modern asocial or individualist account of human nature which helps him to bridge the apparent abyss between individualism and citizen virtue. The natural desires and the human faculties as a whole are not fixed in their character, but have a certain malleability, or as Rousseau puts it rather ironically, they have a certain quality of "perfectibility."[31] In other words, human nature is indeterminate and at the same time capable of transforming itself. The objects that satisfy desire vary with the condition of the "faculties" of both desiring and knowing, and only a certain self-regarding or self-consciousness is a persistent feature throughout all changes. This position is already found, stated less radically, in earlier modern thinkers; it is a natural corollary of the indefiniteness of human desire, which itself belongs to a modern denial of teleology.[32] Rousseau advances farther in this direction than his predecessors, both through his account of the cause (or complex of causes) of this indeterminacy and through his suggestion that through an understanding of this causality, man possesses greater prospects of modifying his condition (for good or ill) than any previous thinker had supposed.

The causal account of malleability or perfectibility has these premises: (1) the denial of a strong instinctual determination in human nature; (2) the view that human reason, aided by imagination (or actually constituted by it), has an inventive capacity for the creation of new "ideas" of objects of desire; (3) the assumption that the invention of such ideas can modify the character of human desire; (4) the view that reason or imagination is itself malleable and not governed by predetermined potentialities; (5) the assumption that the impetus or force that propels the development of the rational powers is the passions, which are themselves modified by these powers.

From this set of premises follows a view of reason and passion as mutually determining. A further consequence is that reasoning, imagining, and speech are acquired, not innate powers, and that the present condition of their development is not to be considered their final form. No one can say that any human being of the past or the present, however virtuous, has become all that a human being can be. At the same time, this lack of teleology means that we lack the notion of a final form, which would enable us to measure the progress mankind has made from its origins. No notion of a perfect state or perfect development can be abstracted from the human faculties. Hence the irony present in the term *perfectibility*.

This account of the human faculties sheds light on a striking and disturbing consideration—that past epochs of human history have had no clear plan or goal for the perfecting of human powers, and that history is thus largely a spectacle of haphazard and blundering "evolution." Rousseau's account shows why this must be the case. The rational powers are modifiable, but not autonomous. They have no capacity for a comprehensive reflection on their own goals and limits. They cannot distance themselves from the instrumental nexus in which they are enmeshed, and thus they cannot acquire an overview of the mechanism that governs human development. Rousseau, however, comes close to asserting that he has such an overview; he has understood better than anyone else, he claims, the causal mechanism behind human history. Yet by his own account, Rousseau owes his privileged viewpoint to the accidents of history rather than to extraordinary powers of detached reflection, that is, the powers of an autonomous reason.[33]

With this modification of modern individualism, in reality a radicalizing of it, Rousseau argues that the transformation of natural man into the citizen is possible because human nature is malleable. Or one can say that Rousseau transposed the basic paradox into human nature itself; human nature has the capacity to become the "other of itself." Whereas this account of man can offer some help to Rousseau in describing the sources of citizen virtue, it opens up another possibility which is ultimately of greater importance to him. If human nature is modifiable, and that modifiability includes the acquisition of reason, then the original man, postulated as a kind of "ideal limit" in a reconstruction of the beginnings, must be prerational. And if original man is prerational, he must also be prepassionate. For while original human nature must have certain instincts or abiding appetites, it will not have desires directed toward objects qualified by attributes of imagination or reason. The modification of desire by imagination gives occasion for temporary affects (fear, anger) with imaginary objects, but more important, it makes possible the passions (love, hatred, envy, revenge, etc.) characterized by both intensity and longevity. Thus in passion, the intensity of momentary affects is prolonged indefinitely because of the "ideal" character of its objects. This has momentous consequences for human life. By means of the passions, human life departs from instinctual regularity and determination in ways that cannot be foreseen; it does so not momentarily, but with persistence and with deliberate pursuit of "arbitrary" objects.

The causality producing the passions is equivalent to the set of conditions that makes "selfhood" possible. Thus it is only as a rational being connecting past, present, and future together into a continuous experience of self that a human being can have the awareness of nonimmediate and "ideal" goods and evils that are the objects of passions. Such capacity to connect the experience of time into a whole (a "self") is basic to what Rousseau means by "reason." According to the argument about human modifiability, this capacity is absent in the original man, who lacks all self-awareness and responds only to immediate pleasure and pain. Having no memory of injury or benefit and no anticipation of victory or defeat, he cannot harbor the basic passions that are all connected with amour-propre and the sense of self in relation to others over time. With the acquisition of the power to project the sense of a continuous self into the past and future (which cannot rest upon the mere association of memories), human experience undergoes a remarkable, and ominous, expansion. Hope, anxiety, regret, longing, with all their versatility and arbitrariness, join the immediate responses of fear, joy, and anger in the human psychic repertory. The life of a human being becomes very much one of living "outside onself" and is exposed to hitherto unknown possibilities of experiencing good and evil.[34]

Rousseau thus argues that many of the evils that his modern predecessors thought were inherent in man's original nature were acquired at the same time that the powers of reasoning and imagining were acquired. Thus the destructive forms of human selfishness should not be considered natural to man. Original man was moved only by momentary feelings and irritations, by objects immediately present to him, and by weak instinctual drives that propelled him to act for his survival. While he was thoroughly selfish, he was not dangerously so. Since his desires did not extend beyond the simplest needs, he did not have desires connected with the comparison of his overall condition (in terms of wealth, power, intelligence, beauty, etc.) with that of others. Lacking a conception of self, he could not compare himself to other selves and thus could have no ideas of superiority and inferiority. He could not anticipate, or even be concerned with, the good or bad opinion of others, for he had no need of others and no conception of their worth or utility to himself. Having no motive to strive for their favor, he lived without ambition, industry, or suspicion of others. Without knowing that he did so, he lived wholly for himself and had no pangs of guilt arising from this fact.

The natural condition appears to have been one of relative peace, serenity, and physical well-being, when compared with the social condition and its "artificial" passions. Having primary regard still for his own good, the social being always looks "outside himself" for the satisfaction of desire. Reason has not made social man superior morally to natural man, but has only made him more dependent on others for the satisfaction of his needs. At the same time, the expansion of his desires by reason and imagination has rendered his own powers insufficient to satisfy his desires and given him a motive for guile, hypocrisy, and all the vices of social life unknown in the natural state. The one new need that dominates his life and makes his powers insufficient to himself is wholly unnatural—the need to acquire the good opinion of other human beings.

This Rousseauian analysis radicalizes modern individualism so as to undermine one of its basic assumptions—that the natural passionateness of original man compelled him, employing a calculative intellect and sober industry, to leave an anxious and uncomfortable state and to give up his natural freedom for the sake of the security and mutual constraints of a social order. Depriving original human nature of its motives for leaving the presocial condition, Rousseau can suggest only that a series of natural accidents once set in motion the latent powers of reason and imagination, thereby creating the passions and the inconveniences of a decayed state of nature. The "progress" that then follows, in the invention of families, societies, laws, and arts, has neither inevitability nor clear superiority to the earliest times.[35]

One could consider this whole view the outcome of a very consequent reflection on what the modern instrumentality of reason entails. Rousseau shows it has a way of undermining itself and of pointing beyond itself. Thus the modern rejection of reason's autonomy was buttressed by the "nominalist" view that the proper object of reason, the universal, is only the association of particulars or of sensations. But nonetheless, early modern thinkers persisted in treating the universal "human nature" as substantial and reliable, and as immediately known to natural man such that he acted fearfully, proudly, suspiciously, and so forth, in relation to the humanity of other humans. Yet if reason is instrumental to sensation and desire, its capacity to form such a universal must be derived and cannot be considered ultimate. Rousseau proposes that natural man possessed no such universals at all and that somehow a power was acquired that could account for the later acquisition of universals—the power to think "I." The "I think" could be called a peculiar concrete universal, connecting past, present, and future into one whole and making all other universals possible. It is the primary form for the creation of all ideas of class, or "general ideas." The unity of the self is the basis of all unity.

That unity makes possible the comparison of one self with other selves, and since it is not "given" but somehow acquired, human sociality is also acquired. Rousseau points to the inseparability in analysis of the acquisition of the form of unity, the "I," and the acquisition of speech. To apprehend any kind of universality (including the "I" itself) seems to presuppose the use of language. But to regard speech as primordial is to regard reason as primordial, which runs contrary to the basic premise of its being acquired. Yet to account for the origin of language one must presuppose the "I" as the original form for all universals, and thus one is caught in a circular argument. Rousseau's confession that he sees no escape from this circle is one of the major instances of his showing how instrumentalism tends to undermine itself if carried through consistently. Indeed his argument points toward the "idealist" replacement of modern sensationalist nominalism by the primordial spontaneity of the "I think" as the creative source of all universality in thought.[36]

Whether or not Kant's notion of a primordial "I think" as the "unity of apperception" implicit in all judging received some provocation from this passage in the Second Discourse, it is certain that Kant's notion addresses a similar difficulty. But it is also clear that Kant's insistence on the pure and original spontaneity of this "I think" puts him at a great distance from Rousseau's line of speculation about natural man. For Kant, the fundamental rational faculties, human self-awareness, and sociality are not derivable from prior sources. Kant does not rule out the evolution and appearance in prehistory of the human rational powers; he simply denies that we possess any scientific or philosophic means to present a coherent account of such evolution. Otherwise Kant is in basic agreement with Rousseau that the emergence, however it occurred, of the "I" and its power to apprehend universals was an event of earth-shattering proportions. It permanently severed the bonds between human life and the rest of nature. Through that event the human species became empowered to invent designs and to pursue imagined goals having no relation to the regularity of the natural order. Man began to make his own "rules" while not being in full control of how he devised those rules or of what consequences flowed from them. He produced an increasingly complex mode of existence in which new evils arose to accompany every new good he instituted. As Kant writes, an abyss of indefinite extent was opened up by the appearance of freedom in the world.[37] While not agreeing with Rousseau on the question of reason as autonomous power, Kant is here nevertheless in accord with Rousseau on the limitless character of the peculiar human capacity to extend desires and "ideal" projects.[38]

Put otherwise, Kant discovers in Rousseau's thinking the very rigorous disclosure of the ultimate human consequences of the modern rejection of classical teleology, and the classical version of reason's autonomy. The power of human reason to create new general ideas that have no metaphysical foundation in a permanent natural order entails that reason can supplement arbitrarily any given order or create a wholly artificial order. Such a power would pose no problems in human life if human reason could also create the power to satisfy the demands that arise from its construction of new objects of desire. But our reason is "finite" and dependent on a given set of natural limitations for its proper functioning; by instituting new objects of desire, it tends only to deepen that dependence. Thus as a social being, man becomes more dependent on others as the scope of his projects increases. The "perfectibility" of our species results in a loss of natural freedom even if it brings certain gains in other respects. The earlier modern thinkers had not seen that their own principles point to this analysis, and they had not seen the dangerous possibilities lurking in their own accounts of human life. Now the possible anarchical consequences of the self-conscious employment of such principles in the ordering of human life must be met with appropriate palliatives. What is needed, in fact, is a recovery on a wholly novel basis of certain ideas of the structure of the soul, and educational and moral doctrines to further the structuring of a healthy soul. The human soul will lose all shape, depth, and the power to govern itself if the riotous growth of desires and needs is allowed to destroy all simplicity, and if the soul does not relearn to subject itself to the rule of law.

Within Rousseau's thought, the natural state as an "ideal" of

absolute freedom and simplicity would seem to be an attractive solution to this problem. Yet it is an elusive and even chimerical ideal, by
Rousseau's own account. Any human being in quest of the peace of
the original solitary condition is already corrupted; the more he
strives to realize the ideal, the farther away from it he feels. Rousseau
vividly portrays how this experience is an ever-renewed source of
anguish in his life.[39] Some form of social and moral dependence is the
fate of all humans. Accordingly it is necessary to devise ideals of political life and of educational formation that bring the soul as close as
possible within the social condition toward the ideal of natural freedom, while not expecting a pure freedom ever to be achieved. There
is no contradiction between Rousseau's statements that social life always involves enslavement and his praises of social and moral freedom. The latter can be honored insofar as it brings human life out of
the very worst servitude and somewhat closer to natural freedom.[40]
Very real difficulties then arise for Rousseau in his efforts to establish
a soul structure for social man, without any assumptions that reason
is an autonomous power.

It is this difficulty that compels Kant to devise a new account of
rational autonomy—one that accepts Rousseau's basic arguments that
the inventive and projective power of reason has no determinate
natural end or telos. In the next chapter we see, in the watershed
Remarks of 1764–65, how Kant's effort develops in constant relation
to the insights of Rousseau. Surely this is an effort to find a way back
to some elements of an ancient account of an ordered soul, and of a
highest good provided by it, which Kant sees as demanded by Rousseau's analysis. The failure to address this teleological problem is
what Kant experiences as a serious lack in the other modern philosophers, even when they uphold certain ideas of a stringent morality
based on moral or sympathetic feelings.[41]

3

Kant's Discovery of a Solution, 1764–65

History, Nature, and Perfection

The *Remarks* provides us with the line of argumentation that leads from Rousseau's account of the problems of reason to Kant's conception of practical reason and of its role within the whole of philosophy. On the analysis of both thinkers, reason is the principal source of human ills. Each thinker responds to this circumstance with an argument for how a humanly constructed "ideal" can offer a structure to the soul and a teleological ordering of its rational and inclinational elements. Kant in this period arrives at the first insights of his transcendental approach in philosophy, since for the first time he sees that reason imposes an alienating dialectic upon itself, and he sees the possibility of devising "ideal" solutions to this dialectic. Both this dialectic and its resolution rest on an account of reason as a spontaneous source of a priori principles (of a "synthetic" nature) that condition reason's activity and supply the framework for its orderly (or faulty) development. Thus the transcendental approach to reason emerges from the dialogue with Rousseau that has been preserved by the *Remarks* for the research of posterity, perhaps accidentally.[1]

In the *Remarks* one finds both an extraordinary high praise of Rousseau, full of optimism about the possibilities disclosed by his discoveries, and a somber recognition of the gravity of the problems exposed by him. Kant declares that Rousseau as discoverer is comparable to Newton. The epochal natural philosopher uncovered "order and regularity combined with simplicity," where before only disorderly variety in the natural phenomena was visible. Rousseau as inquirer into human nature "discovered for the first time, beneath the acquired multiplicity of human forms, the deeply concealed nature of man and the hidden law whose observation justifies Providence" (58.12–59.3).[2] Just as awareness of disorderly variety provoked Newton to search for ordered simplicity in nature, or just as the failure of earlier quests to detect order had to precede the discovery of true order, so Rousseau was first confronted with disorder in human phenomena. The "multiplicity of acquired human forms" had been mistakenly identified with human nature itself, before Rousseau disclosed the true law of human nature. From the standpoint of Rousseau's discovery, one can now see that what was previously held to be natural in man is in fact artificial or the product of culture. The "hidden law" is the account of human reason that includes its perfectibility, from which one learns that culture indefinitely transforms nature rather than perfecting determinate potentials in it. Rousseau's experience of the acquired disorders of reason in modern culture, or of the alienating effects of modern reason, forced on him his insight into this "law." "Since human nature has now acquired such an impoverished form, its natural bases have become dubious and unrecognizable" (47.13–48.7). Put in other terms, Rousseau's insight was that past inquirers into human nature had not returned to the true state of nature and thus had knowledge only of humanity as historical accident had revealed it to them.[3] Nevertheless, Rousseau's insight itself was the fruit of historical accident to the extent that his modern circumstances made it available to him.

One aspect of the abiding law which the extreme conditions of modern times help to reveal is the necessity for human characteristics to deteriorate from their proper vocations in the social condition. Wars, luxury, oppression, slavery, and even religion and science are signs of this deterioration; they are either immediate symptoms of it or they arise as attempts to correct it (78.4–6). With respect to this deterioration, "our present regime" offers unique human dangers and opportunities, for in it "virtue becomes ever more necessary and also ever more impossible" (98.9–10). The current extremity of decline enables one to have insight into the law of deterioration and thus to establish for the first time in history a true science of the acquisition of virtue. "If there is indeed a science that man needs, it is one that teaches him to fulfill properly his appointed place in creation and to learn what he must do to be a human being" (45.17–20). But various "deceptive attractions have unobservedly removed man from his proper place," and the human species needs instruction to call it back to the "condition of a human" (45.20–46.3).

Through its remarkable advances in reason and culture, the human species has acquired attributes that "glitter," but that also "spread corruption" and disturb the natural order. Thus it has "stepped outside the circle of humanity and has become nothing, creating a void that spreads its corruption to the adjacent parts" of nature (41.19–30). Yet this bleak situation can shock a thinker into recognizing that the whole aim of science is to make man more at home in the world appropriate to him (7.8–11). His recognition that theoretical science culminates in a true art of acquiring virtue is inseparable from the insight, afforded by the present decline, that human nature is not fixed and determinate. For the latter insight is equivalent to seeing that human excellence and well-being rest upon art. Again the Rousseauian discovery resembles the Newtonian one: in each case the thinker had to distance himself from nature, as the wisdom and common sense of past ages had represented it, in order to have his vision of the "hidden law" (120.11–21.2).[4]

Because the discovery of the science of virtue is made possible by the deterioration of man in the modern age, it is "vulgar opinion that earlier times were better" than the present (119.22–24). It is not Rousseau's purpose to expound the simpleminded doctrine that the presocial condition was blissful, and that mankind should now return to the forests. Although it can be maintained that "the ancients were closer to nature than we are" (71.19–20), it is nonetheless true that primitive simplicity or the relative simplicity of antiquity is defective. Such simplicity is unaware of the dangers accompanying the developments of culture that modern life has experienced. Thus antiquity was not in a position to formulate the true science that teaches how virtuous simplicity is to be achieved under all possible conditions, even the most extreme corruption and luxury. Innocence is not the same as virtue; in the natural condition "one can be good without virtue and rational without science." Virtue arises when it is necessary, in times of corruption when "social relations bring forth so many unnatural desires," and when the sciences flourish as well (11.9–13). Modern times, bringing about the most extreme point of corruption, also enable us to discover the "Archimedean point" upon which virtue can be grounded under all possible conditions.[5]

Kant claims that the chief aim of Rousseau's *Emile* is to actualize the highest human perfection. "The education of Rousseau is the sole means to restore the flower of civil society," for "laws are of no avail" to this end in the present age of increasing luxury, hatred betweeen the classes, and constant warfare (175.5–12). In other terms, the goal of Rousseau's education is to promote virtuous freedom. "The chief aim of Rousseau is for education to have the character of freedom and to produce a free human being" (167.3–4). The foundation of Rousseau's effort is his new notion of freedom; the whole difficulty of restoring mankind to a sound condition lies in understanding this *crux metaphysicorum*. Two fundamental questions appear to have answers in this notion of freedom: (1) What is the abiding essence or nature of man that endures through all the "acquired forms" of the history of culture? (2) What is the highest virtue or perfection to which humanity can aspire?

The first of these questions is raised in the following way: "Every-thing goes past in flux; the changing tastes, the diverse forms of hu-manity make the whole play of things uncertain and deceptive. Where can I find the firm point of nature that man cannot overthrow and that can offer him the markers to the shore that will sustain him?" (46.11–15). What is sought is a principle of motivation to virtue that will be effective universally and that accordingly belongs to, or even defines, the human essence. "The question is whether I shall find the fulcrum point outside this world or in this world, in order to set the affects in motion. In answer: I find it in the state of nature, that is, of freedom" (56.3–5). Freedom provides the answer to both questions; it is what endures in humanity through all histori-cal change, and it is also the ground of human perfections. It can offer these answers as a "this-worldly" principle, and thus it suggests a way of confirming the moral view of the world without recourse to dogmatic theology or metaphysics. The modern emancipatory project can be salvaged because "freedom, in the genuine sense (moral and not metaphysical) is the highest principle of all virtue and also of all happiness" (31.10–12).

At this moment of the most immediate power of Rousseau over Kant, the latter temporarily adopts the voice of the former, as his partner in an imaginary dialogue. "Freedom" as "the state of nature" seems now to be an answer to his questions, because "the state of nature" is only an idea, not an empirical condition. It is an idea of man that removes all the accidental attributes, and it can act as a stan-dard for evaluating the present condition of man. "If one evaluates the happiness of the savage, it is not in order to return to the forests, but in order to determine what one has lost while in other respects one has made gains" (31.17–19). Unlike a standard one tries to ab-stract from the various attempts to perfect man in society, which all have a certain accidental and arbitrary quality, this standard is valid everywhere and always. At the same time, there is always a powerful motive within the human soul to strive for freedom. Through a men-tal experiment that takes man back to primordial simplicity, one can uncover an idea of freedom that manages at once to be a universal essence and an ideal of perfection. The ideal is that of *Emile*: "to re-main a man of nature in society," to avoid the acquisition of the arbi-trary, accidental, alienating desires of social life, while still being a citizen (31.19–24).

Rousseau seems to have found a way to reinterpret the modern principle of freedom so as to achieve two things: (1) to account for the alienating consequences of human progress, since as "free," man al-ters his nature in ways that thwart his hopes and desires; (2) to uncover a power in the human soul that will motivate, confirm, and sanction the virtuous effort to acquire authority over the passions and thus to attain something of the wholeness and unity with himself that the idea of the natural man represents. According to (1) the human essence is an unhappy one, but according to (2) it has the power to redeem itself, to have salvation without recourse to the superhuman as the agent of salvation. Providence can be justified, for the human species' effort to emancipate itself need not be tragic.

The reinterpretation of freedom entails that it is now doubtful that natural inclinations or passions are what guide us toward freedom or virtue. History shows that the rational pursuit of the satisfaction of inclinations or passions has not led to that end. Whether the striving for freedom can be seen as a natural inclination, one that exists before the development of reason and that endures through that development, is a question causing Kant much difficulty in the *Remarks*. Rousseau's thinking on this in *Emile* is itself very complex. Kant's reflections mirror that complexity, as they sinuously find their way toward a notion of freedom as the autonomy of self-legislative reason, divorced from natural inclinations.

Emile as a child is free and innocent, not virtuous. He needs no knowledge of virtue or freedom, as an uncorrupted presocial being. It is when he is no longer a child that he must have the desire to be free. Nature by itself would not ensure that in the midst of social corruption, Emile would have this desire, or that this desire if present would overpower other attractions. Emile's tutor takes the place of all natural teleology. The tutor's first task is negative—to prevent the acquisition of amour-propre and other passions; if this task is performed successfully, Emile's nature will tend to take the right course (17.27–30, 25.3–7, 28.13–15, 122.7–10). Even so, the moral virtue of the adult, which secures his freedom of mind, cannot rest on a spontaneous love of freedom alone. The power of the surrounding corruptions has to be combatted by a conscious representation, or aim (*Zweck*), that supports the virtuous life, and this aim may have to include the idea of a reward in the next life (17.16–25).[6] In any case, Emile's adult virtue has to consist in "seeking to be free of [acquired] inclinations and learning to dispense with them gladly" (77.24–78.3). But to enforce and motivate this quest and this learning, Emile has to be guided by a powerful idea or set of ideas that he does not have naturally. Emile's soul must be structured by visions of perfection, which are the work of an architectonic artist of the soul. The problem for Kant is whether it is acceptable that the supreme legislator of Emile's soul is the reason of another human being, and not Emile.

Although the status of Rousseau's idea of virtue is in many ways troublesome to Kant, there is no doubt that Rousseau thoroughly persuades him that virtue is not grounded on natural benevolent or sympathetic inclinations. As a principle that must order and rule over inclination, virtue must have some ideal or rational origin. Rousseau's own arguments about the historical development of reason have convinced Kant that moral reason cannot be merely instrumental to nature. Indeed the overwhelming power of the passions generated in social life by the advance of reason therein requires something equally powerful as a counterpoise, and this cannot be found in the weak and unreliable natural inclinations. The idea of "man in his perfection," no longer based on natural potentialities, is an idea of "restored nature," one of absolute freedom that is, at least initially, a negative idea (153.15–22).[7] It is unlike the natural freedom of earlier modern doctrines in that it does not arise simply from spontaneous impulses (148.6–7), and it requires greater "artifice," or more disregard of empirical human nature as known from ordinary experience, in order to grasp its ideal character.[8] Kant writes of the "morally constructed [gekunstelte] man" who "surpasses the nature of man" (60.1–3). The ideal of freedom for the rational and social being is altogether different from the idea of the mere savage.

Yet one can see how far Kant takes the rational construction of an idea of virtue away from the spirit of *Emile* when one sees how he compares the "wise sufficiency" of Emile's virtue (77.13–23) with a kind of Socratic wisdom. Simplicity is either ignorant and innocent or rational and wise (180.16–17), and Socrates is the model of wise simplicity. He needs little because he has knowledge that he can dispense with much (77.6–12). The wise simplicity of the free and virtuous man is, at the highest level, a kind of science (7.8–11). Kant suggests that human perfection is a conscious and consistent willing of an ideal, or a "good will" (138.10–16), and that the philosophic life is not distinct from seeking the perfection of the will. The highest concern of theory or science is practical, and the true basis of moral virtue is a form of theory or science.[9] It is not at all Rousseau's intention to provide a single moral ideal or rational construction of virtue, or to propose that there is but one form of human perfection. But Kant's thoughts clearly tend in this direction, and he finds the strongest support for proceeding in this direction, he believes, from Rousseau. For the latter has shown how altogether problematic, and yet also necessary, is the teleological consummation of reason, in a new legislation of the order of the soul. And in Kant's view, Rousseau has shown that this order, which can be achieved only through a certain kind of willing, is also the sole possible good for human beings.

Will, Reason, and Spontaneity

The notion of "will" must be more closely examined. Since all evils have arisen from the acquisition of alienating needs (which acquisition was for the most part not conscious), and the good will consists in the willing of an ideal of perfection based on the construction of the state of absolute freedom, one can say that all good and all evil arise from the human will—from its unconscious or conscious willing. Nature itself does not give rise to whatever makes life hateful or virtue difficult (45.6–8). Providence is praiseworthy, for in accordance with Providence, all things are in a condition of natural simplicity and soundness, prior to human corruption of them. Complaints about Providence arise only because humans misjudge its plan according to illusory notions of the good or because they have perverted the natural order with their depravity (57.22–58.11). Kant writes that "I suffer no evil other than what I bring upon myself," and thus there are no grounds for complaint against Providence (68.17–22).[10] The attainment of a "moral world," a world that has recovered its original natural wholeness, is in principle possible for the virtuous will (16.4–5).

These questions arise: What is the character of the will that wills such perfection? What is its connection with moral obligation? What is its relation to reason? We have seen that Kant's doubts of 1762, about the grounding of morals and natural theology in feeling, have been resolved by Rousseau in favor of denying the grounding in feeling. Now Rousseau also suggests a positive approach—of replacing feeling by the rational will. A certain form of rational judgment is inherent in any willing directed to freedom or the overcoming of alienation. Kant takes Rousseau to be disclosing an internal logic for the will's effectiveness. This internal logic defines a practical reason that, like moral feeling, is not guided by theoretical apprehension of the good, but which all the same is a form of reason. It is surely evident by now that Rousseau has no place for the theoretical apprehension of a natural order that precedes willing and guides it to the good. Insofar as the absolute freedom of the natural state corresponds to the order sought by the will, the will is determined by a construction and not by something known from experience or theoretically apprehended. That construction is the will's own proposal to itself, born in the experience of progressive human self-alienation, of the "ideal" corrective to that experience.

One could consider this ideal to be the "limit" case, certainly beyond all experience, of an absolute equilibrium between human desire and human powers to satisfy desire. That equilibrium defines "natural man." Human reason and imagination are such as to prevent the complete attainment of this limit, but not to prevent a perpetual approach to it. Whether the human will is to strive toward this ideal is not an arbitrary matter, but a necessity. The alternative to willing this approach is an endless erosion of human freedom, in an endless expansion of desire beyond human powers to satisfy desire. Hence there is an ineluctable "logic," of a practical sort, which Rousseau is the first to discover: a logic within human willing that compels it to construct and to strive to approach the ideal of equilibrium. Rousseau discovers (as part of his "law") that the human will is really a form of practical reason that gives itself structure, goal, and incentive, without borrowing any of these from any superhuman or external source. Once again, the discovery of the "law" rests on the historical experience of the limitless modifiability (and corruptibility) of reason and will, although the law postulates a goal outside all historical experience. In Kant's language, this goal is "supersensible," without being in any traditional sense "metaphysical." It is not theoretically cognizable and not part of the empirical natural order; hence it is unlike all ancient "ideals." Rousseau offers the key to a new kind of metaphysics.

The new metaphysics of the will achieves three things at once: (1) it offers a formula whereby the soul structures itself, without recourse to any "dogmatic" principles; (2) it offers a principle of moral obligation, through the idea of seeking the maximum of freedom for all wills as a condition for achieving one's own; (3) and it offers a "formal" principle untainted by the contingencies of inclination or cultural distinctions, while nonetheless providing an incentive for its observance. Structure, obligation, and motive all arise from the inner dynamics of the will and the unavoidable logic of its self-restitution. Surely a principal text for Kant's derivation of this moral metaphysics qua logic of the will is the *Social Contract*, for that work offers the principle whereby the self-inflicted bondage of man to his own creation—the social order—can be made legitimate, the "general will" of the body of citizens. If the individual subordinates his own will, unconditionally, to the united will of all, and to no particular wills, he gives back his will to himself, to the degree that this is possible in the social condition of dependence. The will obeys a law it gives itself; or at least the alien power it obeys is more nearly its "own," being of a universal character, than if the alien power expressed a particular (and arbitrary) desire. The citizen, seeing that the alternative to submission to the general will is utter bondage, alienation, and the destruction of his will, is compelled to obey the "logic" of the self-preservation of the will. The citizen ascribes to the "formal" and absolute validity of the decisions of the general will; the "form" of the choice of ends (unquestioned right of the majority decision) ensures the goodness of the choice, regardless of its content. Thus the new principle offers self-preserving structure, absolute and formal validity, and incentive, all at one time, to the will.[11]

One must not neglect the facts that Kant would have found this account of the general will in *Emile*[12] and that he reinterpreted the intent of Rousseau's new principle in the light of the vision of human perfection he believed *Emile* to be offering. In effect, Kant conflates the political principle of legitimacy with the structure of the soul, formed according to the ideal construction of man's natural state, that Emile is to acquire through his long education. In Rousseau's view, the general will by itself may preserve the will from total alienation by the forces of political life, but it will not by itself give the soul the structure of an inwardly free and self-ruling being. Indeed, in Rousseau's conception, the efficacy of the principle of subordination to the general will derives from passion: the force of the desire for self-preservation. It neither presupposes nor effects a habituation of that passion, beyond what is necessary for the purposes of political life and the limited degree of freedom attainable in it. But attractive to Kant in the general will is the emphasis on self-legislation, or its independent and "untutored" quality (although here Kant abstracts from the role of the legislator).[13] Kant's conflation would provide every human being, as possessing a rational will, with a principle inherent in that will for providing itself with the autonomous soul structure of Emile. Every human being thus has within itself the "idea" of the supreme legislator who restores the soul to soundness and wholeness without the need for Emile's tutor, that is, for any "dogmatic" authorities whatsoever.

Rousseau's sole concern in the "general will" is with a politically effective notion of self-consistent willing on the social level, which surely assumes that human beings are very far from the natural state and will not ever "return" there. The general will only serves to limit the acquired and corrupted desires for the sake of a stable and minimally "arbitrary" form of political life, and it employs the force of the least harmful of the passions to achieve this aim—self-preservation. It is surely the least "optimistic" of all the Rousseauian "ideas" of how to improve the human condition, and yet it is the one that has the widest practical application. At the same time, it is in a way the most "metaphysical" of all Rousseauian "ideas": its greater abstraction from the condition of particular souls, natures, temperaments, and their possibilities for achieving higher forms of life makes it the best candidate among the ideas for being foundational in a new "moral metaphysics." When Kant uses it for this purpose and achieves the extraordinary abstraction of his account of philosophy as wholly moral, and of morality as wholly philosophical, we uncover a clue to the meaning of later German metaphysics as well as to that of Kant. The German systems, as logics of the will's recovery of itself from alienation, are based on the mutual penetration of politics and first philosophy, with the result of the disappearance of the distinctive nature of each.[14]

In accordance with his collapsing of the distinctions between the ideas of the ordinary citizen, the perfectly educated free man, and the philosopher, Kant draws attention to a difference between his "procedure" and Rousseau's: "Rousseau. He proceeds synthetically and begins from the natural man. I proceed analytically and begin from the morally formed [*gesittete*] man" (14.5–6). On the assumption that immediate awareness and effectiveness of the moral ideal must be ascribed to every human being, Kant believes that one can begin with the will of the cultivated and socialized human being and find the ideal implicit in it. That is, the aforementioned logic of practical reason is assumed to be operative in every human will. That assumption essentially defines the procedure of the first part of the *Foundations of the Metaphysics of Morals*.[15]

Kant seems to gather that Rousseau instead assumes that socialized man's acquisition of passions is a great obstacle to his awareness of the ideal of freedom, not to mention that it is an obstacle to its effectiveness as a motive. Thus Rousseau cannot proceed analytically, insofar as he cannot begin with the moral ideal as already actually the object of the human will, and then analyze the "conditions" of its real effectiveness. Rather, beginning on the one hand with the ideal as it has been constructed by the philosopher (in rare and fortunate circumstances) and on the other hand with human beings as they are, corrupted by reason and society, he must try to create a "synthesis." In this synthesis (or various syntheses) he conceives ways to bring historical and corrupt humanity into closer proximity to the ideal. Rousseau's procedure has to give more importance, and more cautious regard, to the variety of circumstances found in the given human "material," which will limit the effectiveness of the ideal. And he cannot assume that his diverse syntheses will result in a set of moral prescriptions applying uniformly to all human circumstances. The account of the citizen in the best regime, the account of the ideally educated ordinary man, and the solitary thinker or philosopher are different "syntheses." This is not to deny that for Rousseau, too, the "ideal" is not an empirical or historical fact. It is also not to deny that Rousseau in his syntheses looks for an internal "logic" of willing that ensures the effectiveness of the ideal, *once* it is somehow made known to, and inculcated in, the soul.

Rousseau's synthetic procedure, in the case of Emile's education, consists in very elaborate and artificial stratagems of putting into place the social and rational elements in the soul, without disturbing the fragile core of naturalness and freedom with which the child begins. At the start Emile simply *is* free, but at the end of the process he must *will* to remain free. Kant rejects the alleged necessity for such an elaborate education, which prevents Rousseau from offering projects for universal education along the lines of *Emile*. Moral education must make use of rational and moral capacities universally latent in human nature, and which have tendencies to be actual without excessive labors from institutions and educators (29.4–16).[16] Kant's confidence in the fundamental reliability of common reason is certainly in some ways shaken by Rousseau's view of the development of reason in the modern age. But Rousseau's deeper reservations about human reformability, and his darker views about humanity's future, are among the sources of the "bewilderment" Kant often experiences when reading him (43.13–44.5).[17]

The *Remarks* for the first time in the Kantian corpus assigns to reason attributes of spontaneity, freedom, and dignity that continue to hold in all later writings. Spontaneity appears in a human power of self-determination that cannot subordinate itself to the will of another without self-contradiction. One who alienates his own will makes himself a slave and contemptible (66.1–10). This spontaneous power provides the definition of the state of nature as the condition in which this power is exercized absolutely, without restriction. In that condition all wills are equal, fully independent of each other, and no will encounters any occasion for limiting its spontaneity. However, the original state of nature deteriorates and human wills become mutually dependent. Therefore social man must seek legal safeguards that prevent dependence from becoming slavery and, furthermore, must limit the passions that deepen the dependence and predispose the will to alienate itself, in exchanging satisfaction for freedom.

The spontaneous willing of man presupposes reason, for it presupposes a sense of self. The "I" is the source of willing inasmuch as willing is concerned, in various ways, with ownership. "The body is mine because it is a part of my I and is moved by my will" (66.11–12). Being moved by the will and being part of the "I" are the same. Thus for something to be willed means that it is "owned" by the "I." This is why the will cannot alienate itself, that is, become the property of another will, without contradiction. The source of ownership cannot give itself another owner than itself. The most fundamental right of ownership is not the right to external property, but the right to own the source of all ownership—the "I" and the will that is its extension. This most fundamental right is in fact the source of all right and therewith of all morality and duty, for the first duty is to respect the fundamental right of ownership to the source of all ownership. "One must not perform actions out of obedience to another human that one can perform out of inner motives" (66.7–9). The "I" is the source of the "ought," whereas bodily or animal need by itself gives rise to no "ought," for animal desire does not give rise to ownership.[18]

If, as in Rousseau's natural state, there is not yet an "I," then there also exists no "right" and no ownership. Rousseau's radicalizing of the natural state undercuts the earlier modern accounts of original man's motives for leaving the state of nature in the pursuit of rights he possessed from the start. If acquiring an "I" and the need of ownership is not natural, and to be lamented, then property rights are not truly natural. The original spontaneity of the "I" is present in Kant's account, whereas it is not in Rousseau's. For Kant there is from the start a basis for rights and thus for "dignity" in the observation of them, that is lacking in Rousseau. "Perfectibility" in Rousseau's description of original man does not imply spontaneity in Kant's sense. Alienation for Rousseau *begins* as soon as man has an "I," and a sense of ownership, for then he has a self that is defined through relations to other selves. Respecting the dignity of the "I" cannot be the most basic good, for it would be better to have no "I" at all. However, once man has acquired a self and the amour-propre that goes with it he will experience the loss of self-rule as the greatest of evils. Kant supposes that this is experienced as the greatest of evils from the dawn of human existence.[19]

The "I" and its willing in Kant must not be confused with the hylomorphic soul in ancient soul doctrines. The "I" is only an immediate certainty in consciousness that confirms itself through the activity of appropriating. It relates to the body and the external world as things to be mastered and modified. The "I" is a not an indwelling formative power, responsible for growth, nutrition, desire, movement, thought. Yet its essence is desire, in the form of the desire for autonomy or being owner of itself. It decidedly has no interest in being the "indwelling form " of the body, although it cannot be conceived in total separation from the body either. In being confirmed through the activities of appropriating, it requires a body and an external world. For the same reason, the "I" is always exposed to the threat of alienation. Precisely because the "I" is not a separate substance, yet demands autonomy, it cannot preserve itself in the realm of pure thought and is compelled to confront the reality of other "I"'s.

It has a dependent mode of existence (it is not a divine mind), and its search for autonomy leads it toward either tyranny or the "moral world," as possible answers to the quest for absolute self-rule.[20]

The solution of tyranny over others is excluded, for it perpetrates the greatest of horrors; there is "nothing more horrendous" than a human experiencing subjection to the will of another, and hence no fear of man is more natural than fear of servitude (88.3–12). Without reflection, every human chooses death over servitude (92.9–14). Servitude takes on a more terrible aspect for Rousseau and Kant than for the earlier modern thinkers, at the same time that the unnaturalness of the human will and its possibilities for limitless arbitrariness are more emphasized. Nonhuman nature by contrast exhibits regularity, even in its harshness to man; whim or illusion governs the human will, making it unpredictable (164.12–65.3 and 94.12–13). The wills of other humans elude my will and frustrate its rightful demand to absolute self-rule. The will of another belongs to him as mine belongs to me; hence it is not another thing in nature. "Because the perpetrator of my misfortune has reason, he is far more skillful at tormenting me than all of the elements" (91.9–93.13). Hobbes said it was the uncertainties of the state of nature that make the orderly tyranny in the civil state preferable to natural chaos; under this tyranny human passions become more regular. But there is no beneficent tyranny if arbitrariness is intrinsic to human willing as such and if the social condition even augments it, as Rousseau and Kant argue.

The obverse side of the greater emphasis on human arbitrariness is the belief, in Rousseau and Kant, that the human will or reason has greater possibilities of "transcending" mere nature. This transnatural possibility is more appealing to Kant, who shows no interest in Rousseau's idea of transcending the condition of willing and reasoning altogether. The spontaneity of the human will points to man's being a "complete being." This completeness consists in the capacity of the "I" to form the continuous self, stretching through time, and thereby making possible the uniquely human and rational quest for "happiness" as a whole of satisfaction. Only the spontaneous self-projection of the "I" allows this to occur (149.1–7 and 136.13–14). At the same time, the "I" thereby makes possible forms of pain and frustration unknown to other animals. An injury inflicted on man is potentially one that endures for a lifetime, since the "I" remembers. Humans willfully inflict harm on each other, knowing that they cause not only momentary pain but also lasting insult. To deprive another of the power of self-rule is the ultimate insult, directly attacking the "I" which makes one "complete." If the "I" dissolves, so does humanness (93.14–25 and 94.1–3). All forms of dependence tend to dissolve the "I," but dependence on humans especially does so. It is this greater stress on the unnaturalness of the will, both for good and evil, that compels the doctrine of rights after Rousseau and Kant to claim the failure of "natural right" doctrines and to speak only of "human rights." It is not difficult to see that the stress on that unnaturalness is at the heart of the crisis in reason exposed by Rousseau.[21]

The Analysis of Passion:
Honor and Benevolence

By imputing to human nature under all conditions a certain rationality, Kant also imputes to it a concern with dignity or honor. Servitude is regarded with horror because it contradicts the dignity of a rational being. But the striving for autonomy and the concern with dignity at its root are ambiguous. The striving for independence easily forges new bonds of dependence, since the quest for honor that is due a rational being easily gives way to a quest for honor that exceeds what is due. The nonpassionate self-esteem of the free and rational being can easily degenerate into a passion for honor that enslaves mind and body. The intrinsically human concern with honor is in fact the weak point in human reason and is the most evident sign of its dialectical character.[22]

It is in the spirit of *Emile* that Kant attempts to define a just sentiment or feeling of honor grounded solely on awareness of humanity in oneself and compatible with natural simplicity. Rousseau's aim of creating in Emile a limited concern with honor, to fortify his social and benevolent impulses, is clearly precarious. Kant looks for a rock-solid basis in human rationality for a nonpassionate honor; he restricts honor to a species characteristic. All honor rests on a sense of distinction, and honor is inescapably bound up with human self-consciousness; thus a concern with distinction belongs inevitably to all human endeavor. Yet Kant's views on the absoluteness of the "I"'s demands for autonomy render the concern with distinction dangerous and inherently tending to the tyrannical. In other terms, the absoluteness of that demand reflects an absolute gulf separating the human will from the rest of nature, and at the same time it makes the existence of distinctions between human wills insufferable. The only legitimate, and endurable, form that the striving for honor can take is pride in being human, or rather in not being subhuman. Yet since this honor cannot really be either won or lost, and since it abstracts from the obvious concern of humans for recognition from fellow humans for distinctions had in relation to *them*, it does not correspond to the kind of honor that for the most part engages the intense passion and interest of human beings.

We have already noted that Rousseau gives very little scope to pride or honor in the natural state; what there is of it is not passionate and not accorded the immense importance Kant ascribes to a primordial sense of dignity. What Kant ascribes to man in his earliest condition would in Rousseau's eyes be a passion and therefore suspect. Any strong form of amour-propre is characteristic of social man, his dependence on others, and it is regrettable. Kant's version of a strong and original amour-propre, in the form of "metaphysical honor" deriving from man's position within nature, would strike Rousseau as both a misunderstanding of the nature of honor and as offering no practical solution to the problems it causes.

Rousseau's psychology rests on the assumption that any intense form of human self-regard is connected with regard for other humans. It does not make sense to ascribe an intense self-regard to man as a solitary being, and it does not make sense to think it will remain in a nonpassionate form, once implanted. Kant himself is aware of an inherent ambiguity in the human sense of dignity, but is more confident than he might be that his rather "philosophical" version of honor is both universally effective and well grounded. One can trace his eagerness to grasp at this solution back to his original concern with justifying the moral man's view of the world. The "honor" of interest to Kant is really the "recognition," not by gods but by reason contemplating its situation in the whole, of the supreme worth of the virtuous will. Kant, like his modern predecessors, is aware that this demand for recognition is at the root of religious belief and that it readily supports dogmatism and fanaticism. Somewhat wishfully, therefore, Kant turns to his notion of "sound common reason" to find there only a "moral" interest in a recognition that is appropriate to man as rational: the self-ruling will (if kept free of corruption) will not look for divine rewards, but only for the reward of self-esteem. The fundamental Kantian project of reconciling human emancipation with the sacred and the noble comes again into view.

Therefore Kant's discussions of honor in the *Remarks* are of great interest, for they throw much light on Kant's approach to the teleological problem, in its version as the problem of satisfying reason's demand for a justification of the moral view of the universe. The "moral world" or the restored state of nature corresponds to the idea of a human wholeness or simplicity wherein all "ideal" concerns of man are limited to the maintenance of freedom and the flight from any injury to dignity; other anxieties and passions are unknown (121.15–22.6). A form of moral self-esteem operates in man, independent of the esteem of others. This idea of the natural state clearly transforms Rousseau's version wherein natural man is "good" but wholly without virtue. It hardly needs to be said that Rousseau does not intend his version to be a justification of the moral view of the universe.[23]

Following his analytical approach to discovering the presence of the "ideal" in the developed reason of social man, Kant thinks a line can be drawn between a limited concern with honor intrinsic to reason in its sound condition, and passionate and unlimited pursuit of honor that appears only when man has misused reason. Thus nature has planted in man neither "an immediate inclination to acquire" more than what is sufficient for basic subsistence nor "an immediate drive to honor" (17.5–11). Both drives exist only in the condition of "universal luxury," for only in that condition can excess honors and goods appear to be useful to one. The defining feature of the state of luxury is the fact that in that state human desire is mediated and determined by the opinions of others (166.10–17). Indeed that mediation is what distinguishes passion from mere inclination or desire. Passions are directed toward acquiring "goods of illusion," or goods whose value is more determined by the prevailing opinion of their goodness than by their actual utility to the individual. The driving force behind passion is principally the desire to acquire the high regard of others, by means of acquiring things that these others highly regard. The principal root of passion is therefore a drive toward honor granted by other humans (55.1–6, 163.2–3). This drive is not natural to man, for naturally man seeks only the honor or dignity he can give himself (160.20–22).

Kant suggests but does not directly state what it is that keeps the natural concern with honor limited and what it is that compels the acquired concern with honor to be unlimited. The source of natural honor does not elude the control of the "I," for it arises directly from the "I"'s sense of its own free activity. Honor sought through the opinions of others, by contrast, eludes the control of the "I." One who demands the certainty of being honored by others has embarked on a limitless and futile quest, for the opinions and wills of others are capricious and unpredictable. All the same, the tendency of man to embark on this quest is to some degree built into the natural situation. For every "I" in the natural situation seeks to be the absolute owner and master of itself, but finds itself confronted by other "I"s, upon whom, for various reasons, it is dependent. To win the good opinion of these others is a crucial means to gaining some mastery over these others and thus to securing the genuine good of freedom for oneself. All the same, Kant wishes to maintain that the independent form of self-esteem does not immediately degenerate into the striving for the esteem of others, and it defines an ideal condition approachable by social man. All natural inclinations are indeed good: "There is no immediate inclination to morally bad actions, but there is an immediate inclination to good ones" (18.10–11).

From the standpoint of original man's benevolence or philanthropy, it would appear that original man's indifference to the opinion of others must result in a rather passive virtue. He does little for others to gain their approval, and he is equally unconcerned with winning advantages over others (146.10–11). His self-love is always active, but it does not have the exclusive character of the corrupt self-love of social man; the natural man takes no interest in preventing others from being loved or esteemed more than himself (183.25–28). The primary good he seeks is his own freedom. He thus has an interest in being regarded as an equal, for that secures his freedom (162.13–15). Insofar as he has a natural concern with receiving honor from others, it is only with the minimal honor of being regarded as a human being equal to others by dint of reason (55.10–14). He naturally defends himself against attempts to subvert his freedom and against insults to his dignity (60.12–61.4, 163.1).

Yet one must concede the presence of instability in the original condition, if one does not abstract from human empirical characteristics, and if one considers what forces were in the natural state that would prevent it from ever being the "ideal" condition. Various forms of scarcity would give rise to mutual dependence and, thereby, to the concern with "opinion." Above all, sexual desire does not permit humans to remain self-sufficient and solitary, the more so since human sexual desire by nature has a certain unlimitedness; it is not strictly instinctual and not powerful only during mating seasons. Thus sexual desire is the most powerful impetus to acquiring the passion for honor (163.2–64.6, 165.15–16, 192.18–21).[24] In sum, the combination of the demand for autonomy grounded in rational spontaneity, the mutual dependence created by natural scarcity, and the unlimited character of the sexual dependency in particular is an explosive one that already exists in the natural state, tending to undermine its tranquillity and stability. Again Kant is more willing than Rousseau to admit elements of human rationality and sociality into the account of an original condition. In some respects, as in admitting a certain natural diffidence (a fear of inequality), Kant comes closer to Hobbes. Nonetheless Kant holds that prior to the creation of luxurious conditions this natural diffidence does not normally result in aggression or war (74.3–6, 102.12–3.7, 106.14–7.6).

The effort to distinguish between two forms of honor arises directly out of Kant's acceptance of the primary thrust of Rousseau's argument against earlier moral thinkers: neither sociality nor any inclinations that presuppose sociality (as regard for "opinion") are the basis of the true human goods, but only freedom. Moral virtue, the structure of the soul, human perfection—all derive, at least "ideally," from freedom. In Kant's transformation of Rousseau, freedom is itself grounded on an original rationality that has as concomitant aspects certain sociable inclinations.[25] All the same, Kant does not ground moral virtue itself on those inclinations. And more generally, those inclinations are a source of enduring and grave dangers to freedom and virtue. Thus the ethics of sociable feelings has not taken into account the role that reason plays in such feelings, of rendering them modifiable and highly volatile. Rousseau, far from offering Kant another version of *Gefühlsethik*, as has been claimed, has shown Kant the basic flaw of all such ethics.[26]

Although Kant still occasionally uses the term "moral feeling" in the *Remarks*, it is clear that he does not mean by it (as in the *Observations*) an underived love of humanity, but a feeling derived from the perfection of a free will.[27] Yet on the issue of "derivation" there is still a deep divide between Rousseau and Kant. Whereas the two agree that there are no underived moral feelings, for Kant there is such a thing as an original moral interest and motive, grounded in the freedom of the will. Whatever original moral or quasi-moral motives may exist in the state of nature for Rousseau (thus compassion), they lose their force with the growth of passions and the emergence of a complex way of life.[28]

Even so, Kant appears to have learned from Rousseau a subtle criticism of compassion and philanthropy, in terms of the effect that the cultivation of such feelings often has on character in the social condition. Only in the condition of "luxury" is the feeling of compassion nurtured as something good in itself. But this is a perversion of the natural order of things. Compassion is useful only as a spur to effective action; when cultivated for its own sake, it takes the place of action. Indeed, it weakens the capacity for virtuous action, since the man who fills his imagination with the sufferings of others is necessarily in a state of idleness and luxury, and thus is inclined to think others are suffering when they lack the luxury to which he is accustomed. His compassion reflects his own acquired and imaginary needs, and one who has more needs is less able to act. The philanthropist, on the other hand, is inclined to believe he has greater power to help others than is the case; his self-importance reflects again an overly cultivated imagination. Since he will experience that his real powers of benefaction fall far behind his imagined powers, he is likely to lose the simple pleasure in performing good deeds. Unlike the natural man, whose performance of good deeds corresponds to his real powers, the philanthropist pursues a "chimerical" and "fantastic" idea of virtue (25.11–15, 56.7–11, 173.1–15, 134.23–35.9).

The emphasis on freedom and equality in the natural state is incompatible with giving much importance to compassion as the basis of virtue. Where humans regard each other as equal, they are not likely to feel strong motives to benefit one another. On the other hand, the power of the individual to be a benefactor is greater in that state because needs are fewer. Benevolence tends to arise spontaneously from a feeling of power to help one who is weaker; it goes with a certain self-esteem for being powerful. The natural man will think less often, or not at all, about what he should be doing for others, but when he does act for others it is with greater pleasure and effectiveness (36.13–23, 162.4–9, 166.5–7). Kant develops here, in various ways, Rousseau's theme that the "powerful is the good" or that the condition of fewest needs conduces to benevolent action, for it is the condition in which self-sufficiency provides strength (4.15).[29] This is consistent with the view that self-interested feelings are older and more powerful than philanthropic ones (172.27–29).

The critical treatment of compassion and philanthropy not only underlines the rejection of moral sense ethics, but also points to a central feature of the rationality that replaces feeling as the foundational moral principle. Compassion and philanthropy, as products of the imagination in the state of "luxury," are instances of the loss of original or "ideal" equilibrium between desire and power. That loss is what makes virtue "ever more necessary and also ever more impossible" in the luxurious condition. The loss is caused, however, by the growth and progress of reason. At this point one can define the difference between Kant and Rousseau in the following way: for Kant, reason not only brings about the loss of equilibrium but also is in principle wholly capable of restoring it. Indeed, reason correctly understood is the original or ideal equilibrium itself, which reason itself has abandoned in an original error (or "sin"). Another way of putting this is to say that reason is identical with the sphere of justice and injustice, and justice for Kant is the foundation of the greatest good.

Justice and Equality

As "right" (*ius*), rather than as the habit or perpetual will to act justly (*iustitia*), justice can be defined formally as the correspondence between merit and reward, or between moral worth and conditions promoting happiness. It is Kant's view, and not Rousseau's, that happiness must always be considered, in the context of justice, as the appropriate completion of moral worth. Happiness should be sought only as that which is "owed" to one, for one's virtue.[30] The highest development of science is the determination of what is just for the human powers as a whole, that is, what is appropriate for the condition of a human being (7.8–11, 45.17–46.3). In other terms, the highest science determines the virtues or capacities of the human powers, and the completion that is appropriate or owed to them. With respect to the human powers, justice is the attained condition of identity between the completion for which they are suited and the goods or objects they possess. But the human powers thus far in their empirical history have attained mostly false and illusory goods that do not correspond to the true completion of these powers. Human history is mostly a spectacle of injustice.

If nature, wholly apart from the human will, were responsible for this failure, humanity would have little or no right to complain. But the complaint can properly arise that the human powers still lack what is "owed" to them—their true completion—if the fault lies in these powers themselves. For a demand for the just distribution of rewards is meaningful only if the distributor is capable of giving the reward. Nature in itself, wholly apart from reason's legislation, certainly cannot respond to the human complaint; it cannot distribute what it is incapable of giving. Rousseau points out that the human experience of injustice and frustration is the fault of the human powers themselves.[31] They have abandoned an original equality between their true capacities and their desires. Kant argues, more confidently than Rousseau, that what the human powers have abandoned, they should be able to restore. Very strikingly, the insight that reason alone introduces injustice into the world becomes the basis, in Kant, for the argument that the world as a whole is ordered toward justice.

It is a human tendency to have false conceptions of human powers and the attainable goods, and to abandon the just condition of equality between powers and conceptions of the good. One must go back to the original situation of man to understand this tendency, which is unlike any tendency in other animals. The tendency is partly due to the fact that original man, with his minimal development of reason, cannot yet know what his powers are; therefore he cannot know what is beyond those powers. He lacks the "science" of the extent of his powers, which could protect him from false steps and which can be acquired only after many false steps have been taken. Unlike other animals, the human species needs to know its powers in order to use them well; due to the lack of an instinctual determination for those powers, the human species naturally uses them in arbitrary or unhelpful ways. The human powers learn about themselves only through the consequences of their operation.

This offers some insight into what "knowledge" is for man. If the condition of justice is one of equality between power and desire, it is necessarily an ignorant condition. The natural man, being just, cannot know what justice in the fullest sense is. Having done little to advance his powers, he encounters few cases of disharmony between his desire to rule himself and the conditions of life. Only the unusual attempts of other humans to subjugate his will give him some sense of injustice and, therewith, of justice. Therefore knowledge of justice is the result of injustice; social man has knowledge of it because he is unjust. The distinction between the states of nature and of society is the expression of the fundamental disjunction between being and knowing—between being just and having knowledge of justice.

Knowledge alienates the knower from wholeness and being. Thus to be a knower is to be profoundly unjust. The philosopher is moved by this perplexity, but in striving to have more understanding of justice, he becomes ever more unjust. In striving to be just, he strives to be what he is not and cannot be. The state of nature, as an "ideal" that can never be real, is what is assumed for the sake of any knowledge, since the gulf between the real and the ideal is the condition of all knowing. Rousseau is more daunted by this gulf than Kant. The latter would argue that we can acquire knowledge of the limits of our powers and bring our desires into an accord with them that approaches ideal justice. It is possible and even necessary, first to learn what injustice is through the "dialectical" excesses of reason and then to withdraw from our injustice, within the barriers defined by an account of reason's powers. The *Remarks* introduces the idea of a science of the limits of reason's powers as the highest science (77.6–12, 181.1–4).

The injustice of social man consists in the fact that he has acquired desires that exceed his own powers and that thus have destroyed his self-sufficiency. His external servitude reflects an inner inequality. So long as the individual is sufficient to his own needs, he is equal to himself and free. Thus natural inequalities of strength, intelligence, and beauty mean nothing in the natural state, so long as the natural equality of each with himself persists. Such natural inequalities become objects of praise, blame, envy, and desire only when each human being is in need of others in order to maintain equality with himself, through them. But in that case each human being is truly less than himself. This is the real problem of conventional inequality.[32] By the analysis given above, the problem of conventional inequality appears in all efforts to increase knowledge. The desire to know is in tension with the absolute demand of the "I" to own itself and to be its own master. Yet the desire arises out of the same demand. Man has both a spontaneous "I," with no apparent determinate telos, and a dependent nature. Because he is this combination, both his equality with himself and his freedom are inherently unstable.

These observations on justice and equality throw light on the account of moral feeling in the *Remarks*. The replacement of the natural order of freedom and equality by the social order of dependence and conventional inequality has grave implications for the status of justice in the human soul (14.1–4, 40.1–3). In the theoretical ideal of the natural man there are no unjust inclinations; social dependence brings with it unjust inclinations and the need for rules of justice. Certainly spontaneous natural benevolence will no longer suffice in the social condition for the fulfillment of duties to others. And the need for an order within one's own soul, and for a principle to govern the inclinations, is something wholly new. For the first time man needs an ideal of perfection. Man does not know what perfection is until he loses it (again, this is what the "natural state" means). The rules that will direct man to his perfection are not derivable from "taking pleasure immediately in the well-being of others," that is, from moral sense (144.5–6). A more reliable source of moral motivation is "an immediate pleasure in the possible application of our powers to help others" (144.6–7). This pleasure is actually the enjoyment of a certain self-esteem: "We have reason to believe that what the sympathetic instincts of compassion and benevolence are supposed to achieve is actually derived from a self-estimation of the soul and its great strivings to ameliorate others' ills" (144.12–16). Morality is grounded in pride of being the author of prosperity for others. This origin alone is truly consistent with self-sufficiency and freedom. Moral rules, whatever they are, must be derived from this origin.[33]

"Sympathy is an instinct that is effective only on rare and very important occasions" and can by no means ground a universally effective morality (145.14–15). Feeling as a passive or pathetic principle is far less effective and powerful than the pleasure that arises from ourselves as active and free agents. The feeling of the latter sort is moral feeling (145.6–8). It is identical with "the greatest inner perfection arising from the subordination of all our powers and receptivities, under a free will" (145.16–18). Pleasure taken in the free will's activity manages to sustain natural freedom, to supply a widely effective motive, and to provide a principle for the internal structure of the soul, all at once. It is a pleasure (like moral feeling in the later writings) which does not precede, but must follow, the will's activity. Moral feeling is a form of receptivity to one's own spontaneity; it expresses perfect equality of the "I" to itself.

As was already noted, Rousseau suggested that a well-monitored amour-propre, directed at one's powers to help others, might be the force behind a morality consistent with natural freedom. The commentators who turn only to the general will (i.e., Rousseau's version of the generalizing of the will) for Rousseau's contribution to Kant's moral principle miss this essential ingredient of Kant's debt to Rousseau. What they miss is not trivial. The principle of the perfection of a free active will is the answer to a question: how is the will of social and dependent man to govern itself so as to approach ideal equality with itself, and thus to approach original justice? The background of this question is again the Rousseauian discovery that reason per se is the self-alienating source of human ills, and that to understand what reason is, and how human wholeness might be restored, one must be guided by the idea of the natural state. In other words, such an extraordinary inquiry is needed, which abandons so much "common sense," if we are to learn how human freedom is not to annihilate itself.

It is then from here that one can gather the sense of Kant's employment of the general will. For the identification by the individual of his will with an ideal universal will provides a "rule" for the active subordination of his inclinations to the free will. In other words, for human beings as dependent and "corrupt," a principle is needed which will reduce the dependency on inclinations (others' and one's own) and thus give maximum room for the free will to be the source of internal perfection. Rousseau asserts something similar about the general will: "Each, in giving himself to all, gives himself to nobody," for in union with all, each obeys himself. Kant writes, "this will contains now the merely personal will as well as the universal will, in other words, man contemplates himself in consensus with the universal will" (145.21–23). Without this self-contemplation within an ideal principle, dependent man may very well desire to perfect himself in active freedom, but pursue this end in a random and self-defeating way. Through abiding by the rule of universalization, he can bring his will into unity with itself and give it unobstructed freedom to experience its original perfection.[34]

The Kantian principle can seem wholly contrived if we do not know what problems it is trying to solve. It is indeed a forced combination of a political rule of legitimacy and a precarious soul structure of an "ideal" individual, both grounded in the spontaneity of a common reason assumed to be interested above all in securing inner freedom. But its purpose is clear now. Whereas the reason of man with its wayward and dialectical spontaneity has no assurance of maintaining its freedom and dignity through a rule or law provided by nature, human beings, or God, it can find such assurance through the self-imposed law that makes the will equal to itself and able to rejoice in its power of free action. That assurance has no other source. Virtue does in a sense have its own reward, and the question of justifying the moral view of the world can be answered affirmatively (174.1–2). Modern emancipatory reason has its theodicy.

Common Reason and the End of Science

The theodicy of the *Remarks* is an account of the free will that supports the belief, or hope, that the rational spontaneity seeking autonomy will not forever enslave itself to its own ideals (or illusions), but can, through self-legislation, restore itself to true freedom in the equality of power and desire. This means that the will can give itself a teleological ordering (a final goal of perfection) that is not "dogmatic." It means that modern freedom and the need for teleology can be reconciled or, in other words, that modern freedom can have an appropriate "sanction" from new forms of the noble and the sacred. It suggests that the self-legislative will is a new metaphysical principle that can supply meaning to the ultimate aspirations of reason for a satisfying account of the whole. And finally, this theodicy offers the glimmer of a hope that the employment of scientific reason for the sake of emancipating humanity may be able to justify itself, rationally, through the definition of a rational telos. Scientific reason need not undermine itself through the fact that it serves only an irrational telos, one whose goodness it is unable to establish.

The principle of freedom that has all of this promise was described above as a kind of logic of the self-ruling and self-unifying will. This use of the term "logic" was meant to make us think of the "transcendental logic" of theoretical cognition, which Kant discovers some years after the *Remarks*. For just as the logic of the will preserves it from extreme anarchy and alienation, the later transcendental logic of cognition brings to an end the dialectic of speculation and restores reason to harmony with itself. In other words, the transcendental logic helps to fulfill the program announced in the *Remarks*—of establishing a science that restores humanity to its genuine roots, or to its just situation, within creation. Kant discovers in the *Remarks* that the problem for all of reason is one of justice. As the critical writings declare, even for speculation the central question is one of "rights,"

of *quid juris*.[35] All basic questions are ones of justice only because nature does not strictly determine an end for the human powers, and
therefore those powers have both a "right" and a "duty" to determine
an end for themselves.

The relation between the moral teachings of the *Remarks* and the
first beginnings of the speculative critique is illuminated by the very
Rousseauian meditations in the *Remarks* on the problems of modern
progress. The present condition of science and philosophy is indeed
one of the prime indicators of the loss of "natural bases" and of the
"impoverished form" of humanity in the modern world. The progress of the arts and sciences has not been guided by the wisdom that
declares that "the final end of the sciences is to find the vocation of
man" (175.29). Although this progress has wrought amazing technical improvements that seem to increase human mastery over the elements and the human situation as a whole, "man is the corrupter of
nature, not its master" (91.13). The root of the difficulty is, again,
inequality—between human conceptions of the good or final end,
and the actual human powers. The goods for which men are striving,
through scientific and technical progress, are not those for which
their faculties are suited. Modern emancipatory science has thus
lacked guidance from human self-knowledge.

Perhaps most disturbingly, the moral doctrines that underlie and
promote the technical advance actually encourage self-ignorance since
they present an instrumental view of reason. The basis of that view
is that the good is the pleasant and that the pleasant is in no way
determined by reason. Yet if the good is the pleasant, then the good
is equivalent to what appears to be good. "Appearance" and "opinion" alone are the reigning forces in society. "The corruption of our
time comes down to the fact that no one desires for himself to be truly
contented and good, but everyone is satisfied to seem to be both"
(84.10–11). The only good known to the present age is the "good of
illusion," which "consists in seeking out only the opinion of what is
good, whereas the reality is regarded indifferently or indeed hated"
(55.1–6). Similarly, the age is dominated by "moral illusion" which
"consists in one's taking the opinion of a possible moral perfection for
the reality"(172.25–26). The modern liberal doctrine that the ultimate
good is simply identical with whatever the individual takes it to be
encourages, not surprisingly, spiritual debasement and enslavement.
For "appearance" or "opinion" almost never means the individual's
own experience, but majority opinion. The advance of science as furthered by the "opinion" of the good means the increasing power of
"opinion" over individuals and the loss of autonomy.

The corruption in the relation of the sciences to society is immediately evident in the motives of those who pursue the sciences. "The greater part of those who adorn themselves with science do not achieve the improvement of the understanding but attain only a certain perversity thereof," and they use the sciences as "instruments of vanity" (39.20–24). As they seek only various forms of pleasure through their scientific activity, they are hindered from attaining genuine insight, for "if enjoyment from the sciences should be the motive for pursuing them, then it does not matter whether one attains truth or error" (175.26–27). The modern sciences can be reformed and reach genuine truth only through a revolution in their end. Agreement on the practical end of science is a condition for overcoming speculative error as well as for improving the general moral condition of society.

Yet the problems that are so apparent in the modern sciences are to a certain extent intrinsic to science. In the first place science is, like war, servitude, and religion a consequence of human "deterioration"; science arises partly because man forgets his true vocation and partly because science is needed to help him remember it (78.4–6). Science is capable of bringing about a certain "lessening of the evil it has itself produced" (39.24–27).[36] Indeed the scientific knowledge of his vocation that man needs, or the knowledge of justice, has to be the result of the loss or forgetting of that vocation. But initially science mostly leads astray. The powers of human understanding are directed toward a goal that cannot be achieved within this life, with the result that one who is preoccupied with science "mans his post poorly" (38.5–10). There is some doubt as to whether the concern with science is even natural. That we take pleasure in science is not proof of its naturalness, since we can get pleasure from artificial things (38.3–5). And in general the pursuit of science fails to meet the criteria for what is "natural": (1) that it be in accordance with human necessities; and (2) that it be the common property of mankind, and not only of a few humans who oppress all the rest (35.1–4). But the sciences take long epochs to develop; they have been the preserve of but a few epochs and nations, and their success depends on good fortune (37.11–38.2). The undue estimation of the arts and sciences does not "belong to the ends of nature and disturbs the harmony of nature" (37.5–6). The highest aim of science must be to bring itself into accord with the ends of nature, that is, human nature. But that will require that science estimate its own worth properly in the light of its true end.

In accordance with the given definition of the "natural," science that naturalizes itself must establish a new and healthy relation with universal common reason. Given modern corruption of human reason in general, science must first recall common reason to its own principles. Science will recall it to "simplicity" and to awareness of the essential needs of man (6.6–11). The restored or uncorrupted "sound understanding" then provides the corrective to wayward speculation. Science should employ a "method of doubt" with respect to speculative thought in order to defend the sound understanding (175.13–20). "One must teach the young to honor the common understanding on moral as well as logical grounds" (44.6–7), because the common understanding points to both the moral end of science and the correct theoretical methods of science.[37]

In sum, the *Remarks* introduces the Kantian conception of science, according to which the most urgent task of science is to bring its striving for knowledge into agreement with the true end of humanity, which is found in the moral will of common reason or the freedom it seeks. At the present time science, whether as purely speculative or as instrumental to the pleasant and the passions, pursues ends that cannot fail to deepen the dependency of the human species on artificial and merely apparent goods. Yet the true good that must direct science is not to be found by theoretical means, through speculative knowledge of the natural order. Since human reason has a doubtful telos in any external order, the true good of human reason is found within itself, in its internal legislation of a harmonious order. The final "object" that can satisfy reason's quest, and at the same time give it internal order, is something that it must give itself.[38]

This necessity is connected with the circumstance that science necessarily, for long epochs, must be "corrupt" before it can be "sound." Human reason did not originally appear in the world with knowledge of its end, and nature did not fix an end for it to follow, like a somnambulist. Its self-knowledge, most deeply, is that it lacks such a fixed end; but it had to acquire that knowledge somehow, and it had to wander through the labyrinth of dogmatisms to do so. When reason at last discovers its true goal within itself, it can arrive at a just definition of first principles. "One can say that metaphysics is the science of the limits of human reason" because the first principles are not to be found in an order external to reason's activity (181.1–4).[39] Reason justly limits its account of first principles to the elaboration of its internal logic. This, as we have seen, is a logic demanding autonomy, and its power is evident in the universal longing for freedom. It is not the preserve of philosophers.

These considerations help us to understand, on more than an "emotional" level, what Kant has in mind when he says that Rousseau made clear to him why the philosopher cannot regard himself better than the common man (176.1–4). The emancipation of humanity must be a sacred project in order to succeed on its own terms. And the philosophical striving for the whole will be forever unhappy and frustrated if the world supports only the instrumental use of reason for mastery. But emancipation is a sacred project only if the human will is sacred or if "to honor mankind" is basic to the meaning of Enlightenment. Furthermore, if the sacred self-legislative will proves to be the sole source of intelligible unity within reason's principles, the metaphysician finds therein the "whole" which he seeks. He can be reconciled and end the war of his reason against its own limits. This is what Kant means when he declares that Rousseau "turned him around" and gave him several reasons "to honor mankind" (44.8–16).

4

The Origins of
Modern Moral Idealism, 1765–80

The Unity of Freedom and Nature
as Ideal Goal

In the *Remarks* one can discern the first indications of the "idealist" distinction between freedom and nature, and one can discern there the Rousseauian basis of the distinction. The terms *freedom* and *nature* are not yet clearly aligned into the fundamental contrast that tends to hold in Kant's later writings. All the same, the principles behind the distinction have been enunciated, and they arise out of Kant's transformation of Rousseau's treatment of reason. The transformation does not wholly distort Rousseau's thought. It builds upon some aspects of that thought which are accurately and faithfully preserved by Kant. Certain of the most fundamental attributes of *reason* according to Rousseau are of utmost importance for what one could call a shift in the center of gravity in Kant's thinking about reason: from a center that is primarily analytical, logical, and cognitive, to one that is primarily synthesizing, spontaneous, and practical. *Reason* begins to stand for, above all else, the fact that human powers are not defined by a natural order, although those powers have decided limits.[1] As we shall see, the combination of lack of definition and presence of limits characterizes the relation of freedom and nature, which is one of complementary tension and not one of mere disjunction.

The combination comes to view in Rousseau through the discussion of the ambiguity of reason; it has powers that are both wondrous and dreadful. The capacity of reason to create new ideas, to constitute the "I" of selfhood, to give rise to speech, and to devise projects that disregard or even defy the order of nature that limits other animals elevates human life to new heights, but at the same time exposes it to illusions and dangers unknown to the rest of nature. Human life is the victim of its own designs, for the projects invented by human reason almost always outstrip the real human powers of actualization. There is an inherently tyrannical bent to the development of these powers, and the tyrant is the most enslaved of all beings because he defies nature in his quest for superiority. In other terms, as man becomes more fascinated with his powers of inventing and pursuing "ideal" projects, he becomes less able to know himself; self-knowledge is the hardest of all knowledge to acquire.

The perplexity is not at all diminished by the assumption Rousseau makes—that reason is not truly a self-determining power, autonomous of the passions. The creation of new ideas is always propelled by the passions, which have themselves a limitless character. Reason *is* passion, most basically, and passion dominates human life as an uncontrolled and indeterminate force. Its force gathers mysteriously (like a power emerging out of nothing) through its own actions, since the products of the passions (ideas and imaginings) extend and complicate desire. In this way human life tends to "alienate" and enslave itself to its own creations. This circumstance reveals the unmistakable limits of reason, or of the whole of human inventing, projecting, and pursuing of "ideals" that can be called "reason."

It may be surprising at first to discover that this rather dark picture of human reason lies behind the Kantian account of freedom, with its elevating moral idealism. Yet after the concession is made to the "elevating" reading of Kant—that Kant ultimately cannot accept the Rousseauian identification of reason and passion—basic components of the dark picture remain. Just as strongly as Rousseau, Kant stresses the tendency of reason to abandon all forms of order and "simplicity." The nonteleological character of reason in Kant poses the same threats of "alienation." But just as there is in Rousseau some optimism grounded on the supposition that man is the creator of the principal evils befalling him, so in Kant the "dialectical" nature of reason becomes the basis for hitherto unimagined projects for moral reformation. Just as there appears to be no limit to human self-enslavement, there appears to be no limit to progress toward freedom.[2] Kant's greater hopes about such progress are, as has been noted, supported by an account of reason as spontaneous and self-determining. All the same, it must be kept in mind that reason cannot create this progress by mere fiat. The rational construction of the "ideal," and the unity of powers projected in it, is not an arbitrary one. Indeed in Kant's account of reason's discovery and pursuit of its ultimate end, reason must constantly struggle against a tendency to misunderstand itself and even to undermine itself. In fact his account of that end makes sense only as emerging out of reflections on such a tendency.

The end that reason postulates as its ideal of perfection, in the *Remarks*, is described in terms of "nature." This end, we have seen, is the idea of a recovered simplicity and order that is inspired by features of Rousseau's state of nature. The terminology of "nature" can mislead one as to the radicality of the departure of the new end of reason from all earlier notions of nature. The new idea of nature is not the structure of an empirical order, nor is it the characteristically modern reconstruction of the world in terms of notions immediately available to consciousness. For Rousseau and the Kant of the *Remarks*, "nature" is an idea that reason must postulate as the original unity that makes intelligible the persisting reality of reason's self-alienating unfolding. While it is a mere "idea," it is not on that account willful or arbitrary. There is only *one* idea that can underlie the process of reason's unfolding and explain why that unfolding is the source of evils—the idea of a never-experienced equality of desire and power, and of its abandonment. While Rousseau does not pretend that this idea is actually present in the consciousness of empirical human beings, except through a theoretical inquiry such as his own, Kant believes that such an ordering idea must be present in the actual willing of human beings, explaining the will's inherent tendency toward a moral adoption of universal maxims. In this way he begins a novel kind of "analysis" towards transcendental conditions of "factual" features of consciousness, replacing earlier modern forms of analysis.

Therefore the new idea of nature is an idea of freedom. Precisely because it is not an empirical concept of nature, and does not belong to the realm of the senses or perception, it is a first principle of a new metaphysical sort that applies only to the will, or reason. Not long after the *Remarks*, Kant begins to contrast the metaphysical realm of the will, or freedom, with that of the causal order of empirical nature given to the senses. At that point it is necessary for him largely to abandon the terminology of "nature" when speaking of the former realm. Yet in the writings of the "critical" period Kant will on several occasions refer to the goal of fulfilling the "nature" of the rational powers, and thus use the language of nature to describe what can actually belong only to the realm of freedom and the nonempirical ideals the free will postulates. In such cases the language of nature is reflecting the Rousseauian origin of the doctrine of freedom. Yet the "state of nature" itself acquires for Kant only a juridical and legal sense.[3]

It still remains the case that the idea of freedom, or of the original unity of the will with itself, retains an important relation to nature in the older and more familiar sense of "human nature." That is, human nature, as including crucially the dependence of man as rational upon an external world, through the senses and desires, is a presupposition of the new idea. The dependency of the individual on external nature and crucially on other members of his species is presupposed in passion and in the problems created when reason's spontaneity extends and intensifies the passions. Without that presupposition there would be no meaning in the idea of the will's recovery of unity with itself, and there could be no pressure of an inherent "logic" to universalize the will in order to regain the original unity.[4] The compound in human nature of spontaneity and receptivity is the condition for reason's coming into conflict with itself and of its striving toward unity in the prideful self-conquest that affords "dignity" to its existence. This is not to deny that the formal unity of the will is a "pure" motive that is underived from any of the natural dependencies, and that in a special way, the idea of "form" in the case of the will's unity is able to provide "content," in the sense of a motive and an object to be willed.[5]

Later we shall see how the mode of thought initiated in the *Remarks* becomes the Kantian way of seeking first principles in both the practical and the theoretical uses of reason. For in both realms, a primordial duality in reason's powers (of spontaneity and receptivity) is the starting point for formulating an ideal condition that corrects the tendency of reason to dialectic and that also constitutes the conditions making the "normal" and nondialectical functioning of reason possible. This mode of inquiry, in other terms, defines the context of "possible" functioning of reason. The definition provides the essential foundation for the future striving of the human species to bring its employment of reason into agreement with this context, and thus to bring to an end the self-subverting dialectic of reason on all planes—speculative, moral, and cultural.

Yet the approach of Kant to the complete formulation of this systematic foundation for the human self-correction of reason is gradual and long, as befits an undertaking of such dimensions. The present chapter charts essential steps that mark the way. Whereas the *Remarks* provides the core of the problem of reason, and the germ of the basic structure of its solution, it takes Kant more than a decade to understand how that germ is to unfold into a whole account of theoretical and practical reason in their unity and difference. We return to the observation Kant makes around 1769 that the practical sciences are "first in intention" in philosophy and the theoretical are "first in execution." The path to the whole critical "propaedeutic" in an account of the structure and limits of reason's speculative use is guided by an idea of the practical telos. The goal was evident well before all the means to it were.

Having examined the *Remarks*, one should now expect to find that the subsequent effort of Kant to bring theoretical reason into accord with that telos is more complex than the account in the familar text-book version. That is, the issue is not solely that of resolving the conflict between free causation required by morality and deterministic causation required by the sciences of nature. This is a primary, but perhaps only the most popular and accessible, version of the self-alienation of reason. It would be the one primary version of the problem only if all the difficulties in the whole culture of reason focused upon the questions that arise directly from the assumptions immediately underlying the Newtonian scientist's account of the laws of natural phenomena. Yet this is hardly the case, as becomes immediately evident from the facts that "metaphysics" comprehends much more than those questions and that the "foundational" reflection must turn on what is common to the whole array of metaphysical questions. Furthermore, the self-subversion of reason takes on forms in the areas of politics, religion, and aesthetics wherein the freedom/determinism issue is not relevant or wherein it is at least secondary to the main form of "dialectic." [6]

The *Remarks* offers a rich perspective on the question of the practical and moral end of philosophy. Reason's tendency to self-subversion takes on as many forms as there are uses of reason. The problematic relation of the receptive or dependent side of human nature to its spontaneous or freely projective side characterizes reason in all its forms. The way toward a final ordering of reason that brings about a harmonious relation defines the whole task of philosophy. That task is at bottom "practical" or moral because the self-ordering of reason is actually a problem of justice: reason is itself (and not a fixed natural order) responsible for its disorder. Kant believes he has acquired this astounding "analytical" insight from Rousseau's "synthetic" argument—that the "ideal" of such self-ordering is not a mere "chimera" and arbitrary postulation, because some degree of actual and effective order within reason must be presupposed for any of its operations. To uncover by a special analysis the conditions of that order offers us a notion of an ideal of the total ordering of reason's faculties, which can guide historical humanity in its future striving for wholeness.

Thus the actual moral autonomy or self-rule of ordinary reason is a perfection that points beyond itself to a yet higher degree of perfection: one of total subordination of reason to its internally legislated unity. The real and effective freedom in the human soul has an ideal basis that, when elaborated, is the ideal of a whole and completed humanity. It is an ideal in which the "natural" side of man and the "free" side no longer conflict or cause the subversion of reason's activity. Thus in the years immediately following the *Remarks*, Kant outlines the content of this ideal of the unity of freedom and nature, and begins to deliberate on how reason as a whole is to be criticized, so as to support its actualization. Already in the 1760s, the final task of philosophy, as the definitive solution of reason's fundamental perplexities, is presented as a "historical" task: reason achieves its "end" only through the united striving of the human species in a practical project of achieving "justice" toward itself. The origins of the critical philosophy are then to be found in a new "idealism" that is inseparable from regarding the problem of reason as historical and "cultural." Indeed, reason is identical with culture—the whole of the striving to realize free self-unity.[7]

After 1764 Kant begins to refer to the ideal unity of freedom and nature as "the highest good," and he also begins to define this ideal in an explicit argumentation with ancient accounts of the highest good. It is clear that for Kant this ideal unity is not a mere addendum to the chief moral principle, but essential to its meaning. It expresses the final consummation of the human striving for freedom that is implicit in the moral law itself. Reason must postulate the ideal unity because reason cannot regard either moral virtue or happiness as the whole or sufficient good. Since the ultimate problem of human life is that of the rational will achieving a just relation with itself, it is evident that both virtue and happiness (corresponding to the spontaneous and receptive powers) must be achieved in a manner consonant with such justice. Quite simply, both must be grounded in freedom. Happiness pursued with abject subservience to natural inclinations is surely incompatible with the perfection of the free self-ruling will. Happiness must be pursued in a perfectly just manner—one appropriate to a moral being. On the other hand, virtue by itself is insufficient, especially if virtue tends to cause suffering to the natural inclinations. The attainment of a wholly free and self-governing existence is not possible if inclination should forever be opposed to the advance of virtue; instead virtue points to the total end of the "alienating" consequences of the will. Unhappiness caused by the advance of virtue would have to be a sign of a defect in willing (since nature itself institutes no evils for man) and hence a sign of persisting "injustice" in the human condition.[8]

Difficulties that stand in the way of achieving this ideal are enormous. In the first place it becomes clear to Kant that earlier philosophers who concerned themselves with defining the manner in which virtue and happiness are dependent on each other have all been in error. Kant will later speak of a "dialectic of practical reason" that arises from natural misunderstanding of this dependence. Yet once that error is dispelled and other theoretical issues settled, the practical efforts of the human species in achieving the ideal still encounter serious problems. If by postulation, the perplexities of human life have been self-imposed through ages of the growth of reason and sociality, the overcoming of these perplexities must take countless ages of united striving by the whole species.[9] As we shall see, Kant's final word on the possibility of achieving the ideal does not rest with a theological solution. For Kant traces the origin of human evils back to "culture," to basic disproportions in human rational nature, that were "ideally" instituted by the will. For this reason the impossibility of achieving the ideal would have to show that the human species is unlovable. This certainly would not be the consequence, if permanent human defects instituted by nature or God made the achieving impossible. For in that case, if any thing would follow, it would be that nature or God is unlovable.[10] Only the human species, not nature apart from it or God, stands in a relation of justice to the human species.[11]

For the way in which Kant's account of this telos for theoretical inquiry and all uses of reason takes shape in a dialogue with ancient thinkers and in further dialogue with Rousseauian ideas, we must turn to the ethical writings of the period 1765–80.

The Failures of Ancient Moral Idealism

It should not be surprising if the first reflections of Kant on the nature of the "ideal" or "idea" of reason occur in the context of discussions of the tensions between reason and culture, on the one side, and happiness and nature, on the other.[12] For the Kantian notions of "idea" (the abstract goal of humanity) and "ideal" (the projected realization of the goal in individual beings) have Rousseauian roots.[13] Although the *Remarks* itself does not often and conspicuously use these terms, it presents the theoretical considerations to which these words will shortly apply, as fixed technical terms, in subsequent writings.[14] The natural state, not being an empirical condition, is a "standard" for the judging of the human condition (31.13–24). It lies outside the natural order as past common sense and science have understood nature (120.11–21.2), representing a "greatest inner perfection" to be achieved by the will alone, in its free subordination to universal law (145.6–25). The natural state of the will's equality with itself, translated into a goal for social and rational man governing himself by rules, represents an "idea" whose projected embodiment in an individual is an "ideal." Kantian "ideas" abstract from all natural teleology and are pure constructions of reason that are, nonetheless, universally valid and nonarbitrary.[15]

The fact that there are both Rousseauian and ancient origins for Kant's use of "idea" is not a mere coincidence. From the *Remarks* one discerns a return, in limited respects, to ancient accounts of moral virtue and human perfection. Rousseau inspires this return in several ways. He plays a large role in disillusioning Kant with the basing of virtue on either passion or sentiment and in moving Kant toward the noninstrumental account of reason as autonomous law-giving. Kantian moral virtue begins to resemble the autarchy of the wise man in Epicurean and Stoic ethics, who achieves independence of fortune, convention, and unnatural desires or passions through the discipline of reason, the latter forming itself according to conceptions of the natural life and its requirements. The emphasis in both Rousseau and Kant on basing moral virtue in a discipline of the will and on education could strike one as more ancient than modern. Certainly Rousseau makes a much warranted protest against the tendency of modern moral teaching to hand over the development and well-being of the individual to the forces of passion and interest, and to gauge the "worth" of the individual solely in terms of his contribution to the progress of society toward stability and prosperity. In this context we should hardly need to be reminded that Rousseau's hearkening back to ancient models is not restricted to an admiration of citizen virtue in the ancient polis or republic. Rousseau's concern with defining a structure of the soul that gives a foundation to independence from common opinion and a kind of autarchy surely has other ancient sources of a more philosophic sort. We have noted that Kant, however, is more confident than Rousseau about the immediate accessibility and universalizability of this more "philosophic" virtue.

When Kant, around 1764–65, begins to characterize human moral perfection in terms of the highest good or summum bonum and makes constant reference to the ancient doctrines of the highest good while defining his own, he does so under the aegis of Rousseau. The fact that all doctrines of the highest good are described as "ideals" in the novel sense that derives from Rousseau is philosophically the most significant point. Of a more circumstantial nature there is the fact that Rousseau is frequently mentioned (or Rousseauian terms such as "natural man") in the midst of the comparison of ancient doctrines. In fact Rousseau is the sole modern thinker who has this honor. Furthermore, the frequent references to ancient moral ideals begin in 1764–65, the period of the *Remarks* and of the intense reading of Rousseau; there are few references before these dates. Finally, Kant expressly calls Rousseau a kind of "ancient," and with evident reference to *Emile* he writes that "Rousseau's book helps us to improve upon the ancients."[16] Such evidence has led to the scholarly judgment of Rousseau's importance for Kant's new interest in the mid-1760s in ancient moral doctrines.[17]

Thus Kant sees himself as taking his cue from Rousseau in reviving the ancient controversy about the nature of the complete good that is the end of all human efforts at living well. Kant does not fail to note that the modern philosophers have neglected the question of the highest good; his praise of Rousseau as a kind of ancient is not meant loosely, but conveys that a genuine revival of a primary theme absent from modern thought is occurring in Rousseau. The modern philosophers, Kant notes, restrict themselves to the question of the "criterion" of moral judgment; the question of the perfection or telos of man is dropped. Where a notion of "perfection" does arise, as in Wolff, Kant complains that it is employed in an "abstract" and "formal" manner.[18] Of course Kant very well understands why the notion of the highest good has disappeared from modern discourse: all premodern notions of the highest good are in some way or another "dogmatic" and incompatible with the indeterminacy of the natural good or happiness that seems to be required by both the modern scientific account of nature and the modern liberal project of emancipating humanity. Thus modern moralists talk mostly about the "criterion of judgment" because they assume that the question of the human good must be reducible to the uncovering of the explicit or implicit inclinations or "senses" of the good present universally in common reason. The consideration of the perfect or complete good points to an authoritative goal that supersedes the individual's determination of his *own* good or his own powers of judgment. It also has the connotation of assuming a questionable harmony between the natural whole and human striving.

The revival of the highest good thus had to overcome the formidable obstacles posed by these modern arguments, whose force Kant basically accepts. Rousseau's success in the revival then points to a very high praise for him: he is the synthesis of Newton and Socrates. The Rousseauian revival is compatible with modern philosophy—with the indeterminacy of nature as required by science and individualism. This then is what is extraordinary about the new "idea" of perfection in Rousseau: it is not dogmatic, and yet at the same time it is prescriptive and not merely subjective. More strongly, it is a new sort of metaphysical first principle that thus indicates how modern philosophy may be able, on its own ground, to offer a first principle to rival ancient metaphysics. Rousseau "improves on" and does not merely revive the ancients. Finally, the effort to revive a Socratic inquiry into the complete good is not the result merely of sympathy with the ancient world. Rousseau shows that it is a necessity for modern philosophy itself to renew this inquiry, since the lack of clarity about its telos is endangering the success of the modern emancipatory project. The radicalizing of the modern principles will uncover a doctrine of the highest good as their necessary presupposition, without which those principles collapse upon themselves. Thus Kant's sudden interest in evaluating ancient discussions of the highest good is not an antiquarian one and is not secondary to the main question that has assumed crisis proportions: How is modern rationality to preserve itself through an adequate definition of its end?

All the same, one may wonder why Kant pays so much regard to the ancient doctrines if Rousseau offers a superior version of what they would offer. All the ancient doctrines assume what Rousseau rightly denies—that there is a given natural telos for man, and that the theoretical intellect can grasp what that telos is. Nonetheless there is a defect in Rousseau. The status and meaning of reason are very unclear in Rousseau, and the great merit of the new idea of perfection (its basis in freedom) has doubtful support in reason. By contrast, the ancient schools have all taken up the question of how reason is to ground the good. More specifically, they argue from the assumption, made in various ways, that man is a dual being and that the complete good must be defined in terms of that duality. In other words, the problem of the highest good is to find the right condition of reason and appetite, or of virtue and happiness. Rousseau has found a modern way to describe that duality—as the duality of freedom and nature, or of culture and nature. Unfortunately he has not made clear how the first term in the duality (freedom or culture) is anchored in reason as a spontaneous and autonomous power. Since there are no modern accounts of reason to help Kant at this juncture, he looks to the ancients for further assistance. This is not to retract the conclusion drawn earlier from the *Remarks*—that Rousseau provides the crucial insight for a new doctrine of practical reason, through his new "logic" of the self-limiting and self-unifying will. It is to say that Kant believes he must take that insight a step farther and elaborate it in terms of the fundamental duality in human nature (of spontaneous and receptive powers) that, from Kant's standpoint, Rousseau's own doctrine requires but does not employ.

The various doctrines of the highest good in the ancient schools are construed by Kant as aiming at one final good—at the combination of the maximum of human autonomy with a minimum of dependence on desires and passions that do not correspond to genuine needs. A version of this final good was mentioned in the *Remarks*, where perfection is described in terms of a maximum of power for active benevolence and a minumum of needs (146.2–9). Rousseau prescribes such a combination for Emile; there is an inverse proportion between our power for acting well and the extent of our needs. Thus Rousseau shows that our power to be free and self-ruling cannot be considered in abstraction from the condition of our desires and needs. And indeed he shows how, rather paradoxically, our modern culture of freedom tends to extend those needs in a way that is harmful to freedom. His argument demonstrates that modern man requires a conception of his whole life that will shape desires and needs in a way that is consistent with being free; a new telos is required. The moral principle of autonomous self-legislation cannot disregard the condition of the inclinations and desires, even though it does not take its "motive" from them. If the culture of freedom that promotes autonomy is simultaneously extending the needs that undermine autonomy—which is now the case—then free rationality must have regard for a "totality" of the human condition in which the progress toward freedom transpires consistently.

The perspective Rousseau offers on the theme of the highest good is a novel one emphasizing the historical and modifiable character of the human faculties. Kant brings that perspective, which is alien to the ancient authors, to bear upon his evaluation of ancient thought, while at the same time he tries to reintroduce elements of ancient reason into a modern context. The outcome is an essential element of the foundation of modern moral idealism—a doctrine of historical reason and its ideal telos. Various aspects of the new approach to reason come to light through Kant's judgments on the ancient forms of idealism.

Numerous reflections from the *Nachlass* discuss the Cynical, Epicurean, and Stoical accounts of the highest good or "moral ideal." These schools variously evince something praiseworthy: a concern with the maximum of virtue or capacity for "good action" grounded on freedom of the will under rational guidance.[19] They argue that virtue is the principal source of human happiness or perfection and that reason is the principal source of both; they rightly stress that human beings acquire the principles of virtue without divine assistance.[20] The Cynics strive toward "simplicity" in the minimum of desire, from which a maximum of happiness is alleged to result, since pain is caused by excess of desire.[21] The Epicurean notion is a positive one of the greatest pleasure rather than a negative one of reducing pain, but it too approaches happiness through reason and prudence in the quest for a moderate way of life. The Stoics identify the greatest good with a morally striving will. Neither the minimum of pain nor pleasure achieved through moderation is the direct goal, since pain is natural and evil is conquered by fortitude, not by moderation alone.

Each school analyzes the complete good in terms of maxima in the use of reason or will and minima in the condition of desire. In the case of the Cynics and Epicureans the maximum good results from a minimum in desiring; in the case of the Stoics the maximum of virtue in willing is itself the good.[22]

All of the ancient ideals furthermore assume the dualism of rational and desiring faculties; that dualism structures the search for maxima and minima. For the maximum of rational freedom and the minimum of desire are present in each account, although in some cases the maximum is only the means and in other cases (the Stoic) it is itself the end. The problem of the complete good, it can be said in general, is to establish the right proportion between basically heterogeneous elements of human nature that tend to be in a wrong proportion. This proportion is not fixed by instinct, and the tendency of each element is to disregard, or be ignorant of, its proper relation to the other element. Desire tends to ignore reason; reason in its turn, knowing it should rule desire, needs training and experience in order to do so.[23] Kant thus admires the ancients for their upholding the dualism of faculties and for realizing that the unity or the harmony of these faculties is a major, perhaps the major, problem of human life.[24]

On the other hand, Kant's treatment of this dualism betrays modern presuppositions, and especially Rousseauian ones. In the first place, there is the complete absence in his account of the ancient schools of any reference to the relation of the human soul and its virtue to cosmological principles—an absence particularly notable in the case of the Epicurean and Stoic doctrines. This absence is related to the characterization of virtue in terms of maxima and minima. For that mode of analysis is related to the understanding of the perfection of the human condition as a condition of equality between the powers of willing (or reason) and desiring; such equality is only an "ideal" and is not part of human empirical life or experience.[25] It certainly cannot be abstracted or otherwise known directly from the actual operation of human powers. We recall that the Rousseauian insight that perfection must have such an "ideal" character follows from the radically nonteleological view of those powers, such that their actual operation can result only in limitless striving and its "alienating" consequences. The empirical order of nature, nature as we can know it theoretically and scientifically, provides no basis for the completion or satisfaction of that striving. The ancient doctrines must be restated without any cosmological elements. The limitlessness of the human faculties can attain a satisfactory limit only through the construction of "extremes" that have no existence in the empirical order. This is the rational construction of a nonexistent "nature."

The Rousseauian analysis of the human problem discussed the ine-quality of powers as their unavoidable "real" condition, but did not postulate a "real" duality of powers to explain it. That postulation is the basis of Kant's renewal of the ancients; by means of it, he hopes that a real approach to ideal unity is possible (whereas Rousseau has in a sense only an ideal approach to ideal unity). If the problem in Rousseau is that he lacks a dualistic basis for ideal unity, the problem in the ancients is that they lack the "ideal" understanding of the unity to be achieved through dualism. They assume, as "dogmatists," that there is a given, natural telos for the powers, knowable theoretically.[26] Their theoretical failure is that they do not grasp the historical and modifiable character of the powers whose obverse side is their limit-lessness. That failure has the immediate practical consequence that the ancient moral principles have doubtful effectiveness. A few ex-amples of Kant's criticisms reveal the related theoretical and practical failures.

Of the principal schools reviewed, the Stoic gives the largest role to the free rational will, in Kant's understanding, and is the "truest in pure morality." Yet of all the doctrines the Stoic is the least appropri-ate to human nature and thus is "incorrect *in concreto*"; it is the doc-trine that is hardest to apply or make effective.[27] Of the Epicurean doctrine the opposite is said: it is the most effective in application to human nature but is "morally false" when judged by the "pure rule" of morality; it contains no teaching of genuine virtue.[28] Interestingly, the Cynical doctrine is "theoretically correct" and is closely allied to Rousseau's "ideal of an artificial education." All the same it has not adequately defined the end of moral life, for its notions of naturalness and simplicity provide only a "doctrine of means."[29] Presumably it fails to grasp that freedom of the will is the true end and content of the idea of natural simplicity. All these criticisms seem to point to-ward one general criticism: the ancients make "chimerae" out of their ideals, through neglecting, it seems, either the true *end* of morality or the *conditions* for the effectiveness of the moral rule.[30] As a result, the ancient doctrines are "mere theories of moral philosophy" that do not translate into effective forms of practice.[31]

The criticism of ineffectiveness, which in various forms occurs throughout modern "realist" attacks on ancient thought, would seem hard to reconcile with Kant's emphasis on the "purity" of the moral rule and the new "idealism" based on it.[32] Furthermore it seems to apply chiefly to the Stoics, who on the other hand come closest to Kant's concern with the pure moral will. Yet apparently the Stoics lack some important insight into human nature, without which they are unable to prescribe a version of the pure ideal which can be truly effective. And the Epicurean effective appeal to pleasure and the inclinations is also chimerical because of, presumably, the same lack of insight. That lack cannot be simply the lack of the "pure rule," if the deficiency is the same for all the schools, since the Stoics are not wanting on that point.

One acquires some insight into the alleged common deficiency of the ancients from reflections that point to the strengths of Rousseau's account of human nature. Briefly, the essential point is the failure of the ancients to realize that the rational powers of man are as much the cause of disequilibrium as they are the source of possible order in the soul. The ancient view of reason is too optimistic. Now it is of utmost importance to realize that when Kant makes this charge, he does not indicate that, after all, he agrees with an earlier modern view of reason as instrumental to passion. Reason's spontaneity and its distinctness from the receptive faculties were, in Kant's view, anticipated, if obscurely, by the ancients. Yet the ancients did not see how wayward and problematic is the "progress" of that rational spontaneity in the realm of culture. They relied on a form of reason that was assumed to be well embedded within a natural teleological order. Hence the pure reason of the Stoics is, as much as the impure prudence of the Epicureans, insufficiently armed against the dangers that arise from reason itself. The enemy is not solely (or even properly) the inclinations or the excesses of desire.[33] Stated in other terms, the ancients did not possess knowledge of the historical character of the rational powers, which has been exposed so dramatically by Rousseau.

A couple of reflections mentioning Rousseau, or thoughts clearly ascribable to him, help to make clear that such is the critique of the ancients. One reflections lists four deficiencies of earlier moral thinking.[34] In the fourth the ancients are mentioned specifically. Kant complains of (1) neglect of the difference between natural and morally or socially formed (*gesittete*) man; (2) confusion of the pragmatic with the moral; (3) neglect of "the moral as such, without regard for what is peculiar to a human being and its situation"; and (4) the error of the ancients who "confounded natural law with ethics." Points (1) and (3) are linked to Rousseau's discovery that earlier moralists took man as they knew him, formed by their culture and its accidents, to be humanity's essence. That error is corrected by the discovery of man's historical essence.From it follows the conclusion that one cannot proceed "empirically" in ethics and abstract from man as history has made him, what the human potentials are. Yet this is what the ancients (and not only they) have done. Their theoretical failure entailed that they could not have seen the "ideal" character of virtue or perfection; hence they confounded natural law with true ethics (4). From this flows another failure, this time of a practical nature: the ancients could not arrive at moral principles that are truly prescriptive and obliging for all human beings under all circumstances (2).

What Kant does not care to state about the ancients is that they knew they were not providing a universally prescriptive ethics. They acknowledged that the achievement of excellence is conditioned by circumstances that often lie beyond human control. This is stated perhaps more emphatically by Plato and Aristotle than by the later schools that are more attractive to Kant.[35] Antiquity had not yet embarked on the emancipatory project to make such conditions irrelevant to the human attainment of the good or to conquer such conditions and free humanity from the dominion of nature and chance. Rousseau and Kant, who are profoundly in accord with that modern project, nevertheless believe they uncover defects in human rationality that make its achievement very difficult. To conquer those defects means to advance the emancipatory project; it does not mean to return to an ancient standpoint. But in their view it may mean that one can combine modern freedom with what is most valuable in ancient thought.

The severity of the rejection of the ancient standpoint comes out clearly in another reflection that mentions *Emile*.[36] The reflection has a heading: "The order of considering human nature is as follows." Among the points Kant raises are: (1) "the natural indeterminacy in the kind and proportion of human powers and inclinations, and the potential of human nature for taking on every kind of form"; (2) the human vocation and "whether man's estate consists in simplicity or in the highest culture of his powers and the greatest satisfaction of his desires"; (3) the natural purpose of the human powers and "whether the sciences necessarily belong" to that purpose; (4) "the art or culture of the powers and inclinations that most accords with nature," considered in the light of the moral education in *Emile*. The first point, not stated as a question, points to what is problematic in all the other points: whether the human essence is natural.[37] The difficulty, indeed the impossibility, of answering that question in the affirmative explains why the highest good of man must be considered in the light of the tension between "culture" (the actual unhappy unfolding of the human powers) and "nature" (as the postulated ideal of perfect unfolding).

Morality as System

Although the ancient ideals are to be radically transformed by the historical account of reason, Kant continues to employ surveys of ancient doctrines as a way of introducing the topics of the highest good and the ideal of reason. He does this both in the course of ethics lectures, delivered between 1775 and 1780, and in the *Critique of Practical Reason*.[38] The discussion in the lectures is closely related to the discussions in the *Remarks* and reflections of the 1760s, and thus we turn briefly to them for further instruction about the original intent of the highest good in Kant. The topic is broached in a section "On the Moral Systems of the Ancients," where it is strikingly brought into relation with the notion of "system." The use of this terminology for discussing the highest good is not new in 1775,[39] but the very prominent juxtaposing of "system," "ideal," and "highest good" in the lectures suggests that Kant has a more defined and articulated view of how moral perfection serves as the final end of reason as a whole, conceived as "system." Indeed the notion of a system of all the rational strivings of man, united in one concept as their telos, appears to be emerging as the central consideration of all philosophy.

The idea of a system of reason that unites the principles of freedom and nature, and whose realization in history functions as the ultimate telos of all rational strivings, is clearly adumbrated in the idea of the highest good as found in the ethical writings between 1765 and 1781. Indeed the discussions there could not lead one to suppose that the idea of the highest good is a minor issue, secondary to the meaning of morality as well as to reason as a whole. Furthermore, since we have seen how any account of human perfection has to come to terms with the historical and indeterminate character of reason in "culture," we are prepared to find that more lies behind the problem of the highest good than may at first be apparent. In the ethics lectures, the "system" of the unity of happiness and virtue that is required by morality might seem to be self-contained and to have no relation to a wider system of reason as a whole. But two important writings that precede the lectures, the *Dreams of a Spirit-Seer Explained by the Dreams of Metaphysics* of 1766, and the *Dissertation on the Sensible and Intelligible Worlds* of 1770, indicate that a larger role must be assigned to the highest end of reason as defined by morality.[40]

In anticipation we can note that the following features are found in the emerging system of reason that is equivalent to the fully elaborated idea of the highest good. (1) The achievement of the complete good takes the form of an endless approach to the realization of a "moral world" that unites maximum virtue with happiness for all rational beings. (2) The same moral world is understood to be an "effect" of human free will and not a gift of divine grace, even though the mechanism whereby it is to be achieved surpasses theoretical insight and must be conceived with the help of postulates. (3) An essential precondition for the approach to the reality of this ideal is the harmony of all rational wills under self-imposed laws, and such harmony rests on the enactment of political, educational, and religious reforms within human history.

With respect to this least feature, it is of first importance to note that it presupposes the mutual dependence of rational wills as having a sensible character; it therefore presupposes the problems in the development of reason and culture that arise from that dependence. In other words, in a subtle and understated way, all of the accounts of the final end of reason assume human sociality and the problems related to it. On reflection, that is hardly surprising since the highest good is the idea of the unification of the two sides of man's being, and these come into conflict crucially because man (as both free and dependent) is social.[41] One question that concerns us is how such reciprocal dependence of humans is of importance to "pure" morality, which seems to abstract from such conditions that are, apparently, "external" to the internal self-determination of the pure will. Another is how the highest good as "effect" of the will is, in some way, produced by human actions in history. And third, we need to know how such a worldly "effect" relates to the otherworldly dimension of moral history, which rests on postulations of God and immortality.

The ethics lectures introduce the highest goood as a moral "system" that has been conceived in diverse ways by the ancient philosophers. In the first place, the highest good is an ideal: "We may call this *summum bonum* an ideal, that is, the highest conceivable standard by which everything is to be judged and weighed."[42] All judging of things with respect to some possible perfection requires "archetypes" to guide the judging; such an archetype is an ideal that never permits full actualization. But an archetype is not merely a criterion of judgment. It is also a notion of a reality (infinitely distant) to be attained by our striving.[43] Thus "archetype" refers properly to an object of the will (its intended effect) and not to an object of cognition. The object in question is that of a most perfect world in which rational beings are both happy and worthy of happiness. It corresponds to the unity of virtue and happiness that the ancients said could be achieved only through a free will. Furthermore, the object that is judged by the archetype of the perfect world or highest good is our actual world and the condition of man in it. The "ideal" is not wholly severed from the actual world but rather represents the standard to which human efforts constantly refer, as they strive to bring the actual world to perfection. The archetype serves as a standard for the judging of our actions and their relations to their intended effects.

The perfect world to which all our strivings refer as their goal must include happiness, because from a purely rational standpoint, a world in which virtuous beings are unhappy is repugnant. However, since the ancients were correct in asserting that "happiness springs from man's freedom of will," it seems that the perfect world will somehow, as a whole, be the effect of human freedom. Perhaps the only world that is wholly satisfying to reason is one that reflects reason's activity and in which happiness is the product of reason and not merely a gift of fortune or grace.[44] In any case, the ethics lectures leave no doubt that the highest good is understood as an object to be achieved by human efforts: "The ultimate destiny of the human race is the greatest moral perfection, provided that it is achieved through human freedom, whereby alone man is capable of the greatest happiness. God might have made men perfect and given to each his portion of happiness. But happiness would not then have derived from the inner principle of the world, for the inner principle of the world is freedom."[45] The worldly character of the human destiny becomes clear from Kant's discussion of the role that states, princes, and educational institutions must play in its attainment.

In the light of this conception of the ideal or system of morality one must evaluate Kant's criticism in the ethics lectures of all the ancient ideals, which criticism is related to the charge that these ideals are "chimerical" or merely "theory." The criticism is that "the ancients had no conception of any higher moral perfection than such as could emanate from human nature."[46] This applies to all the schools, even the Stoics, insofar as all ancient ethics aim at a natural end or perfection, and lack true insight into freedom or into reason as striving beyond everything merely natural. As we saw, it is the ancient neglect of the unnaturalness of human reason that undermines the true effectiveness of their ideals. Somewhat paradoxically, the ancient optimism about reason's "naturalness" results in a morality of limited ambitions (being restricted to an elite with gifted natures or fortunate circumstances) and to an underestimation of what reason understood as freedom can accomplish, in the way of achieving universal goals for the whole species.

The true intent of Kant's criticims is not to say that the ancients are eudaemonists or that they offer only "impure" motives to the moral will. Indeed, the Stoics exaggerate the human capacity to disregard happiness and to find satisfaction in individual virtuous willing alone. This exaggeration is part of their unwarranted optimism. One can again say that "ineffectiveness" is central to the charge of excessive reliance on nature.[47] Indeed, the human will needs an incentive in an idea of happiness resulting from the free and extraordinary transnatural efforts of the human species. Only a united project of achieving perfection on the part of mankind (a project of conquering nature) can result in a happiness "justly" apportioned to the strivings of the moral will. What the ancients offer as compensation for virtue is, for Kant, paltry. The pure ideal of the Stoics is insufficiently universal, comprehensive, and elevating to motivate and guide human efforts toward the free condition of wholeness and unity of the will with itself.

All the same, the true ideal is a worldly one insofar as it is to be the product of human freedom. And it is with this in mind that one must interpret the favorable remarks on Christianity that conclude the discussion of ancient ideals. The Christian ideal, which is one of holiness, is praised for resting on the purest morality and, at the same time, for giving the strongest motivation to the will among all ideals. That powerful motive is its promise of "happiness beyond this world," which is certainly something the ancient natural ideals do not promise. Nonetheless the Christian ideal is criticized because "it is humanly unattainable and bases itself on the belief in divine aid."[48] Thus the highest moral ideal would combine the strengths of Christianity and antiquity; it would propose the loftiest object of universal perfection, transcending the limits of the merely given situation of man, but it would insist on the human will's sole responsibility for reaching that perfection.[49] This synthesis, however, is not derived from the two premodern elements, but uses those elements to secure and render more attractive a distinctively modern account of the ideal. For both premodern elements are unaware of the true meaning of autonomy and its basis. They do not see that the primary dangers to human life arise from the limitlessness of the free will (perhaps classical antiquity being more wanting here), and they do not see how the same will is also capable of infinite projects of reform, with its unaided powers.

That the highest good is an ideal of universal perfection and that as a "system" it encompasses the strivings of all rational wills thus emerge from the ethics lectures. Later we see how this universality arises from the conditioning of the individual's striving for perfection by the progress of the whole species. This is a major theme of several "critical" writings after 1781. Yet its origins are in the account of culture in the 1760s, and the conditioning is already indicated in Kant's first published work to discuss the new ideal of a moral world based on freedom—the *Dreams of a Spirit-Seer*. This work, the first to display the consequences of the absorption of Rousseau's revolution, is notable for three other features: (1) it is the first work of Kant to offer a description of a will that is "pure" and of a morality that arises solely from the universal voice of moral reason, rather than from moral sense; (2) it introduces the doctrine of the practical end of all philosophy and rational inquiry, as determined by pure morality; (3) it elaborates the definition of metaphysics introduced in the *Remarks* as the "science of the limits of reason," whose aim is to defend common moral reason against distortions by speculative thought. The new science provides unobstructed room not only for the primary rules of morality but just as importantly for the striving of the system of rational wills toward its ideal completion. This essay begins to show clearly how the novel view of the practical end of reason determines the nature of theoretical inquiry. But, as was observed by some of Kant's contemporaries, the essay is puzzlingly ambiguous and leaves the reader uncertain of its verdict on theoretical reason's competence.[50]

The account of the moral world as a system of wills in the *Dreams* rests on the morality of the "simple heart." The prescriptions of a pure morality, present in every human being, give rise to a "moral faith," with its component doctrines of divine governance of the world and immortality of the soul.[51] Theoretical inquiry has the function of supporting the validity of these doctrines. Moreover, theoretical investigation discloses that reason cannot argue against the possible reality of a hypothesis concerning the "systematic constitution of a spiritual world"; this hypothesis, which is merely possible from a scientific or theoretical standpoint, acquires a "probable demonstration" from an "actual and generally admitted observation" taken from moral experience.[52] Kant now introduces a mode of argument characteristic of his "critical" thought: moral experience points to a realm of hypotheses that elude theoretical validation, but that also transcend theoretical confutation, as theory itself stringently can show. Thus morality opens up the possibility of a metaphysics of a new sort, concerned with objects produced by or implied by the activity of a free will ("noumenal" objects) and transcending the whole realm of sense ("phenomena") to which theoretical science is limited.[53]

The "generally admitted observation" that occasions the hypothesis is this: in contradiction to the impulses of self-love there are certain "powers" in the human heart that compel human beings to direct their concerns toward the well-being of others. These "powers" seem to lie outside the human heart and to reside in a "foreign will" that restricts the otherwise unlimited self-love of man. The effect of such power is to cause a feeling that the "drives" of human beings need some "focus" outside the individual, in the universal good. Such a feeling of necessitation ("moral feeling") is a mere appearance, which the human mind surmises is derived from some higher cause inaccessible to its cognition.[54] Hypotheses about this causation are theoretically permissible, and one in particular recommends itself from a moral standpoint. Our experience of a need to "harmonize with a universal will" as the "focus" of our strivings is by hypothesis the effect of a real interaction of spiritual natures. These are acting through human willing to bring about a "moral unity and systematic constitution" of all rational wills, "according to purely spiritual laws."[55]

The experience of a compulsion to place the focus of our strivings in a universal will surely recalls the identification of the individual will with the universal will in the *Remarks*, which there, too, is the ground of moral feeling and also the sole source of self-consistency in human willing. As in the *Remarks*, the principle of a universal will (or "system of spirits") provides a basis for morality that must be distinguished from self-love and to that extent is like a "foreign will" acting on the inclinations. The point, again, is that one has to look away from empirical human nature, toward a rational "ideal," to grasp what can ground true freedom and self-consistency in the will. The source of morality is not, as in ancient (and early modern) doctrines, part of that nature.

Such considerations enable us to place the apparently rather wild "spiritualism" of this hypothesis in the proper perspective. It is not altogether certain that the hypothesis requires that the spiritual realm be composed of wholly intelligible beings, distinct from human wills. Indeed, the hypothesis may be incoherent if the spiritual realm is understood in that way. For the hypothesis requires that the spiritual cause of our striving also be the goal of that striving, that is, something attainable "ideally" by the human will. To be precise, the feeling of necessitation spurs the human will to strive for a certain effect in the world—the instituting of just relations between virtuous willing and happiness for rational beings in general. The striving of the will does indeed encounter a disturbing lack of just accord between "moral and physical relations for men here on earth." And moral striving is frustrated by the recognition that "the morality of actions cannot have its full effect in the corporeal life of man according to the order of nature," that is, according to the natural laws of mechanism.[56] Accordingly, as the final end of moral striving, human reason must postulate an ideal world in which just proportion is achieved. But it is supposedly a realm of pure spiritual natures which is acting "through us" to bring about a world that is, as "ideal," identical with their own—a systematic constitution of wills governed only by pure moral laws.

Now Kant insists that his hypothesis in moral theology does not make an appeal to miraculous causes; he asserts the principle that postulations about theological matters must be made in accordance with the requirements and goals of earthly strivings. And thus he remarks that our earthly striving and the achievement of its final goal must be a "continuous whole according to the order of nature." If this is so, the spiritual natures that work through the human will are not separate from it but immanent in it and striving in it toward the creation of the moral world. It is hard to see that the "realm of spiritual natures" means anything more than reason's "ideal" and its power to motivate human striving. For only then can the source and the goal of willing be the same or continuous. (If the spiritual natures as a separate world were both source and goal, it would be hard, if not impossible, to conceive how that world could be the "effect" of human willing.)[57]

Such adjustments of the meaning of "spiritual nature" seem required in order to avoid a "fanatical" interpretation of Kant's hypothesis. Furthermore, they are in accord with the style of the essay, which is at once playful and reserved.[58] Nevertheless the hypothesis remains obscure; in particular it seems that the "continuous whole according to the order of nature" must rest on something other than the laws of nature governing phenomena. This notion of "order" seems to point toward Kant's investigations into hidden harmonies between the phenomenal order of nature and an intelligible substrate, and thus into a possible more comprensive notion of "nature" that includes the ideal workings of moral reason.[59] But more generally, one can say that the hypothesis is of interest for its implied presentation of the highest good as the ideal unification of the two aspects of human nature (freedom and inclination), which is to be achieved solely through human striving. It thus points to the new Kantian notion of "system," understood as an ideal end of unification to be furthered by all the human rational strivings.

The *Dreams* introduces the morality of postulations, for the scope of human striving is one of infinite futurity. The concern with immortality is thus grounded in human reason.[60] But accordingly any postulations of an afterlife have to be consistent with reason or with pure morality. In other words, morality cannot be grounded in the hope of rewards to be received in an afterlife. On the contrary, the afterlife and all doctrines of moral theology must be grounded in the unconditioned precepts of morality, as the postulation of conditions for the achieving of the object required by those precepts. The moral doctrine of the *Remarks* and the hypothesis of the *Dreams* taken together suggest that immortality or infinite futurity is inseparable from the foundation of the new moral metaphysics of freedom because that metaphysics is not one of separate and actual substances. Rather, it is a metaphysics of the unification of the strivings of finite reason according to the "logic" of the will, which is inherently an infinite project. This does not preclude that Kant's philosophy, as a moral metaphysics, is an attempt to come to terms with human mortality. Indeed it may be the greatest "interest" of this supposedly "disinterested" morality to provide a confirmation of the human need for a sense of "worth" within the natural whole, which means nothing less than to answer the question of what death means for a self-conscious and free being such as man. To provide an answer to that question is unavoidable for any philosophy that dares to be responsible for the whole human condition.

Socratic Metaphysics as Science of the End and the Limit of Reason

While the *Dreams* essay suggests a possible moral system embracing the free will and phenomenal nature, brought into a just relation through the united strivings of human beings, it also suggests that such a system determines the just employment of moral and theoretical reason, and their proper relation. The first foundations are laid here for a system of reason that comprehends all uses of reason and that is not restricted to morality. Yet these foundations are laid under the aegis of morality; the moral strivings of reason result in a projection of the outlines of a final ideal "whole," comprehending all the human faculties and bringing them to consummation in relations of harmony. Morality provides the telos, the prior "intention," that guides the progress of philosophy. Therefore moral principles are the true first causes, and the whole that is defined by them is the true whole. Put in other terms, the true "whole," which all past philosophy has sought to define and know but which it has misunderstood in "dogmatic" fashion, is the wholeness of the human faculties, their just and self-consistent relations. In grasping that this is the true whole of concern to his reason, man returns to his proper place within creation, abandoning the chimerical ambitions of past philosophy and practice that have only undermined his humanity.[61]

We have seen that Kant was confronted with certain fundamental teleological problems in modern emancipatory philosophy and that, in a fashion consistent with the "antidogmatic" intent of modern philosophy, he sought the required telos for philosophy in a form of universal common reason. But common reason could not be understood as passionate or "sentimental," due to the discovery of the dynamical character of reason. The only satisfactory account of common reason is the spontaneous logic of the self-limiting will. Now we have also seen that as providing the telos for all uses of reason, that logic contains implicitly an ideal of perfection, that is, of the full and harmonious development of all human faculties. But it is the *Dreams* essay which offers for the first time a view of how that idea of a "whole" of perfection would determine specifically a notion of theoretical metaphysics and speculative inquiry.

In the first place, we should expect to find that common moral reason is the primary source of metaphysical questions; its demands determine the agenda for speculative inquiry. Thus Kant writes that the interest of moral reason in a future world, in which its strivings for the ideal can be realized, is this primary source: "The questions about spiritual natures, about freedom and predestination and our future condition, are what originally set all the powers of the understanding in motion, and due to their preeminence men are drawn into the contests of speculation."[62] This moral origin of metaphysics is of utmost importance for indicating the true *end* of theoretical inquiry. The common reason has a surer grasp of that end than the speculative thinker, who tries to corrupt the common reason. "The vanity of science likes to excuse its occupations with the pretext of their importance," since dogmatic science claims that speculative knowledge of God and the soul is needed for the grounding of morality.[63] But the pure simple morality of common reason knows better and, without "detour" through theories, bases the moral disposition on its immediately available precepts.

The common reason's sound tendency to reject theory is not only important for the "purity" of morality, but it is also a clue to the nature and status of theory. It is not only the case that common morality does not have to learn first truths from theory; it is also the case that the theorists have to learn first truths from common morality. To put this point most accurately, one has to say more than just that the theorists have a primary duty to defend or at least not destroy the common moral understanding. Beyond this, they learn the true end of their own activity, and more specifically, they learn why they should be satisfied with the *limits* of their striving for knowledge, from common reason. Theoretical inquiry will, in any case, encounter its limits in ultimate perplexities.[64] But from theory alone one cannot understand why these limits are good. For this instruction is needed from common reason, which tells the speculative thinker that insight into highest realities is not necessary, and is even distracting, to a firm grasp of the ultimate end of human life.

The coincidence of the sound moral grasp of the end of reason and the speculative thinker's discovery of the limits of insight defines what Kant calls "Socratic wisdom." Such wisdom, having experience of both the basic moral truths and the possibilities of theoretical insight, is capable of "selecting from among the countless tasks facing us, those whose solution concerns humanity."[65] In other words, such wisdom can perform the ultimate teleological function within reason—legislating reason's final end and requiring theory to be subservient to that end. That requirement is not arbitrary tyranny, Kant believes, because it is beneficial to theory. Without this guidance from Socratic wisdom, theory simply persists in the frustrating exercise of seeking what it cannot know or at least of desiring what it cannot have. Socratic moral wisdom, in other words, directs reason away from dialectical pursuits and toward a self-consistent use of reason.[66] It does so not only through displaying the factual boundaries of inquiry, but also through demonstrating why reason should be content with those boundaries. It supplies an ultimate end and justification for reason's condition. And it does so by arguing that theory's alleged need for knowledge of first causes is factitious and self-inflicted. Speculative thought can attain a satisfying equality between its desire and its actual power, through bringing the former into a wise accord with knowledge of the latter.

The true metaphysical "whole" is precisely this attainment of accord within the human rational powers. The Socratic thinker is needed for bringing it about; common moral reason, which points to the end, and inquiry, which discovers limits, tend not to address each other very well. Yet to be really satisfying to reason, the common moral reason has to supply something equivalent to the articulated knowledge of first causes that theory has sought. Morality's mere assertion that theory need not be concerned with such knowledge will not suffice. And as we have seen, according to Kant common reason has a genuine need for metaphysical realities, albeit determined from a purely practical standpoint. The various discussions of the *Dreams* and of contemporary reflections allow one to surmise that the "moral world" as the system of freedom and nature corresponds to that highest object, of a practical character, that reason seeks. The striving for this object is what enables reason to come into accord with itself and be a true whole.

The *Dreams* essay, the first theoretical treatise after the *Remarks*, makes public the definition of metaphysics as "the science of the limits of human reason," which was first used in the *Remarks*.[67] The full elaboration of that definition is the *Critique of Pure Reason*.[68] From the "precritical" writings we are examining, it becomes evident that a certain complementarity and mutual dependence of moral telos and theoretical account of limits are foundational to the emerging "critique." Theoretical inquiry needs an "end," not only to orient its efforts but to establish their goodness, especially when their "limits" become apparent. The moral end needs the account of limits not only to establish the autonomy of moral precepts from the rival claims of dogmatic thought, but to ground its precepts. It must come into a fruitful cooperation with theory, for only then can the moral end of reason take its rightful place as the true whole that satisfies the strivings of theory. Morality and theory together form a system of the new "Socratic" kind.

Since the notions of "end" and "limit" are not intelligible in this system apart from each other, the full definition of metaphysics is "science of the end and of the limit of reason."[69] That definition, with its presuppositions and its implications, is the theme of numerous reflections in the *Nachlass* from the later 1760s to about 1780.[70] The line of argumentation in these reflections culminates in Kant's mature account of philosophy as the architectonic science whose highest task is a form of legislation.[71]Proceeding from the idea of moral telos, philosophy moves as it were in a circle, legislating the conditions in reason necessary for achieving the telos.[72] Thus such legislation entails a duality—that of "end" and of conditions, means, or instruments for attaining the end. The inner duality within first philosophy or metaphysics is characterized by dualities besides that of "science of end" and "science of limits." Such dualities are "positive" and "negative" science, "doctrinal" and "zetetic" science, and "organon" and "propaedeutic."

As "negative," theoretical inquiry establishes its own limits and secures the "positive" doctrines of morality and religion.[73] Whereas morality provides "doctrine" or even (in a favorable sense) "dogma" for reason, theory's role is to be "zetetic," or skeptical, in circumscribing the sphere in which knowledge can be justly "extended."[74] But the most significant duality is the last: organon and propaedeutic. The revolution in the meaning of philosophy that Kant's account of reason proposes is summed up in the fact that morality or practice becomes the true "organon" for extending reason's grasp of first causes, whereas theory itself is only a "propaedeutic" to this organon.[75] As propaedeutic, theory has only a corrective, disciplinary, or canonical function and is not properly "extensional," in the knowledge of first causes. Theory is in a sense only an instrument—one that serves morality or practice. This sense of "instrumental" is, however, to be distinguished from all earlier notions of speculative method or reason as the instrument of insight into the natures of things.[76] Criticism shows that such an instrument of insight (insofar as one is possible) is provided only by morality.

The preeminence of the concerns of morality within philosophy is repeatedly asserted in the *Nachlass*. Metaphysical questions arise from common reason, whose moral concerns alone give metaphysics whatever worth and necessity it has.[77] The chief questions, relating to God, freedom, and a future life, are of such importance because answering them "will secure the ground of our conduct and the principles of life."[78] Since the true core of metaphysics is such questions, metaphysics has greater urgency than other sciences; the pursuit of knowledge for its own sake is decried as a corruption of reason. All other sciences must be pursued for the sake of metaphysics.[79] Numerous reflections assert that metaphysics, as concerned with man's final end, is the only truly necessary science.[80] The differentiation between these grades of necessity is the source of the difference between the true philosopher, who as lawgiver determines the final end of humanity, and the "rational artificer" who constructs systems of knowledge without reference to the final end.[81]

From such considerations one might tend to draw a wrong conclusion—that the common reason is a wholly unproblematic guide to the end of reason. It is true that Kant in various ways often makes the claim that "the culture of sound reason," uncorrupted by speculation, is the touchstone for all the arts and sciences.[82] But the urgent moral questions of the same common reason lead the "natural use of reason" to the very "limit of the world," thus compelling it to conceive the world as whole and even to think of what is beyond the world.[83] Because of pressures to speculate inherent in morality, common reason is exposed to the errors of "enthusiasm" and of groundless hypotheses about the supersensible; it is then the natural prey of "subtle reasoners" who promote false doctrines and unbelief.[84] Yet Kant asserts that this weakness of common reason is less one of unclarity about the ends of action than one of a lack of "logical perfection" in grasping their theoretical implications; the critical thinker's "duty" is to bring his logical art to the support of the sound moral tendencies of common reason.[85]

The principal benefaction that the philosopher performs is a determination of boundaries; he prevents the speculative thinkers from extending merely material or phenomenal concepts into the realm of ends, and thereby he guarantees the freedom of morals and religion from theoretical subversion.[86] The requirement of keeping "ends" apart from the realm of "theory" is what makes philosophy so very distinct from science (and is related to freedom's radical distinctness from nature). The philosopher has a primary obligation to understand that his activity is wholly different from sciences of discovery, such as mathematics and natural philosophy.[87] The vocation of humanity is not discoverable by any such science; the human vocation is not simply given to man by his nature and consists rather in a certain kind of self-legislation. Philosophy is only the most comprehensive and self-conscious version of that legislation, but it is very liable to the temptation to think of itself as a science of discovery.[88]

In keeping with this account of the task of philosophy, theoretical inquiry is primarily self-knowledge; it is a thorough and methodical observance of the inability of our scientific concepts of objects to determine knowledge of ends.[89] Yet human reason has natural tendencies to ignore this fundamental restriction on the use of such concepts and thus has tendencies to misjudge its powers. Reason has need of a "disciplinary master," without which it "confuses the sound understanding" and grows "wildly, without bearing blossoms or fruit."[90] It seems that the Kantian "gadfly" to self-knowledge resembles a Hobbesian tyrant more than a Socratic questioner. This is because the self-knowledge required of us must clearly allow the principle of freedom to dominate over nature; without that domination, the natural tendencies of the human faculties will harvest only chaos. The true calling of philosophy is to legislate unity where otherwise disunity reigns.[91] This calling has sanctioning not from the will to power of higher men, but from the simple and lucid, if fragile, voice of common reason.

The Dialectic of the Pure Concepts of the Whole

Amid the details of the increasingly complex account of reason that emerges from the writings of 1765–80, one should not lose sight of a guiding thread first appearing in the *Remarks*. This again is the Rousseauian discovery that all the ills experienced by man as rational have their origin in the misrelation of human powers, for which misrelation those powers alone are responsible. That misrelation can arise because man as rational has a certain indeterminacy of essence, and empirical nature does not limit the use and misuse of these powers. Understood as "freedom," that same indeterminacy offers the possibility of a supreme legislation by a free rationality that orders the human powers in a final and satisfactory way.

One can best grasp the import of Kant's argument for an inherently "dialectical" character of speculative reason with the help of this thread. In the reflections we have already observed Kant speaking of a tendency of speculative reason, unless disciplined by "criticism," to confound itself by coming into conflict with moral reason.[92] Kant considers this a self-confounding: earlier thinkers did not claim that a rejection of common moral reason was a self-destruction of reason, even if they did not approve of the rejection. But because Kant has argued that the the moral will is the true foundation of reason and the sole possible source of the unity of reason with itself, he must argue that whatever endangers moral reason endangers reason itself.

Now Kant further argues that the moral strivings of reason point to an idea of the "whole," which as a practical project, represents a satisfactory completion of those strivings. But when the cognitive faculties of reason come into play, as they naturally do, in an attempt to conceive this whole through a total cognition of its grounds and limits, they institute a "dialectic" of opposing theses about the whole. Reason as theoretical finds itself unable to prefer one thesis over the other: both are persuasive. This perplexity is injurious to common reason because it concerns ultimate objects (God, the soul, the world) that relate to its moral interests. Yet Kant attempts to show that such perplexity is self-inflicted. As with other problems in reason, it arises from a false relation between powers, which reason itself can correct. Indeed, it arises from a natural tendency of speculative reason to misunderstand itself. While such self-misunderstanding is not willful and is the result of natural error, it is nonetheless in principle reformable.

The error is the false assumption of theoretical reason that it possesses certain a priori or "pure" concepts with which it is able to describe the realm of ultimate ends. To disclose and correct this error becomes Kant's chief object in the investigation of theoretical reason, some time in the late 1760s.[93] This path of inquiry, leading to the three *Critiques*, is the consequent development of Kant's insight into the incapacity of theoretical reason, and nature as known by it, to determine the realm of final ends. The "critical" approach in philosophy is, in other words, the correction of the error of all past culture (including the modern emancipatory one) of looking to nature for the teleological determination of human reason.

The distinctively "critical" approach to the problems of speculative inquiry grounds its problems and their solution in the faculty or power of reason and its relation to itself. Thus according to this approach, metaphysics in its speculative part (as the propaedeutic to the practical part) is above all a "science of the subject" and thus a form of self-knowing.[94] Yet prior to arriving at this characterization, which focuses on the human "subject," Kant saw the problem of speculative metaphysics to be that of bringing about the "agreement of knowledge with itself" in metaphysical matters.[95] This characterization is fundamental to the methodological reflections in the *Prize-Essay* and to its account of the sources for the failure of all past metaphysics to become a genuine science possessing certainty in its premises and deductions comparable to those in mathematics.[96] That failure, Kant argues, is due to a lack of accord between the nature of the concepts of metaphysics and the kinds of methods employed to attain scientific certainty with these concepts. We should examine briefly this account of the failure of metaphysics, since important elements of it are incorporated into the later critical approach.

The *Essay* is the first of Kant's propadeutical writings on metaphysics; in the introduction Kant asserts that his inquiry is not a part of metaphysics, but an investigation into the method of metaphysics, which must precede metaphysics proper.[97] The propaedeutical reflection turns on the distinction between metaphysical and mathematical concepts; concepts must be treated and elaborated by methods appropriate to their peculiar natures. Kant argues that in past forms of metaphysics (surely he refers chiefly to modern forms), mathematical methods of analysis and synthesis have wrongly been applied to metaphysical concepts in an effort to construct metaphysical systems by means of deductions (or syntheses) from primary axioms, postulates, and definitions. Any such effort must fail, for by their nature metaphysical concepts cannot be used as geometrical or quasi-geometrical premises in synthetic arguments.[98] That is, metaphysical concepts are inherently obscure, and they require first of all an analysis into clear and distinct elements. These concepts are given somehow in our experience; the first task of metaphysics is the analysis of the "datum" of a metaphysical concept such as "appetite." By contrast, mathematical concepts are constructed by means of arbitrary definitions and their combinations. Since the human mind stipulates their form and content, they are wholly clear and unambiguous from the start. Hence the mathematician is able rapidly to proceed to the synthetic and deductive stage of argument, and ages ago mathematics was able to establish itself as a true science. But due to the obscurity of its concepts (which is not simply a result of human failings), metaphysics lacks these advantages; it is still struggling to become a science.[99]

Mathematical methods have been prematurely applied in metaphysics, without adequate prior analysis of the metaphysical concepts into their simple elements. This is what suggests itself as the summary of Kant's argument; but this summary does not rule out the possibility that after the necessary analyses have been completed, metaphysics would become a science with synthetic arguments. Yet this summary overlooks Kant's suggestions that metaphysics may not be able to complete its analyses to ultimate simple elements or grounds. Whereas mathematics can begin with a sufficient "explanation" of a particular concept, and metaphysics certainly cannot begin in that way, it is not certain that metaphysical analysis can even terminate in sufficient explanations.

Indeed a metaphysical analysis must look for "immediate certainties" that emerge from a given concept and make deductions from these, with awareness that the immediate certainties are not the full object of the concept or its whole essence. Kant recommends to metaphysicians the procedure of Newton in natural philosophy: he established laws governing natural phenomena without assumptions about the ultimate grounds, causes, or whole essences of the phenomena. In this way he was able to establish an extraordinary degree of certainty in natural philosophy, with no claim, however, to understand nature as a whole, in its ultimate grounds. If metaphysics were to imitate his procedure, it too could create a high degree of certainty in its arguments, although what one would learn from them might be small (as compared to what metaphysicians have hoped to learn). It therefore is not at all apparent that metaphysics will at any future date be a synthetic-deductive science from ultimate simple elements.[100]

The stress on the unavoidable heterogeneity of mathematical and metaphysical concepts in the *Essay* remains a crux of Kant's thinking.[101] Metaphysical concepts, with their inferior evidentiality, must, Kant eventually discovers, be treated by methods wholly different from the traditional "analysis"; at the same time, the possibility of an approach of metaphysics to the condition of a synthetic science becomes all the more remote. That is, metaphysics becomes less a science of invention, construction, and discovery and more one of the self-limitation of reason. In yet other terms, as the core of metaphysics shifts to its practical telos-giving part and away from theoretical inquiry, the latter appears ever more incapable of providing knowledge of the fundamental objects of metaphysics; the problem of the evidence of metaphysical concepts becomes more severe. In the *Essay* Kant presents aspects of his later view on the "discursive" character of metaphysics, but is still far from seeing the radicality of the problem raised by the "pure concepts." Notably the *Essay* says nothing about the origins of metaphysical concepts, the manner in which they are "given" to human reason, or their function within human knowledge. The whole central theme of "subjectivity" has not been raised: metaphysical error arises from lack of agreement of knowledge with itself, but not yet from discord of the "subject" with itself.

An advance toward such an account of the problem of metaphysics is made by the *Dreams* essay, which introduces the task of determining the subjective relation of concepts to the powers of the understanding into the definition of metaphysics.[102] Specifically, it

discusses the subjective need that human reason has for the metaphysical concepts of substance, force, and causality, which is above
all a moral need—the inexorable concerns with the fate of the soul,
God, and freedom, "set all the powers of the understanding" in motion. And further, the essay develops a more articulated and forceful
argument as to why human reason is unable to penetrate into the
inner natures or ultimate grounds of things such that all metaphysics
must be confined within certain limits of reason. The argument resembles that of the *Prize-Essay* in that it concludes that the use of
metaphysical concepts can be nothing more than a characterization of
certain primary relations given in the "data of experience." These relations have immediate certainty without providing insight into first
causes.[103] Yet this later writing more emphatically abjures the possibility of a completed analysis of metaphysical concepts to ultimate
simple elements and proposes for them a pragmatic or practical validity for ordering experience. And in accordance with this view, the
essay looks at metaphysical concepts as primary relata or "syntheses," as in the case of the correlation of cause and effect. Thus the
problem of metaphysical error is no longer discussed in terms of
carrying out the correct form of analysis, but of observing correctly
the implications of the forms of synthesis implicit in metaphysical
concepts.

The background to these views is found in an important observation made in a small treatise falling between the *Prize-Essay* and the
Dreams essay—that metaphysical concepts (force, cause, substance)
express syntheses of distinct concepts which are not reducible by the
law of noncontradiction to relations of identity. Whatever metaphysical necessity they contain is not logical necessity; the notion of an
"effect" is not contained in the notion of a "cause," logically. The
"real ground" expressed by the causal concept must be distinguished
from a logical ground.[104] There is then the difficulty that the real
ground seems to express no metaphysical necessity; logical relations
at this point in Kant's thinking exhaust the whole realm of metaphysically necessary relations. Furthermore, since metaphysical concepts
are not constructible, they lack the evidence of mathematicals; they
acquire their evidence from their relation to experience. At the same
time, they are not derivable or analyzable from experience, since the
latter presupposes their use. Metaphysical concepts, being complex,
are not the termini of analysis into simples, but their complexity is
not grounded in any intelligible necessity.

One is naturally struck by the similarity of these arguments to
Hume's. Evidently Kant, at the time of the *Dreams* essay, is satisfied
with a pragmatic interpretation of metaphysics as merely exhibiting

certain basic principles, somehow "given" with the use of human reason, that order the "data" of sense.[105] This contentment seems to express an indifference or skepticism concerning the possible sources of metaphysical necessity for such principles. Kant presents such agnosticism as compatible with his Socratic wisdom: as regards ultimate grounds, the merely moral and postulative use of concepts of ground is sufficient for reason's highest interest. Indeed, lack of speculative insight into any metaphysical necessity is morally a positive fact, since such insight would render moral self-determination dependent on speculative thought. It is tempting to say that this essay, marking the point of Kant's closest convergence with Hume, evidences the true "dogmatic slumber" from which Kant had to be awakened.

Having reached this point, Kant in the later 1760s finds himself compelled to renew the question of the "subjective origins" of the metaphysical concepts, so as to determine precisely how these concepts are "given" with human reason, and to ascribe to them a certain metaphysical or a priori necessity that is not solely logical. The view that Kant was jarred by Hume alone to take up this inquiry is inadequate. To understand the further direction that Kant's inquiry takes, one first notes that the "subjective need" of a moral nature, which the *Dreams* already ascribes to metaphysical concepts, contains the seed for such inquiry. The Socratic wisdom aims at bringing that subjective need into harmony with the cognitive limits of reason, so as to avoid the corruptions of speculative thought. Kant differs from Hume here in admitting that from a moral standpoint, a certain kind of "metaphysics" of ultimate grounds is desirable and necessary. Therefore the motives for the renewal of Hume's investigation of the origins and validity of metaphysical concepts would have a certain non-Humean and moral character.[106] That is, the inquiry into metaphysical necessity becomes urgent if the *legitimate* need for metaphysics tends to unfold in a "dialectical" way.

From a purely cognitive standpoint, it is not evident immediately that Kant should be dissatisfied with his skepticism. The limited "pragmatic" certainty that theoretical metaphysics attains is perfectly compatible with Newtonian science; Kant himself says his approach to theoretical inquiry is in a Newtonian spirit. The problem of securing some metaphysical necessity for metaphysical concepts emerges from within metaphysics itself (and not in the foundations of natural science), insofar as reason's metaphysical demands for ultimates are inexorable and in some fashion legitimate. Understood as grounded in the sacred and the noble, the metaphysical needs of reason must be satisfied.[107]

The approach to the problem of the metaphysical necessity of the causal judgment, which Kant as "critical" philosopher eventually adopts, is conditioned by a prior understanding of judgment in general, found already in a writing of the early 1760s.[108] The account of judgment in this essay on the forms of the syllogism differs from that of many of Kant's contemporaries and gives a distinctive character to his metaphysical agnosticism concerning causality and other fundamental concepts. In this essay's conclusion, Kant describes the features of human judging that distinguish it from the mere association of impressions in subhuman animals.[109] In any human judgment, there is an implicit awareness, expressed by the copula "is," that a representation in the mind (the predicate-term) is different from, while related to, an object to which it belongs (the subject-term). Thus in human judging no impression or representation is ever regarded in isolation, but is always "judged" to belong to an object that contains it and that contains other representations not mentioned in the judgment as well. That is to say that every human judgment is characterized by its relation to a realm of objects that are independent of the immediate perception; Kant will later call this characteristic "objectivity." By dint of always being implicitly directed to a realm of objects, human judging is unlike the mere association of ideas in lower animals. One can say that from 1762 and on, Kant always ascribes to judging a certain intentionality and that this ascription in no way implies the possibility of human insight into first causes.[110]

The Kantian account of judging includes a view of human reason as spontaneous. Since a judgment regards a representation as distinct from an object, and thus implicitly as a mere attribute, a judgment entails the possibility of comparing attributes and thus of considering the adequacy of the attribute to the object, that is, as a true or false attribution. This human capacity for reflection on the truth of judgements means that the human subject has deliberative distance on its representations and is not immediately determined to act on them. In other words, the human judging capacity points to a certain nondetermination of human action by instinct or impulse, and it indicates the moral superiority of man to other animals. The spontaneity of reason evidenced in the copula ("is") in judgment is crucial to the transcendental arguments of the first *Critique*.[111]

It should be observed that, from the start, this spontaneity distinguishes Kant's treatment of the causal judgment from Hume's treatment. Kant's principal endeavor, in his "answer to Hume," is not to prove the "objectivity" of causal and other judgments; a certain objectivity is the premise of Kant's argumentation and not its result. But Kant eventually, by a regressive argument from this "given" objectivity implicit in all judgments, tries rather to establish the ground of the possibility of this objectivity. His aim in so doing is to locate the realm of valid application of the "pure concept" of cause and the other "pure concepts" of metaphysics. His need to do so arises from another premise that Hume would never grant—that human reason has a necessary and legitimate concern with the determination of supersensible objects, which concern however must be properly defined and "limited." Thus a certain spontaneity of human reason, which Hume cannot allow, is present in the human mind's capacity for objectivity (asserted in 1762) and in its demand for ideas of supersensible grounds (asserted in 1766). Both forms of spontaneity function as primary grounds for Kant's subsequent argumentation.[112]

More precisely, what are the considerations that compel Kant to raise his distinctive question about the ground of objectivity? We turn again to the *Nachlass* reflections where we uncover that the following are decisive: (1) Human reason has a twofold need for the concept of "ground" and its closely related or variant concepts—object, whole, cause, and substance. One need is moral reason's requirement of notions of absolute grounds, which need is clearly for supersensible objects. The other need is for the ordinary concept of "object" that is implicit in any judgment of experience and that lies under the judgement as the "ground" of predication or as the point of focus for the unification of attributes. This notion of ground has valid application only within the realm of sense experience. (2) All past philosophy suffers from deficient clarification and demarcation of these two concepts of ground; that deficiency, furthermore, is rooted in a natural tendency of reason in its speculative use. (3) The required "critical" clarification and demarcation are very elusive and difficult, for they must contend with the fact that they are dealing with pure concepts of a "discursive" character, which do not allow for an intuitive resolution of the question of the scope of their valid application. (4) Yet such a critical undertaking is of utmost urgency, since confusion of the two concepts of ground results in a dialectic that is injurious to the moral interests of reason and thereby to the very possibility of reason itself.

To secure reason's telos and reason's capacity for a confident and nondialectical self-determination, theoretical inquiry (as propaedeutic) must pursue its "boundary-setting" task (already seen as the task of theory by 1766) specifically by determining the spheres of validity for the two concepts of ground (or object, whole, cause, substance). Since one of the concepts is a presupposition of the objectivity of ordinary judgments, a principal phase of the critical defense of reason must be an inquiry into the sources of objectivity. By uncovering the role of the epistemological concept of ground in objectivity, one should be able to determine its true character and distinguish it from the "metaphysical" concept of ground that moral reason postulates in a supersensible realm.

Whereas by 1766 Kant already possesses the elementary distinctions between the experiential object or ground and the supersensible object or ground, and the phenomenal and noumenal realms of their application, he at that time does not see clearly that there is a natural "dialectic" of conflating them, nor does he see what is required by way of "critique" to end the conflation. As Kant remarks, the year 1769 gives him "much light" in these metaphysical matters; it is around then that the four considerations above begin to come into clear focus.[113]

Crucial to the new insights is Kant's discovery of his critical way of distinguishing between the intuitive and discursive elements of human knowledge, which is first published in the *Inaugural Dissertation* of 1770. That distinction advances the critical account of the problem of the metaphysical concepts in these ways: (1) It deepens the discussion in the *Prize-Essay* of the difference between mathematical and metaphysical concepts, and offers a more powerful explanation for the success of mathematical science and for the failures of metaphysics to become science. (2) It offers a more articulate reflection than is found in the *Dreams* essay on why the supersensible strivings of reason to realize an ideal whole cannot be satisfied in the realm of experience. (3) It proposes elements of an account of what reason, speculatively, tries to grasp when it seeks knowledge of the ideal whole and of how that effort is "dialectical."

The new account of the elements of knowledge starts from the description of space and time as intuitive modes of apprehension that are at once both the "forms" of all sensible experience and the mathematizable substrates that make mathematical sciences possible. Their dual function guarantees the universal applicability of mathematics to all experience, thus to "nature" as it "appears" to our faculties. And thereby mathematical science is able to be the true organon for the theoretical extension of human knowledge.[114] Kant's thoughts on the status of space and time and its implications for natural science are what receive most attention from commentators on the discoveries of this period. Yet just as important for the criticism of reason is the way in which "intuitive" apprehension is contrasted with "discursive." Intuitions are per se singulars; as forms of our intuiting, space and time are individual "wholes" that condition all our reception by the senses of particulars. These wholes are prior to their parts, the instances of spatial and temporal quanta. That all instances are actual parts means that space and time are perfectly homogeneous and that whatever is known of any part can be perfectly extrapolated to the whole. This uniformity secures the universality and necessity of mathematical principles throughout all of nature.[115]

That all instances of space and time are genuine parts of the wholes of space and time means that those parts are wholly homogeneous with or "coordinated" with one another and with the wholes. By contrast our conceptual thinking is based on universals, to which particular instances of the universal are "subordinated." That is to say that those instances are not "given" with the universals as their actual parts. All instances of a universal have other universal attributes as well, and hence these instances are not homogeneous with the universal. As a consequence, the instances of the universal are not intuited through the universal. Through acquaintance with a universal, the human mind does not immediately grasp all the individuals that fall under it. Hence the range of applicability of a universal always has a certain indeterminacy; we cannot say, as we can with space and time, what every instance of the universal must be, taken as a whole with all its attributes.

This is a limitation on "discursive" or conceptual knowledge. It entails that knowledge of any particular thing through one of its universal attributes is "mediate" knowledge of that particular, through something it shares with other, indeterminately many, particulars. Space and time prove to be the only attributes of things we can know "immediately," that is, with an absolute grasp of the actuality of all the other instances. Concepts or universals express mere "possibilities," for which it is impossible for us to know, in a prior fashion, the infinitely many possible actualizations.[116] Kant therefore argues that no individual thing, with all its attributes, is knowable intuitively or immediately as a whole (as Leibniz claimed is possible in the ideal case); only a thing's spatial and temporal conditions are wholes that can be apprehended in this way.[117]

The necessary indeterminacy in discursive and conceptual knowing has great consequence for metaphysics, which, if it could be a science, would be a conceptual science. Logic is also conceptual but has been able to establish itself as a science because it considers only the formal relations of concepts and makes no claim (when it stays within its proper bounds) to determine real things and their natures. The latter claim, of course, is the claim of metaphysics.[118] To make good this claim, metaphysicians have been tempted to treat metaphysical concepts as mathematical and hence as intuitively determinable. They have also tried to derive these concepts empirically from sense experience. Both attempts miss the character of the metaphysical concepts, which are a priori but not intuitively determinable.[119]

They somehow underlie all our experience and knowledge of "objects," whatever these may be. Yet it is surely impossible to determine a priori, through the mere concepts of "objects" themselves, what the whole world of objects in all its characteristics must be. Furthermore it is impossible to determine through any a priori concepts the whole nature of any single thing in the world (as a whole of attributes).

Kant has previously dismissed the delusions that arise from conflating metaphysics and mathematics, and has already asserted the spontaneous and "pure" origin of metaphysical concepts. Now he sees that a profounder illusion arises from the kinship between logic and metaphysics as discursive forms of inquiry. Human reason has a need for thinking and determining certain ideal objects, or absolute grounds or wholes; the world as a whole (as the totality of space and time), or absolutely simple first elements (which are indivisible wholes), are prime instances.[120] The world as a whole and simple first parts of the world are conceptual objects; they are "things" that must have attributes distinguishing them from other "things"; they are not merely regions of space and time. They are thus discursively cognizable objects (in principle) and not merely intuitable wholes. But in fact these objects are unrealizable and uncognizable for human reason. Yet since ordinary judging, or the logical use of reason, has no difficulty placing under every judgment the concept of "object," as only partially determined, human reason quite naturally supposes that in the same way, the notion of "object" will apply to the ideal of a completely determined whole. This natural tendency is the source of what Kant eventually calls an "antinomy" in reason.

At first glance the difficulty seems reducible merely to the fact that the intuitions of space and time, in which human reason tries to conceive its absolute wholes, are infinitely extensible and infinitely divisible, and thus by their nature they prevent reason from discovering the ultimate limits of extension and division which it seeks. But if the dialectic of reason amounted only to this, it could be quickly resolved through the exposure of this simple error. Kant would hardly need to undertake the inquiries of reason's criticism in order to show this. As both the *Nachlass* and the Antinomy section in the *Critique* itself demonstrate, the difficulty lies more deeply rooted, and concealed, in human reason. The *Nachlass* materials from between 1769 and 1772 already speak of a conflict between principles of reason, that is, of reason with itself. At issue is not the apparent conflict (indeed, it is not a real conflict) between the character of spatiotemporal intuition and the demands of reason.

Human reason proposes two equally binding rules or principles that govern the way it conceives the whole. One is a rule of reason that "all has a ground" or that when any object is posited some prior object as its ground must be posited. Kant sometimes calls this "the principle of sufficient reason." This principle expresses a stipulation reason gives itself concerning its own activity as a whole, namely, that all its thinking is conditional: our "understanding can posit nothing absolutely" and can posit things "only through a condition."[121] Although the idea or project of thinking the absolute naturally occurs to human reason, it surpasses reason's powers of conceiving. Thus an absolutely necessary first cause, or first being, "cannot be thought" by us.[122] The rule of the conditionality of reason demands that "our reason contains nothing but relations," and hence it cannot grasp something that, standing outside of all relations, is absolutely unconditioned.[123]

The conditionality of human reason must be related to discursivity. It is to be related to the fact that reason, as discursive, can grasp things only through concepts and thus only "mediately."[124] That is, concepts are modes of thinking that only partially determine an object to which they apply; they do not determine unique objects; a concept is a predicate, and all predicates apply to more than one object.[125] This is a consequence of the fact that concepts are dependent for their content on the senses and thus on a passive mode of intuition. If concepts could create their own objects (as a divine mind might create through mere thinking), they could then grasp wholly unique objects. Only under that condition could our reason think an absolutely independent or unconditioned object. Expressed in other terms, that condition would be one in which conceiving and intuiting are identical acts.[126] Thus one can say that the rule of "positing nothing absolutely," which reason prescribes to itself for its conduct of theoretical inquiry, is simply the acknowledgment of the discursive character of reason and the limitations imposed by it. As such, the rule is entirely binding and legitimate. Any abrogation of this rule can mean only that reason fails to understand itself and relate properly to itself.

Yet reason proposes another rule to itself that is equally binding and legitimate, but that appears to be in conflict with the first rule. By its nature reason demands "completeness" in any series of conditions that, either logically or causally, accounts for the existence of a state of affairs. In any series there must be an ultimate first condition which has no prior condition. From the standpoint of the purely logical analysis of concepts, this rule must posit the idea of a completely determined object—one whose attributes are wholly knowable, as the presupposition for the analysis of attributes; this is the notion of the *synthesa completa* of much importance in the schools deriving from Leibniz.[127] But perhaps more fundamental to reason's interest in com-

pleteness is the requirement of a first cause in a series of causal conditions. For Kant there is no doubt that such a requirement is of a
moral and practical nature. The first cause, not having a prior cause,
has the character of freedom; the first in a series, having ultimate
responsibility for the series, is an "ought" determining the course of
things. "The first in a series of causes is always the free will."[128]

This rule or requirement of reason, again a stipulation to itself of
what it must think or presuppose, is the "subjective law of reason, to
assume a first action from which all else follows"; but Kant notes that
"it is just as necessary to assume absolutely that every action has a
ground and that hence there is no first ground."[129] An apparent contradiction exists between the two most fundamental rules of reason.
It should now be clear that the antinomy of freedom and mechanism
is but one, albeit a very important one, of the forms of this contradiction. "An extraordinary confusion arises in the use of our reason from
the conflation of two concepts: everything (singularly regarded) has a
ground; but everything taken together has no ground, and thus
something exists without ground."[130] This statement suggests that
the contradiction is only apparent, arising from a failure of reason to
keep two notions of "ground" separate. One of the notions of ground
properly applies to reason in its discursive activity of determining the
given material of sense (passive intuition) with concepts; according to
this notion, every ground must have a prior ground (or every determination of reason has its own conditions). But there is another notion of ground which in the *Nachlass* (but not always elsewhere)
is called a "real ground." This is a first and unconditioned ground
that by itself can determine the existence of things that follow from it.
Its status is highly problematic: "Reason feels the need for a real
ground yet cannot think such a ground according to its own laws. It
follows that this concept is not objective."[131] Naturally the question
arises: In what realm of reason's activity can this "need" be legiti-
mately satisfied?

Human conceiving, as "discursive" and thus dependent on an
external source for its content, is incapable of grasping any of the
following: the first cause of a series of events; the real ground of existence; the completed synthesis of an object's concept. Such notions,
if they have any realization, must have validity outside the whole
realm of conceptuality. That is, they have no application in the sensible realm, wherein theoretical cognition takes place. The absolute
objects posited by reason's moral and metaphysical needs must simply belong in an extratheoretical space that is empty of cognizable
objects. All the same, reason has a tendency to attempt to realize the
absolute within the conditioned realm of sense.[132] The ground of this

tendency is a natural illusion to which reason is subject, arising from the concept of "object in general" that is implicit in all judging. The universality of this concept for theoretical cognition (which rests on its a priori character) inclines reason to suppose that through this concept it has insight into the nature of objects in all possible worlds, including those absolute objects cognizable only by nonfinite minds. Our reason naturally overlooks the fact that the universality of this concept is not absolute; the "object" that underlies judging has validity only within the context of a finite (discursive) mind's mode of knowing. While this concept has validity as a necessary condition of our knowing, and is thus for our knowing wholly "objective," it is all the same restricted to our mode of knowing and in that respect merely "subjective."

The illusion is otherwise described by Kant as one arising from the nature of logic. The universality of "object in general" is identical with the universality of logic; for "object" underlies all judging, and by "logic" one means only the elaboration of human conceptuality and its rules.[133] Both "object" and "logic," so far as we have insight into their possibility, are limited to the conditions of finite minds. Metaphysics, understood as ontology, has mistakenly claimed that it can give an account of "things in general," without regard to the context of human cognition, and has been led astray by the apparent power of logic to hold outside that context.[134] Logic tends to be "dialectical" in that it seems to provide an organon for the determination of the structure of all possible worlds.[135] Thus to expose and to uproot this error are principal concerns of a criticism of theoretical reason, which thereby establishes the limitation of all the categories implicit in our logic to the conditions of a finite mind. Accordingly this criticism is called "transcendental logic."[136] The inquiries of this logic bring the human "subject" into proper relation with itself by disclosing how metaphysical error emerges from the subject's attempts to satisfy its highest needs within a realm of its own activity wherein that is impossible. This logic must show that the categories or pure concepts connected with the concept of "object" (ground, whole, substance, etc.) cannot be employed theoretically by the moral needs of reason for the absolute, as instruments to determine the absolute. These concepts are irremediably restricted to the sensible realm of finite cognition.[137]

The new account of theoretical philosophy as transcendental logic provides a fulfillment of Kant's design to uncover the source of metaphysical error by means of a "science of the subject." It establishes the form of propaedeutical inquiry that can, in definitive fashion, exclude "theory" or the cognition of nature from the realm of ends, which is now left free for determination by the legislative will. We now turn to the *Dissertation* of 1770 for the indications it offers of this "critical" version of the goal and structure of philosophy.

The argument of this writing is a "methodical" one; it is another propaedeutical inquiry aiming at disclosing the errors of metaphysics that have prevented it from becoming a science. Such an inquiry is not really a proposal of the proper method of metaphysics, but a methodical reflection, prior to metaphysics, that defines the powers of the human subject and therewith the sphere of cognition within which metaphysical certainty is attainable.[138] Fundamental to such a propaedeutic is the uncovering of "illusions of the intellect" arising from an improper "contagion of sensitive cognition with intellectual" or from an improper relation of sensible and intellectual elements of knowledge.[139] The *Dissertation* contains neither a full-fledged account of a dialectic between "laws of reason" (although this idea appears in the contemporary *Nachlass*) nor a deduction of the legitimate use of the pure concepts to bring an end to the dialectic. Nevertheless it contains important aspects of an account of reason as tending to "illusion" in metaphysics and of an account of the limits of human cognition as a response to that tendency.

Part of the propaedeutical inquiry is a clear determination of the differences between metaphysical and mathematical concepts. The account of this difference here goes well beyond the terms of the *Prize-Essay*; it brings attention to the fact that mathematics (and with it, mathematical natural science) derives its high degree of evidentiality from its realizability in the intuitions of space and time, which are the "forms" of sensibility for human cognition. Metaphysical concepts, as we have seen Kant assert at many points, do not have the advantage of intuitability.[140] But now the argument is that the metaphysical concepts, or certain among them, altogether transcend the realm of sense through not being realizable in the intuitive forms of experience. Furthermore, Kant uses the language of "ideas" and "ideals," which appeared first in the ethics reflections, to characterize the transcendent metaphysical concepts. In other words, the concepts of moral idealism are brought more explicitly into relation with the criticism of theoretical reason than in any previous published work.

Kant's argument is that human reason has a need for certain "ideas" of absolute wholes or grounds that transcend and elude any concrete embodiment in sensible intuition. From this many thinkers erroneously conclude that such ideas are in themselves impossible or merely illusory. Against this conclusion, one should propose another account of cognition—that the "laws of intuition" by which we cognize anything given to us in experience are not the condition of things in themselves. Therefore the ideas of absolute wholes or grounds may have some reality beyond the realm of sense.[141] It is, however, a hasty inference from this assertion of Kant to the prevalent view that Kant here defends a version of dogmatic theoretical cognition. Kant notes another error of metaphysicians—that of supposing that the ideas are cognizable intuitively by our human finite minds or that they can be "given" to us as objects of cognition. The errors of "mystical Platonism" are cited here, as are various modern doctrines that deny the heterogeneity of sense and intellect, and that regard sense as only a "confused" form of intellection. According to such doctrines, nothing in principle would prevent an intuitive cognition of an intellectual idea, except the human mind's tendency to confusion or obscurity.[142] But Kant urges that on principle, sense experience and pure intellection of ideas must remain forever disjunct. Mathematical science (the true organon of human knowledge) is based on a clarity and evidence that are peculiar to sense experience and restricted to it; thus "sense" has its own dignity and is not merely an inferior form of intellect. On the other hand, the realization of intellectual ideas in a noumenal realm may perforce not be "theoretical" at all.

The denial of theoretical cognition of the ideas is instrumental to the telos of the propaedeutical argument—the defense of a transsensible employment of the ideas, chiefly for the sake of morality. By securing the possibility of a "noumenal" realization of the ideas, Kant revives "the noblest institution of antiquity"—the discussion of the phenomenal and noumenal realms; it is clear that in antiquity this discussion always served, and now again serves, a moral end.[143] Yet Kant's revival of this institution is a self-conscious transformation of Platonism whereby the ideas are not cognizable objects. Instead they are ideas of the "maximum" or "perfection," and thus of a "criterion" or "common measure" pertaining above all to matters of morality and freedom.[144] This treatise is thus wholly continuous with Kant's movement, begun in 1764–65, along a path toward a practical realization of the human metaphysical interest; it by no means relapses into an earlier "dogmatism," as is sometimes said. Yet the argument of the *Dissertation* is surely understated; it only suggests, but does not proclaim, the "critical" interpretation of the ideas as conceptions of the totality of human practical striving.

Both the movement toward practical metaphysics and the understated character of the treatise emerge from its statements on the "real use" (contrasted with "logical use") of the intellect. Kant permits only two applications of the "real use"—an "elenctic" one that exposes the errors of metaphysics and a "dogmatic" one that permits a noumenal use of ideas as "exemplars." While not denying a theoretical role to ideas explicitly, no such role is described. "God" as well as "moral perfection" are mentioned as two forms of "noumenal perfection"; God is said to be the "theoretical sense" of that perfection. Yet no theoretical function for the idea of God is in any way developed.[145] In the *Nachlass* of this period, there is mention of a use of the idea of God for theoretical cognition, as representing the maximum or goal of cognition, in the form of the unity of natural laws. This is an employment of the idea that is in conformity with the "laws of the understanding," and it is what Kant in the *Critique of Pure Reason* calls a "regulative idea." Kant asserts that the idea of God must always be used in a way that is "relative" to our purposes, that is, its nature is determined by the character of our reason and its requirements.[146] As we have seen, Kant repeatedly asserts that speculative insight into the being of God would not be in accord with those requirements.

Elsewhere the *Dissertation* is more outspoken on the limits of reason. There is the unambiguous assertion that "only through the senses [in passive intuition] is any matter given to us for cognition."[147] Emphatically Kant denies that the human intellect is "archetypal" and thus capable of having supersensible intuitions whereby objects would be given through mere thought.[148] Now from the premises that (1) all human cognition is conditioned by sensible intuition and (2) the ideas of the intellect cannot be given in a sensible intuition, the conclusion very directly follows: (3) such ideas cannot be objects of human cognition. All cognition (human or otherwise) must have an intuitive component wherein something singular is given; in the case of the human mind, the singular can be given only through the passive medium of the senses. The human intellect, so far as it cognizes any singular object, is dependent on the senses. And if the intellect can spontaneously transcend the realm of sense by means of ideas of wholes, it must also acknowledge the impossibility of having cognition of objects corresponding to such ideas.[149] Furthermore, doubt is cast on the ontological status of the pure ideas of the intellect (i.e., on the existence of realities independent of human reason corresponding to them) by the statement that such concepts are not innate but acquired through a process of abstraction—from "laws inherent in the mind (by attending to the mind's actions on the occasion of experience)."[150] While Kant clearly speaks of an a priori status for such concepts (they are not acquired directly from the senses), he proposes for them the "transcendental" status that is much more elaborated in the *Critique* and already at this time discussed in the *Nachlass*: they are rules or principles that reason discovers in itself as the conditions of its own activity.[151]

Indeed, in several respects the *Dissertation* hints toward the transcendental approach to all cognition and all uses of reason, and not only in its introduction of the "pure forms of intuition" and of the noumenal "ideas" as self-regulative principles of reason. For in this work Kant uses such terms as "laws of experience," "laws of phenomena," and "laws" for the combining of subject and predicate in the judgment of a sensibly given object, whereby he clearly refers to an a priori conceptual ordering of the sensibly given that goes beyond what the forms of intuition (space and time) contribute.[152] In other words, the suggestion of "laws of the understanding," which are prescribed through the categories (articulated as rules of synthesis), is already present here. The "laws" in question are not merely logical and not merely intuitive relations. Yet as we saw, Kant in 1762 already made clear that experience rests on the human mind's relation to a realm of "objectivity" that is prescribed by its *own* necessity of simultaneously relating and distinguishing an attribute (representation) from a presupposed object as its "ground." It is not a large step from that view to the account of the presupposed objectivity-structure in terms of "laws" that quite obviously cannot be regarded as acquired from experience (without arguing in a vicious circle).

Therefore it is a misunderstanding of the major problems and intent of the critical philosophy, as well as of the place of the *Dissertation* in its emergence, to argue that the great insight that follows this work is the uncovering of the conceptual structure of the understanding, by way of the system of synthetic a priori judgments that prescribe the form of "objectivity" to the sensibly given material of intuition. Various notions of synthetic "laws of phenomena," resting on presupposed concepts of "object," seem to be present in Kant's thinking after the middle 1760s. The point that must be underlined is that at no point for Kant was metaphysics' central concern to account for ordinary experience (and its judgments). Rather its concern was to give an account of the status of the pure metaphysical concepts. The main task was never "epistemology" in the accepted sense today. Kant did not feel that his primary goal must be to prove the fact of experiential "objectivity" and to demonstrate that it rests on a priori rules or principles. He surely remarked on the great difficulty of demonstrating the latter, in which demonstration the former is a basic presupposition rather than something to be proved. Yet the primary aim of a "deduction" is to establish the objectivity of the pure concepts themselves, not that of the ordinary experience they help to condition. The true problem of reason is a metaphysical one, and critical inquiries serve the ultimate metaphysical need of reason. Ordinary experience, with its presupposition of objectivity, provides the context for solving the metaphysical problem; it is not itself the metaphysical problem, nor does metaphysics have its telos in simply accounting for ordinary experience.

These observations are supported by Kant's discussions of the goals of critical philosophy and the obstacles he had to remove in reaching them. Some letters of the period of the *Dissertation* establish that the problem not yet solved by that writing is the "deduction" of the pure concepts, that is, of the grounds and the nature of their validity and objectivity. Of the *Dissertation* itself, Kant writes that its purpose is to be above all propaedeutical to a moral metaphysics and that it fails (and perhaps was not originally intended) to be the completed propaedeutic. Notably, Kant does not complain that he persists in the treatise of 1770 to present a dogmatic account of theoretical cognition.[153] Furthermore, Kant states that he regards the problem of theoretical cognition of the phenomenal order, by means of the mathematical, to be largely solved in this treatise. The objectivity of concepts in general, and in particular of the foundations of mathematical and natural sciences, is not the remaining issue. The profound perplexity still to be addressed by criticism is to establish how the pure metaphysical concepts, with their "discursive" nature that cannot supply an intuition of singular objects, nevertheless point beyond themselves toward the realm of objects that they condition, and how apart from such conditioning they have no theoretical fulfillment. Since mathematical concepts supply their own intuitions in the formal substrata of space and time, their theoretical fulfillment is not in question; what is more, their necessary validity for objects of experience is secured by the fact that the formal intuitions are also the forms of all sensibly given objects. And with respect to the discursive metaphysical concepts (substance, cause, necessity, existence, etc.), the question is not whether they underlie knowledge of objects, but how they do so. The whole realm of objective experience has to be assumed as given by Kant, for him to pose the main question of the "deduction" at all.[154]

While the conflicting claims of the fundamental "laws of reason" concerning absolute wholes have convinced Kant between 1769 and 1772 that pure concepts can have no theoretical fulfillment if they are understood to refer to completely determined or "absolute" intuitable objects, it is yet another matter to demonstrate how they nonetheless maintain theoretical validity as conditions of the incompletely determinable intuited objects of human "dependent" experience. One must show how their theoretical use is restricted to that context in order to remove forever the temptation to theorize beyond that context. In a letter to J. Bernoulli, written within a year after the first

Critique's publication, Kant remarks how it was just this question of the deduction of the "source" and valid use of the metaphysical concepts that had not been answered by the *Dissertation* and that afterward caused him much difficulty.[155] This is the most difficult of metaphysical questions to answer, for the answer requires that the finite human mind show that the most fundamental conditions of its thought and knowledge (all centered around its "logical" capacities) are limited to that finite context (so far as they remain thinkable by us). If the argument is to proceed consistently with its own claim about "finitude," then the demonstration of limits must take place wholly within the context of finitude.

The ambition of this argument consists in the scope of what it claims can be done wholly within the perspective of "finitude." All of the metaphysical interests of reason, borne out of the human mind's irrepressible concern with the noble and the sacred, must be demonstrably satisfiable within the scope of human finitude, although these interests must press toward infinite objects. It was this ambition that later German idealism said could not be sustained since the "transcendental logic" that seeks to define the limits of logic must thereby transcend them, into the infinite. One can say Kant's idealism marks the high point of a certain effort that has been renewed, but not surpassed, by later phenomenological and hermeneutical definitions of the "horizon" of experience. It would confine the reflection on the absolute (whose meaning and content are ultimately moral), within the sphere of human freedom and practice (or common reason and judgment) that is kept distinct from the speculative noumenal realm. Thus its aim is to render internally consistent a moral interpretation of the modern emancipatory project (as needing a sanction from an "ideal" realm): this is the essence of modern moral idealism. Yet one might argue that both Kant and many of his idealist critics have simply not accepted what one should accept as truth—that common moral reason and its strivings are not internally consistent and never can be, or that the "human world" is not a "system." The undoubtedly attractive and impressive efforts to establish the fact of such a system have, as we have seen, their origin in the transformation of Rousseau—in the idea that self-legislative freedom is the basis of all rationality and the key to its "recovery" of self-consistency.

5

Culture and the Practical Interpretation of the End of Reason, 1781–1800

The Ultimate End of Theoretical Inquiry

If any work has maintained the force of a constant undertow beneath the surface currents of Western culture in the past two centuries, it is the *Critique of Pure Reason*. Yet one might not associate this work with the term *culture*, or suppose that this writing among Kant's writings addresses itself to the task of forming a "culture," unless it be the culture of speculative thinkers and of scientists or theoreticians who take guidance from them in fundamental matters of cognition. But the reader of the *Critique* may miss the point that its inquiries are directed toward a reform of *all* culture, which is to begin with the reform of metaphysics. The latter notably is described as "the perfection of all culture of human reason."[1]

It is widely known that Kant has instigated the later modern way of understanding culture, as the free development of the rational powers that have an "arbitrary" and as yet indeterminate fulfillment. Man alone as free legislator over his powers can prescribe an end or fulfillment to them.[2] But unlike many later modern accounts of culture, Kant's version subordinates the whole of culture to the legislation of philosophic reason. The *Critique* is written to secure and promote a hierarchical ordering implicit in every human reasoner who possesses in germ the idea of philosophy's legislation. The critical philosopher outlines the "architectonic" structure of reason, which the development of reason in the species contains implicitly, but which it does not consciously realize or fully embody. Once it is brought to humanity's awareness through the *Critique*, this outline serves as an "ideal" of a system of the unified rational powers, one that humanity over millennia gradually approaches. The organizing principle of this ideal is the subordination of all theoretical inquiry, and all other culture of human skills and talents, to the ultimate moral end of reason.

We turn to the *Critique* as the primary testament of the "revolution" that Kant sought in the ordering of human interests and powers. This ordering will "secure the true and lasting welfare of the human species," such as Kant declared to be the function of metaphysics at the start of his journey to the critical philosophy. The *Critique* contains the full elaboration of the metaphysical propaedeutic that provides the foundation of something new in the self-understanding of reason, which is neither a new speculative metaphysics nor a new moral philosophy.[3] Rather, the ground is laid for an ultimate flourishing and self-reconciliation of human reason in all of its employments. The first phase of the foundational legislation is "negative"—the removing of obstacles that stand in the way of reason's grasp of its true essence; reason is a self-determining power that alone is responsible for the projection and achievement of humanity's final end. The greater part of the *Critique* is dedicated to this negative task, which is perhaps the more crucial phase of the argument. For the inquiries of critical philosophy proceed from an initial conception of reason, according to which the chief difficulty in reason and all human life is reason's self-obfuscation, in various forms of false "theory," or false accounts of reason's own essence. If the tendency to false theory is disciplined, common reason untrammeled by "sophistry" will advance with sureness toward a moral conception of humanity's end and of the free use of its faculties.

Yet the telos of the negative inquiry is not simply to "level the ground" to make room for a moral philosophy implicit in sound common reason. The positive phase of the foundational legislation includes inquiries and determinations of goals that are wholly in the spirit of common moral reason, but that belong on a speculative plane beyond the grasp of common reason. Taking initial direction from common reason, the critical thinker must reinterpret the highest theoretical strivings of reason in a way that performs justice to their internal requirements, as well as to the requirements of a moral world based on freedom. That reinterpretation results in a "system of reason," which strictly speaking belongs neither to theoretical nor to moral philosophy. Rather, it unfolds the ultimate end of both, within a self-consistent account of reason. At the core of the highest legislation of reason in this "system" is the interpretation of the speculative striving of reason for the whole or the absolute, in terms of practical totality. Only as secured within this whole system of reason is sound moral reason forever protected against the destructive dialectic of "dogmatism." Then it becomes evident that the new system of reason is nothing less than the basis of "culture" in its later modern sense—as the self-sufficient and self-enclosed determination of purpose and final meaning, which borrows no principles from "transcendent" sources, natural or divine. Within this system, any reference of human reason to purportedly transcendent being must be understood in terms of "immanent" functions and requirements of human reason. Herewith Kant claims to satisfy at once the various strivings of human reason that in previous culture have been discordant and unreconciled: morality's need for justification, speculative reason's need for comprehension of the whole, and humanity's discovery in the modern age of its emancipatory goal.

The concluding passages of the *Critique* offer the outline of this system, and thus they propose the basic elements of the positive phase of the new legislation. The central concept of the positive phase is the highest good, as the unification of the diverse strivings of human rational nature. This concept contains, as outlined in the *Critique*, the nucleus of the final ordering, or *telos*, of reason. For this concept we turn to the relatively neglected concluding division, entitled "Doctrine of Method," and especially to two of its chapters, the "Canon of Pure Reason" and the "Architectonic of Pure Reason."[4] The tendency of commentators is to ignore the Architectonic, and to regard the Canon as having only historical interest, as a rudimentary and imperfect version of the "analytic of the principles of practical reason," of which Kant will later provide mature versions in the *Foundations* and *Critique of Practical Reason*.[5] Yet the text itself does not support this view of the Canon's character, intent, and status within Kant's work. The primary intent of this chapter has to be grasped within the whole project of the *Critique*. The Canon's aim is not to provide the foundations of moral philosophy (which aim in fact it explicitly renounces)[6] but the outline of the completion of the metaphysical strivings of reason in a new "system" of reason.

Much of the Canon's discussion is about the ideas of God, freedom, and immortality, as postulates arising from the requirements of pure morality. Thus, regarded as a metaphysical or speculative discussion, the Canon appears to be tangential to the main theoretical topics of the *Critique*; Kant remarks himself how little there is of theoretical usefulness in these ideas. Insofar as the Canon appears to be a moral philosophical discussion, it seems rather misplaced and, furthermore, to suggest "impure" or "heteronomous" versions of morality. Yet Kant asserts that the bases of morality lie outside the purview of the present critical inquiry. And his emphasis on the postulates is not in order to ground morality in "impure" fashion on those postulates rather than on the free self-determining will of pure morality.[7] The Canon belongs to the critique of speculative reason. The emphasis on the postulates would be better understood if it were seen that these practical "ideas" are the successors to the discredited speculative "ideas" of reason's dialectic (God, soul, and world). The theme of the Canon is the theoretical or speculative importance of that replacement from the standpoint of a final "system" of reason.

The opening statements of the Canon help to place it within the argument of the *Critique*. The "Transcendental Analytic" is itself characterized as a "canon," namely, one that determines the correct employment of the theoretical principles of the pure understanding, which are concerned solely with knowledge of phenomena. *Canon* is defined as "the sum-total of *a priori* principles for the correct employment of certain faculties of knowledge."[8] The "Transcendental Dialectic," by contrast, has treated theoretical reason's quest for speculative knowledge of "ideas," and it has shown that since such speculative knowledge is unavailable, there is no "canon" of the theoretical employment of reason here. There can only be a "discipline" of reason's pretensions to find knowledge in the noumenal realm, which discipline is the first chapter of the Doctrine of Method. Yet the present Canon of Pure Reason would seem to reinstate what the Dialectic has discredited, namely, a correct employment of reason in determining objects in the noumenal realm. The same "ideas" that were said to have no cognitive objects before are now said to have objects of a practical nature; the ideas are reinstated, but not from a theoretical standpoint.[9]

Thus the present Canon is continuous with the previous parts of the *Critique* in that it treats of uses of reason that may "form the goal toward which reason is directing its efforts" in speculative inquiry, but which it fails to realize in such inquiry.[10] Certain supersensible objects, of some sort, must be accessible to reason, for "how else can we account for our inextinguishable desire to find firm footing somewhere beyond the limits of experience? Reason has a presentiment of objects which possess a great interest for it."[11] The regulative use of ideas of totality, guiding theoretical inquiry on the purely phenomenal plane to the infinitely distant goal of the complete and unified system of natural laws, could not provide these objects.[12] For the knowledge of phenomenal nature does not satisfy reason's deepest longing. In the present Canon, Kant will not only describe the objects that satisfy that longing, but therewith also bring into the light of day the true raison d'être of the inquiries which before had only obscurely understood their own motivation. Thus the first section of the Canon is entitled "Of the Ultimate End of the Pure Employment of Our Reason."[13]

This section immediately confronts us with a perplexity. It asks why reason imposes on itself such heavy theoretical labors in the effort to gain knowledge of God, the soul, and the world, when such ideas are useless (save in a regulative way) for the theoretical extension of reason?[14] The analytical and dialectical parts of the *Critique* could not, after all, establish even the real possibility of such "ideas"; they could only determine that the possibility of such ideas is not contradicted by the principles of the understanding in its theoretical use, which supports the scientific knowledge of nature.[15] To avoid the conception that reason is driven by a blatant misunderstanding or that reason would have been wiser to look from the start at a merely "practical" interpretation of the ideas, it is important to show a certain continuity or similarity between the speculative interest in these ideas and the practical one. (Indeed it may have been necessary for reason to start with the false speculative interpretation of the ideas before it could discover the true practical one.)

An examination of the three practical ideas (God, freedom, and immortality) reveals something about them illuminative of reason's "real" interest in these ideas. They are not intelligible by themselves, or even as only related to the moral law, on whose basis they are postulated. They point beyond themselves to a single end of all reason, in which they are united. Through these ideas, reason is "impelled by a tendency of its nature" to complete its inquiries in a "self-subsistent whole" which comprehends and transcends phenomenal nature.[16] This "whole" is another name for the final system of reason in which all interests and employments of reason are united. The continuity between speculative and practical uses of the ideas is the concern with a "whole" that is common to both. Thus while renouncing speculative insight into wholes, reason does not abandon all satisfaction of realizing some form of wholeness. And its speculative efforts to know wholes were not merely aberrant and misguided, but involved "presentiments" of its final goal, which is at last achieved through the practical interpretation of the ideas. One can say that the ideas, properly interpreted, form the "whole" that is perhaps the primary theme of Kant's thinking after 1765: reason's unity with itself, through which it rescues itself from the alienation of all abortive past efforts to find satisfaction in nature, and which is grounded on the moral self-legislative will.

Thus Kant states plainly here that the highest "interest of humanity" is practical in character.[17] Elsewhere Kant notes that "in actual fact, reason has only one single interest," which leads to the conclusion that all strivings of reason are guided by and consummated in the practical use of reason.[18] "The whole equipment of reason, in the discipline which may be entitled pure philosophy, is in fact determined with a view to the three above-mentioned problems," namely, God, freedom, and immortality.[19] Yet the adequate understanding of how reason is directed toward these three ideas requires one to note that they form a system of which they are subordinate aspects.[20] It is actually this system, or whole, that constitutes the highest interest and final end of reason; it is also known as the "highest good."

The "ideal of the highest good" is the subject of the second section of the Canon, and it is introduced by a consideration of three questions in which, Kant says, "all the interests of my reason, speculative as well as practical, combine."[21] The three questions in conjunction point to the highest good as the object satisfying all three. "What ought I to do?" is the first question in the order of motives or of the determination of the will. It is answered by the moral law and its concept of duty, and for the sake of the will's accountablity to morality, freedom is postulated. At the same time, the moral law occasions certain hopes for the attainment of happiness proportionate to moral worth. The question "What may I hope?" in its full elaboration is "What may I hope if I do what I ought to do?" Hoping is to be conditioned by moral virtue; one is to hope only for a happiness one is worthy to receive. Since such happiness is not attainable within a lifetime, its possibility rests on the assumptions of an enduring future existence and a supreme being or cause to secure that existence. Accordingly the moral law gives rise to the primary inquiries of speculative reason: "Is there freedom? Is there a future life? Is there a God?" These form the essential core of metaphysics and determine the content of the third basic question: "What can I know?"[22]

The notion of a system of reason, however, is not exhausted by this account of these questions. One sees that the "ought" gives rise to a single comprehensive end governing all our acting, hoping, and inquiring. This is an end that is legislated for us by moral duty and that has no reference to our personal concern with happiness. The end is the idea of a world in which freedom harmonizes universally with a moral distribution of happiness.[23] In other terms, the true object of moral hoping is a "moral world" in which all rational beings have achieved, or are forever making progress toward achieving, the maximum of moral worth (moral freedom) and the corresponding maximum of happiness. Such a world embodies the ideal convergence of the "ought" of freedom and the "is" of nature. Only for the purpose of conceiving that convergence does reason postulate God and a future life. Thus moral reason's need to postulate that ideal convergence is the ground of the inquiries that constitute metaphysics. Through its quest to realize that ideal, reason as it were articulates and systematizes itself. The logic of the pure will unfolds as the logic of the whole system of rational questions and inquiries.

Thus Kant writes that the ideal of the moral world (or highest good) corresponds to "a special kind of systematic unity, namely, the moral."[24] This notion of system grows directly out of the internal requirement of teleology implicit in the free moral will; the will demands the existence of a world in which "the free will of each being is, under moral laws, in complete systematic unity with itself and with the freedom of every other."[25] It must be seen how the full development of this concept of reason's systematic unity with itself entails the achievement of happiness as well as that of moral worth. Surely the demanded "ideal" includes a conception of the sensible world and of the rational will's place within it. The idea of this world must have an "effect" in the sensible world; only as a projected "effect" can it function as an end for the activities of rational beings within the sensible world. Were the highest good conceived wholly noumenally or as separate from the sensible world, it would be impossible to regard it as the approachable goal of our actions. Indeed the moral world is called "the sensible world viewed as being an object of pure reason in its practical employment."[26] Furthermore the actions that might lead to the reality of such a world are called "actions as might be met with in the *history* of mankind"; therefore the principles of pure practical reason that govern such actions can be called "principles of the *possibility of experience*."[27] Neither the teleological function of the end nor the idea of its realization in human finite experience would be thinkable if the moral ideal were truly otherworldly. What is more, there are deeper intimations in the Canon of what systematic unity between freedom and nature might mean and which exclude an account of either moral perfection or happiness as achievable only in a supersensible mode of existence.[28]

The Canon offers some suggestions that the "self-subsistent whole" that reason requires might be realizable immanently, that is, that freedom alone may be responsible for the achievement of the unity of freedom and nature. There are remarks about a "system of self-rewarding morality" wherein free rational beings are the authors of their own happiness.[29] Given his premise of the fundamental heterogeneity of freedom (reason) and nature (inclination), Kant surely does not mean that, in any immediate way, freedom can produce happiness for oneself and others. More indirectly, however, there may be a connection: the rational will's harmony with itself and others may be an essential condition, while not a guarantee, of attaining happiness. While one cannot be directly responsible for another's happiness, the duty to respect the right of another to use his will freely includes, of course, the duty to respect his pursuit of happiness. Indeed the primary duty to secure the legal right (or "external freedom") of others to such pursuit is derived by Kant directly from the moral law; to the extent that the pursuit of happiness is an expression of the free rational will, it has intrinsic moral significance. From such considerations one can argue that the rational ideal of the highest good grounds the transition from pure morality to politics and legality.[30] One can then say that the achievement of the just legal order, as an indispensable condition for the attainment of the highest good, is a central component of the moral world. Insofar as moral progress will issue in such an order, that progress has some "self-rewarding" features. Notably Kant cites Plato's *Republic* as the "idea" of the perfectly just regime and speaks of its self-rewarding character.[31] Furthermore Kant remarks that free agents at some future time may be "the cause of general happiness"; this may come about if "everyone does as he ought."[32] Various statements thus point to an interpretation of the "systematic unity of wills" as containing the possibility of happiness through the freedom of finite rational beings and not simply through the agency of a divine will.[33]

All the same Kant proceeds to observe the difficulty that a just correspondence between virtue and happiness is seemingly not to be expected from the ordinary course of nature, as governed by mechanical laws indifferent to moral purposes. This might seem to entail a complete dismissal of the self-rewarding system of freedom and nature. At least it suggests that one might have to be satisfied with a very attenuated notion of systematic unity, according to which happiness is a mere possibility, wholly beyond theoretical anticipation, but rationally compatible with the idea of the self-consistent willing in the best legal order. Yet one should note Kant's remark that our present understanding of nature does not exhaust all posibilities in the relation of morality to laws of nature.[34] Such considerations illuminate the introduction of a supreme being as the highest original good who secures the highest derivative good—the system of rational wills that includes their happiness.[35] The supreme being is not the highest good in the sense that mystical unity with it is the supreme end of a rational being; it is the highest of causes instrumental to humanity's purpose of attaining its ideal. "Moral theology thus is of immanent use only. It enables us to fulfill our vocation in this present world by showing us how to adapt ourselves to the system of all ends."[36] Furthermore, it seems that one should not conceive the "will" of this supreme cause in anthropomorphic fashion, although its function is wholly anthropocentric.[37] Earlier in the *Critique* the correct account of the deity was said to be "as being a substratum, to us unknown, of the systematic unity, order, and purposivness of the arrangement of the world—an idea that reason is constrained to form as the regulative principle of its investigation of nature."[38] Now a related conception of the deity is introduced to bring the investigation of nature into accord with the final moral purpose of human striving within the sensible world. The postulative and moral use of the deity embraces and gives the final telos to the regulative and theoretical use of the ideas.

Here and elsewhere Kant postulates the possibility of the advancement of the human species toward the reality of the system of virtuous and happy rational beings by forces largely but perhaps not wholly inscrutable to theoretical inspection. The convergence of the sensible world and moral freedom, whereby freedom receives the cosmic sanction of an appropriate happiness, is the postulated "design" of a supreme cause, whose mode of action "in the world of sense is in large part concealed from us."[39] Yet the phrase "in large part" indicates that there is some role for theoretical inquiry in the discovery and description of such forces. Possibly some traces of nature's abetting of man's highest end in the world can be discerned through theory and observation; as subordinated to the task of uncovering such traces, "all investigation of nature tends to take the form of a system of ends."[40] That is, the idea of the systematic unity of nature and freedom in the moral world "leads inevitably also to the purposive unity of all things which constitute this great whole, in accordance with universal laws of nature." [41] Surely then, the postulated idea of happiness in proportion to moral worth is not conceived in total abstraction from the actual sensible and natural condition of humanity, that is, it is not relegated simply to another world. In fact we see that if reason in all its employments is to be a truly unified "system," then the theoretical investigation of empirical nature should have some role in the promotion of the highest moral end. It is not only as a propaedeutic, eliminating the false speculative dialectic, that theoretical inquiry promotes man's worldly goal.

Thus critical theology is to take the form of an effort to unify the various employments of reason in relation to the demands of freedom for the ideal, and not in relation to external commands. Hereby the speculative and practical are united; there is a new account of the whole in which freedom is the highest *arche*; all supersensible realities and causes are understood as subordinated to freedom's essential projects. Even the idea of God is so subordinated. Kant could not state more directly the primacy of the practical in the profoundest sense in which he intends it; the practical determines the direction and even the content of theoretical inquiry. The unity that reason seeks to articulate is "grounded in freedom's own essential nature."[42] Indeed the transcendental enlargement of knowledge is not "the cause but merely the effect of the practical purposiveness which pure reason imposes on us." Also: "What *use* can we make of our under-standing, even in respect of experience, if we do not propose ends to ourselves? But the highest ends are those of morality."[43]

The legislation of the supreme purposive unity of reason by prac-tical reason is not an unprepared announcement of the Canon. As we have seen, the idea of a whole ordered by moral concerns, and form-ing a system that is somehow "continuous" with the order of nature, dates back to the middle 1760s. It remains Kant's notion of the su-preme end of all reason and indeed of all creation; it is still the goal of rational inquiry in the *Critique of Judgment* to uncover traces of the real possibility of the attainment of such a system.[44] The reflection on aesthetic and organic phenomena, but not only on these, is initiated and governed by that goal. One needs also to consider how Kant's philosophizing about politics, history, religion, and the entire realm of "culture" belongs within the context of reflection on the supreme end of reason. The Canon only supplies very broad outlines of that reflection; it remains for the later "critical" writings to provide the detailed working out of the projected system in its positive, postpro-paedeutical phase. But the Canon already indicates the fundamental intent of the whole system: the reinterpretation of all of metaphysics, with its apparently transpractical and speculative goals, as simply supporting the human worldly vocation of recovering reason out of its self-inflicted alienation. Reason's goal is only an "immanent" and practical one—to become "at home" in this world.

Philosophy's "Idea" and Its History

The reinterpretation of metaphysics as practical is carried a few cru-cial steps farther by the following two chapters of the *Critique*'s Doc-trine of Method. The Architectonic of Pure Reason shows that the demand for unity among the uses of reason, as grounded on moral freedom, is intrinsic to the concept or "idea" of philosophy itself; it thus offers further justification for the thesis of the Canon.[45] In the History of Pure Reason, Kant indicates that the idea of philosophy reaches its consummate articulation in "criticism," which is the form of philosophy that overcomes the deficiencies of all previous attempts to erect a systematic or scientific philosophy.[46] It thus shows that the idea of reason's end in the Canon is justified by historical reflection on earlier endeavors in the realm of pure reason. Yet the Architectonic lays an important foundation for the historical reflection of the last chapter in that it discloses why the idea of philosophy could come to full clarity only at the end of a long historical development; it reveals an intrinsic connection between "system" and "history." Reason's demand for completion in a system entails that reason must be essentially historical, at least in important respects.

The demand for system follows, as we have seen, from the circumstance that only unified and systematic knowledge can further the essential end of reason, which is practical: to advance the progress of the human species to a fully self-consistent and self-determining use of reason. To that end, the rational investigation and exploitation of nature (in the sciences that can promote human welfare on many levels) must be subordinated to, and thus unified with, the moral use of reason. In the Architectonic, Kant demonstrates how this systematic "form" of reason in its consummation must follow from the "idea" of philosophy. An "idea" generally determines in a priori fashion a whole schema or form for a body of knowledge (whatever it may be) that is systematic; thus "by a system I understand the unity of the manifold modes of knowledge under one idea."[47] Systematic form is organic and distinguished from a mere aggregate. Organic form displays complementarity (but not homogeneity) among the parts that make up the whole body of knowledge; the whole is not formed by an arbitrary additive procedure. A system is thus characterized by perspicuity of plan and completeness of articulation, as well as by diversity among the internal parts.[48] Kant further states that only systematic knowledge is scientific knowledge in the truest sense. An "architectonic" he defines as a "doctrine of the scientific" in knowledge, or, in other words, as an art of forming systems. With respect to the whole account of all uses of reason, or philosophy, there must be an architectonic that determines the systematic form of such an account. Such an architectonic necessarily looks for the "idea" of the specific field of knowledge, in this case philosophy, that will guide the determination of its systematic form.[49]

Further consideration of the nature of systematic knowledge and its basis in an idea discloses that the completeness, perspicuity, and complementarity of diverse parts must have a teleological foundation of a certain kind. The special relation among the parts of a system, a relation that is not arbitrary and aggregative, must be grounded in their subordination to a necessary organizing end. When such an organizing end is absent, knowledge is merely "technical"; a technical pursuit of knowledge is "in accordance with purposes contingently occasioned," and it results only in a "technical unity" of parts of knowledge accidentally related to one another.[50] Thus true science has an architectonic unity grounded in a purpose that is necessary in the sense that the purpose has a necessary relation to each aspect of the whole body of knowledge. But in the case of the systematic unity of philosophy (the whole of reason) it is clear that the organizing purpose must be necessary in one further sense. This purpose, being the principle that governs all knowledge and uses of reason, cannot be conditional upon some higher form of knowledge or use of reason. Therefore only an unconditional purpose, one necessarily chosen by a rational being, can guide the forming of the system of philosophy. The "idea" governing philosophy will then be found in a highest end that is chosen for itself, absolutely, and that moreover is necessarily chosen.

We have seen Kant argue as early as 1764–65 that nature, as natural inclination, cannot be the source of such an end. For natural purposes, as given by pleasure or desire, are contingent and not rigorously universal; only commands, based on freedom, can give rise to strict universality in the realm of ends. What is more, natural purposes are not intrinsically self-consistent; they can give rise to no reliable "rule" or legislation for the use of the will or of reason. The supreme end that organizes reason must command with strict universality, and it can avoid the dangers of "contingency" only if it commands from an Archimedean point, beyond the reach of nature's partial and "dialectical" tendencies. Such an end, of course, can be given only by pure moral reason. The supreme end (or idea) of philosophy is grounded in freedom (the uncaused cause), which, in order to legislate with strict universality, must be effective in every human reasoner. The idea of philosophy must represent a universal interest; so understood, that idea is the "world concept" (as contrasted with the merely technical and scholastic concept) of philosophy. The world concept "relates to that in which everyone necessarily has an interest." [51] An idea based on a law representing the interest of only certain human beings or nonuniversal needs of the mind cannot govern absolutely. "The sciences are devised from the standpoint of a certain universal interest," [52] and with respect to philosophy in particular, it must be asserted that "the archetype for the estimation of all attempts at philosophizing" is present in every human being. [53]

The one human end that has strict universality and that obliges unconditionally is the teleological principle that moral freedom gives us. Philosophy, as articulated by the "idea" of that end, is above all else moral philosophy, or, more exactly, it is the unification of all uses of reason from the standpoint of moral philosophy. According to Kant, the ancients rightly gave preeminence to moral philosophy on systematic grounds; moral philosophy as the study of man's vocation has "superiority over all other occupations of reason." [54] Moral philosophy here means the determination of the end of man, or of reason, which must include the interpretation of the place of speculation in the human vocation. It is surely not just the foundations of the concept of duty. Thus moral philosophy correctly conceived is identical with philosophy itself, as "the science of the relation of all knowledge to the essential ends of reason," and according to this definition "the philosopher is not a mere artificer but the lawgiver of human reason."[55] The other sciences should be seen as the "instruments" of the philosopher's legislation.[56]

Now it is evident that the idea of philosophy, governing all uses of reason and forming a system from them, has authority over all of culture. Philosophy is the comprehensive legislation of human culture, whose perfection is metaphysics.[57] Yet metaphysics, as we have seen, has propaedeutical and dogmatic phases; the ruling part of metaphysics is the dogmatic telos, and metaphysics in that form has responsibility for the ordering of all human culture. The task of metaphysics has certainly not been completed; metaphysics has barely commenced its proper work. Kant strikingly remarks that our "culture is without plan"; the task of metaphysics is to give it a plan, to make culture a system.[58] Yet the fulfillment of this task has firm foundations in ordinary human reason and is not an alien or arbitrary imposition on humanity. For Kant notes of metaphysics that "the idea of such a science is as old as speculative reason."[59] "Human reason, since it first began to think, or rather reflect, has never been able to dispense with a metaphysics."[60] Whereas one cannot ascribe to every human reasoner an actual engagement in speculative inquiry in the strict sense, one can ascribe to him something even more fundamental from the standpoint of metaphysics—a presentiment of the idea or telos that must govern all uses of reason, hence all of culture.[61]

If the idea of philosophy's system has been present in all human reason implicitly since the earliest times, and if that system is not fully actual until all human reason legislates over itself consciously, in the light of that idea, then it is evident that "system" and "history" are intimately related. From the beginnings of human history, the common reason has tended, in Kant's view, to distinguish pure duty from the promptings of inclination, and has thereby tended to make the correct systematic distinction between freedom and nature, although without consciously elaborating it.[62] Thus the very idea of a pure and universal legislative reason, which is the key to the critical system of reason, makes its first appearance in ordinary morality. For it is in this realm that a motive exists for the separation of a priori principles from empirical ones that does not exist in the merely theoretical contemplation of nature.

Thus human progress in the awareness of the purity of the moral principle was the condition for one of the most momentous of conceptual changes mentioned in the Canon. "We find, in the history of pure reason, that until the moral concepts were sufficiently purified and determined, and until the systematic unity of their ends was understood in accordance with true concepts and from necessary principles, the knowledge of nature, and even quite a considerable development of reason in many other sciences, could give rise to only crude and incoherent concepts of the Deity."[63] The human species has progressed in separating out the pure principle of the will from other motives and has thereby progressed in its conception of the supreme organizing principle of all of nature. Pure reason has a history because pure reason is, above all else, the gradual assertion of the domination of legislative freedom over mere nature. Therefore advances in the awareness of freedom are the profoundest source of advances in metaphysical understanding: the enlargement of metaphysical knowledge is not the cause, but the effect, of the practical purposiveness of reason.

Even from a theoretical standpoint, true metaphysics cannot consist simply of theoretical understanding, but must rest on the ascendancy of freedom over nature; for only this ascendancy enables reason to overcome the dialectic of an impure reason that follows the "leading-strings" of nature. In the Architectonic, Kant stresses once again the importance of that dialectic as the background and condition of critical inquiry. "Human reason, being by its very nature dialectical, can never dispense with such a science [of criticism] which curbs it, and through a scientific and completely convincing self-knowledge, prevents the devastations of which a lawless speculative reason would otherwise quite inevitably be guilty in the field of morals as well as religion."[64] But now that dialectic acquires new significance in light of the "idea" of philosophy. That is, the dialectic belongs to the historical character of reason or, more precisely, to the account of why the idea of philosophy has taken many ages of human progress, by no means even and assured, to reach clarity about the idea. For the emergence of that idea into full consciousness has entailed the following: that reason assert the rule of "law" over its own natural lawless tendencies. That assertion presupposed greater awareness of the scope and responsibility of human freedom. This in turn had its foundation in the voice of pure duty in common reason. But the elevation of human freedom above ancient and tenacious "crude" conceptions of itself involved a certain conquest of nature on many levels that could not occur suddenly and without the participation (largely unconscious) of the whole species. In terms that surely remind us of later German idealism, Kant argues that the idea of philosophy is nothing other than the progress of the whole species toward self-knowledge, wherein the decisive moment is humanity's discovery of its own essence—freedom.

That discovery could not take the form of noting a mere "fact"; it has had to be an actual historical accomplishment, a transformation that is still continuing in the human condition. For the supremacy of freedom has had to establish itself in every use of human reason, that is, in every part of "culture." Kant remarks on the difficulties that have stood in the way of this establishment, which reaches an epochal turning point in the new dispensation of "criticism." The Architectonic treats in particular the problems of finding the correct standpoint in speculative inquiry. Although the true idea of philosophy "lies hidden in reason" like a microscopic "germ," human reason possesses no natural insight into the proper way to cultivate it. Human efforts have groped toward their telos in a largely haphazard fashion. The natural order of inquiry is to begin with a mere "assemblage of materials in a technical manner," guided by an inchoate sense of the "idea," until it "first becomes possible for us to discern the idea in a clearer light and to devise the whole architectonically in accordance with the ends of reason."[65] Notably, reason's theoretical advance toward the rule of systematic self-legislation has to be guided by an accurate notion of the *end* of reason. The true end of reason is grounded in freedom's absolute sovereignty. Lacking guidance from that end, reason will proceed only "technically," that is, "instrumentally." Reason's natural dialectical tendency is to degrade itself to instrument, mere *techne*. This is an unavoidable tendency since insight into the proper form of rational governance is not given to man by nature; it can be acquired only through "practice," the actual exercise of such governance. Again, the true standpoint in metaphysics cannot be attained by purely speculative or contemplative reflection.

Human reason thus begins with a false articulation of philosophy as a confused mass of knowledge, of mixed origin; the pure element of metaphysical knowledge is not yet separated from empirical and mathematical knowledge.[66] The important "revolutions" in philosophy and the sciences consist in reason's making strides forward in awareness of the role of pure (a priori) principles in legislating over the "given" material of sensibility. And as we have seen, perhaps the most difficult step of all has been the last of the revolutions: the separation of metaphysics from the other a priori sciences, logic and mathematics, with which the pure reason of metaphysics so easily confounds itself. For in this revolution, reason has a harder task than before; it makes distinctions *within* the pure sciences and learns to grasp the distinctiveness of the metaphysical concepts. This task goes beyond the legislation of reason over nature, already practiced and understood by Galileo, Newton, and modern natural philosophy (and with which Kant's own revolution is easily confounded). Metaphysics, before "criticism," is misunderstood in either "sensualistic" or "intellectualistic" fashion as either an empirical science or a pure science that as organon extends human knowledge of objects. Both misunderstandings are inevitable and are the source of the disunity and disarray in past philosophy.[67]

The critical insight is that metaphysics is not and cannot be a science of the extension of knowledge at all, but is the self-legislation of reason grounded on its self-knowledge. Since this is identical with reason's attainment of unity with itself, it is the only way to unity among the conflicting doctrines. We have seen that it is identical with reason's discovery of the sole possible source of teleology; the "transcendental" insight is that reason can never be in harmony with itself unless it ceases to look to nature for the highest ground of purposes. Thus metaphysics, the first of the sciences, reasserts its importance within the context of the recent modern disregard of metaphysics because the determination of the highest end of reason has been neglected by modern philosophy. Or one can say that modern philosophy left intact and unexamined the most basic of ancient premises—that nature in some sense gives reason its end. The criticism of that premise is entirely different from any "theoretical" enterprise of the past; it is not a new form of "extending" knowledge, since all such extension assumes guidance from nature. Its problem is not just the "bases of experience," for its theme is the ultimate end that is not intuitable, constructible, or in any way part of experience.

This line of reflection illuminates why the discovery of the critical standpoint must have a long prehistory and why it is conditioned by historical factors. The chapter on the History of Reason concludes that through its repeated failures, philosophy must learn that "the critical path alone is still open."[68] As Kant states in the *Nachlass*, these failures have "necessitated a suspicion of all methods [in metaphysics], and an investigation of the subjective sources."[69] The dialectic of reason is, in other words, the necessary presupposition of the discovery of the final standpoint. This dialectic alone has "preserved the human understanding from complete decay in modern times, in matters of metaphysics," and this reveals that "in such ways the course of nature follows a beautiful, in large part mysterious order, finally reaching perfection even through destruction."[70] It thus seems that nature promotes the overcoming of its own dialectical tendencies through that dialectic, which compels pure reason as freedom to assume the legislative role. Surely nature does not itself provide the final ordering end. Rather, it is "in the order of nature that at the beginning, many forms of knowledge, or at least attempts at understanding, multiply without correct method, and only later are brought under rules."[71] The arrival at correct method and rules, however, rests on the encounter with the necessity to "systematize" all of reason from the standpoint of a final end that can be given only by freedom. Very oddly, a necessity that seems to be a merely empirical vicissitude of history belongs to the essence of pure reason. Yet consideration of the Kantian project and its "idea" shows that it cannot be otherwise. For philosophy enslaves itself to history, its vicissitudes and revelations, when it assumes responsibility for all of human welfare, and even when (or perhaps especially when) it seeks to bring humanity to a "pure" standpoint.

It remains for us to examine how the idea of philosophy takes concrete form in the progress of "culture" as a whole; for the achievement of freedom by the species as a whole is the content of that idea and thus of metaphysics itself. In particular, reason strives toward unity with itself, achievable only if reason is true to its free essence. All of culture, as the realm in which reason distorts or discloses its essence, is of concern to critical metaphysics. Theoretical philosophy can offer only the propaedeutic to the final culture, which propaedeutic itself rests on a certain progress in freedom made by past culture. The fact that reason's attainment of unity with itself has historical conditions that reason at the start of history could neither foresee nor legislate is especially important in the account of culture. The history of culture offers the sobering and invaluable lesson that reason, even as it progresses, is the cause of its own confounding.

Culture's Contradictions and Their Ideal Resolution

Throughout his literary career, Kant reflected on the the problem of the highest good from two perspectives, seeming at first quite distinct, which could be called "religious" and "cultural." In the former reflection, Kant seeks to find useful anticipations in Christian doctrine of the purely rational doctrines of moral religion. In other words, he seeks "signs" that "historical religion" may in crucial ways be preparing humanity for the universal acceptance of purely rational forms of faith; the tenets of such faith are the postulates supporting the human species' purposeful and consistent striving toward realizing its final end (the highest good) on earth. It would be a mistake, however, to suppose that the more obviously worldly and cultural treatment of the same issues is incompatible with, or even secondary compared with, the religious treatment. In this context one cannot disregard Kant's famous caution in the public discussion of religious matters.[72] Furthermore, Kant's departures from orthodoxy (in his reforms of historical religion) are complemented by cultural and political accounts of human progress toward the moral world. These accounts fill some of the lacunae, and offer answers to some of the baffling features, of the apparently wholly religious accounts.

As we have seen, even the supposedly "otherworldly" Canon asserts that moral theology "enables us to fulfill our vocation in the present world," and that the moral world which is the highest object of moral hopes is an idea of the sensible world, viewed as an object of pure practical reason. If the future life is understood as a nonbodily existence, how can it supply a condition for humanity's progress toward the highest good, which certainly includes an idea of the perfecting of human earthly and sensible existence? The notion of the highest good as the totality of ends is necessary only for a being that is both rational and sensible—one for whom the relation between the strivings of sensible nature and of autonomous reason is a problem. Kant in numerous places notes that the attaining of a harmony between those strivings, under the unquestioned supremacy of pure moral reason, is the chief problem to be solved by culture. The cultural perspective on the problem of the highest good offers a clearer view than the religious one of how "happiness in proportion to moral worth" may be a goal attainable by human efforts within the sphere of human institutions and worldly progress. The problem of happiness takes on a more concrete character, and indeed its moral significance can be better grasped, if happiness is not merely the "reward" that a superhuman agency must grant to virtue. In fact, from the cultural perspective one learns how happiness *becomes* a problem for humanity in the first instance. This perspective reveals a certain human responsibility for unhappiness, and that responsibility, in turn, has moral significance.[73]

The argument of this study has pointed to the primacy of the cultural perspective in that it has tried to show that for Kant the whole problem of reason is one of culture; that is, the problem of reason is how free rationality is to relate to nature in a way that is not dialectical. Reason can attain a nondialectical unity with itself only if it does not take its end from nature; that does not entail that reason can ignore the realm of natural ends, however. Metaphysics is the foundational inquiry, as the self-correction of reason, enabling free rationality to come into accord with itself; it is the foundational inquiry establishing the "sound culture" of reason. The problem of the culture of reason has, as we have seen, a principal root in the thought of

Rousseau. Thus Kant since the period of the *Remarks* has considered the whole good of man (and the end of man as rational) in terms of the preservation of freedom within the conditions of civilization, especially modern civilization.[74] Rousseau provided paradigmatic formulations of the problem, which uncovered the deficiencies of all earlier philosophic accounts of the human good: no previous account of man had noted the extent to which free rationality can create novel and "artificial" obstacles to the achievement of virtuous simplicity that must be based on the same free rationality. Thus no previous account had noted the extent to which reason is in conflict with itself.

Yet since reason alone subverts reason, it should be possible for reason to correct itself and attain a higher level of "culture" than any that has been known before. On this assumption, or hope, even the formula "happiness in proportion to moral worth" may not express a goal that is altogether elusive to the worldly efforts of the human species. The idea of happiness may not express only an empty fiction, even if it tends to be the product of the restless vagaries of the imagination, detached from instinctual determination. Indeed it may be possible that reason's self-correction includes a refinement and "criticism" of the idea of happiness, whose outcome would be the pursuit of an improved notion of happiness entailing less subversion of the ends of freedom and virtue than in the past. More positively, it might result in the species' attaining happiness (of a sort) through its free efforts alone. The examination of the history of human culture might shed some light on how certain hidden forces or processes may abet both the negative object of "less subversion" of freedom by nature and the positive object of a harmony between freedom and nature. Thus Kant devotes his speculations on the course of history to the search for "signs" of such progress toward the "ideal" of reason. Hopes for the attainment of the ideal are considerably strengthened if one can argue, on the basis of historical evidence, that the conflicts between freedom and nature are merely of reason's making and that they are not grounded in an intractable natural order.

Many of the Kantian writings and reflections after 1781 are devoted to developing the following theses: that free rationality is the source of human culture—both its ills and ennobling achievements; that the aim of culture is the elevation of man above mere "animality" by reason; and that the future possibilities for the species, contained in that elevation, point to a final "system" in which the human powers are perfected and completed.[75] Human beings in any one generation (even the greatest of human beings) cannot disclose these possibilities; the human powers are historical, and their character is modified by the advances of culture. Thus Kant, even for systematic reasons, needs to reflect on the course of history in order to estimate the potentials and limits of those powers. He learned from Rousseau the error of supposing that man in any given epoch will disclose the potentials and limits of a given "nature." Culture is the sphere of human freedom and thus of human self-transformation; the human powers disclose a "natural indeterminacy in kind and proportion," which, however, can indicate a certain positive and determinate goal if the perspective adopted in viewing these powers is sufficiently comprehensive and historical.[76] The most comprehensive of knowable wholes, in which humanity finds its appropriate "place," is human history.

One can begin with the observation, gathered from even the merely "empirical" study of human history,[77] that the development of free rationality in man is much indebted to the harshness of man's natural situation and thus to certain characteristics of humanity as "finite" and sensible. Man must elevate himself above animality in the sphere of culture through self-imposed forms of "discipline" and "constraint." The subordination of the inclinations to law is a necessity, because the human inclinations are limitless and characterized by a boundless love of freedom; at the same time, the natural situation is one of scarcity and conducive to chaotic competition. The necessity of law is inseparable from human freedom's compulsion to depart from the natural simplicity and regularity of other beings. The arbitrariness of human willing is unlike the perfect spontaneity of divine willing, since the natural or sensible constraints on the former incline human wills to come into conflict with themselves and each other. The need of man to overcome his animality is due to the fact that human willing and desiring is not truly "animalic." Thus the coercive forces resulting in culture and the rule of law are essentially human and not to be confused with mere "mechanism." Since the discipline of social life is a necessary condition for the full development of the moral consciousness, even the highest features of man's humanity owe much to the original coercive forces behind the rule of law. "Everything good and man's progress toward perfection are grounded upon a civil constitution. Yet the latter presupposes discord, scarcity, and the necessity of labor. Adam."[78] "Man is an animal who is in need of, and capable of, discipline by reason," and the external discipline of law precedes and makes possible the inner discipline of virtue, "the compulsion of the inner conscience: morality."[79] Morality seems to be thinkable only for a needy being—one whose desires tend to exceed its powers and which thus comes into conflict with itself. Such a being is a political being.

The hardness of man's natural situation is a factor not only in the

invention of law, but in the human compulsion to industrious activity. And again there is a psychological factor. Human sociality as
well as the competitiveness inherent in a condition of scarcity for beings with limitless desires is at the root of labor. "The chief effect of
the social condition is the compulsion to activity"; human talents are
developed under the stimulation of natural hardship and of the
amour-propre intrinsic to a finite rational being.[80] Because they are
not self-sufficient, men have need of the wills of others in order to
achieve their ends; but since they are free and not easily compelled to
serve the ends of another, their assistance must be won through mutual esteem. The striving to make oneself estimable in the eyes of
others is the principal occasion for the human discovery of free activity as the source of dignity and of a peculiar satisfaction. The true
human vocation comes into view as a result of the combined forces of
natural scarcity, the primordial conflict of wills, and the effort to attain some mastery of the situation through the extension of human
talents. The true vocation is the perfection of freedom: "The pecu-
liarity of humanity is that it must invent all good for itself and create
this good through freedom";[81] "Man shall produce all perfection out
of himself; he must be educated and trained, and thus the species
grows in perfection."[82]

Whereas the end of other species, given to them by instinct, is
merely to reproduce their kind, man's end is "the development of all
talents, the exercise of his whole nature, and the attainment of the
highest self-esteem through establishing concord and rules."[83] One
can see that Kant differs markedly from Rousseau in his account of
natural scarcity and harshness, and of the social intercourse that from
the start incites and fuels the passions. But the two thinkers agree on
the intrinsic link between rationality and the passions, and on the
progressive and limitless widening of the human powers consequent
upon passion. In sum, they agree on fundamental aspects of the relation of reason and "culture."

Culture, in this new account of human powers, opens up the prospect of the gravest difficulties as well as the most inspiring possibilities for the human future. Human neediness, willfulness, and conflict
are the source of much misery and danger; on the other hand, such
discomforts compel man, out of dissatisfaction with himself, to formulate the "ideal" of the beneficent unfolding of his powers.[84] Indeed, man's ills are something for which he has reason to be grateful;
he is forced to discover higher satisfactions in free activity than mere
nature can provide and which are unknown to all other beings. Nature's niggardliness points to man's transnatural source of worth and
contentment; without his free activity, nature itself would lack a final

purpose.[85] Hence freedom is the basis of a theodicy: it is "the order of nature" that "good must arise from evil or, more precisely, that the driving force behind the unfolding of the latent seed of the good, is evil."[86] Again it is clear that nature's order means primarily a certain negative condition that she institutes, provoking the human free exercise of legislative and end-giving reason; nature does not determine the end, but compels man to give himself his end. As in the case of the natural dialectic of reason in its speculative use, a certain natural tendency toward disorder and disequilibrium compels reason to overcome nature and to construct a superior "ideal" order on the basis of freedom. The utility of evil for the good is not an awkward or inconsistent element of "realism" within modern moral idealism, but an essential presupposition of its account of freedom and reason as compensating for nature's deficiencies.

Yet the human effort to achieve an ideal completion of the rational powers necessarily takes the form of a striving to unify freedom with happiness or natural contentment; the theodicean formula of "good through evil" does not, it seems, adequately address that rational hope. Again Kant is Rousseau's student on a crucial matter. Kant asserts that the development of reason and talents necessarily intensifies the opposition between freedom and happiness, incipient even in the earliest times. Social discipline and cultural refinement are ennobling but injurious to human happiness and peace of mind. The rewards of self-esteem through free activity cannot, it seems, justify all the pains connected with progress.

This quandary—the fact that the elevation of man above animality through culture creates new discontents and thereby jeopardizes man's essential rational goal—leads Kant to declare that man is a "contradiction." He further asks "whether it is not the case that all men are in a way disturbed," whether man is not an unstable and "ambiguous being, between the angels and cattle."[87] For it is evident that the quality in man that renders him nearly divine—free rationality—cannot flourish without endangering the animal and vital bases of his existence. And thus the moral ideal of reason must be built on the "realistic" recognition that the well-being of the vital bases must accompany, or be promoted by, the progress of reason, for otherwise free rationality and the moral foundation of human "worth" are themselves endangered. Kant's nonascetic and worldly defense of reason must justify reason against powerful complaints that reason renders man's earthly life miserable and that man would do well to submit his will to the authority of mere "mechanism." Moral exhortation is not the whole, or even the primary, intent of Kant's defense of free rationality. The primary intent is to promote human self-knowledge, which must result in the self-accord of reason and the uncovering of a rational vocation befitting man's true "place" as a finite and sensible, albeit also free and rational, being.[88]

The conflicts between freedom (or reason) and nature (or inclination), generated by the advance of culture, can be stated in terms of a divergence of goals or ends for the species and the individual. For it is primarily as a species that humanity benefits from the growth of reason, whereas the natural or instinctual ends of humanity are primarily of concern to individuals, and these suffer through the rational advance of the species.[89] It should be noted how the presupposed view of "reason" here divorces the ends of reason from the teleological structure and disposition of organic individuals. Kant notes three areas of such conflict: sexual repression, the requirements of scientific progress, and social inequalities. In each area there surfaces a primordial disproportion between human desire and power, intrinsic to the advance of reason. Thus society provides for the natural end of reproducing and maintaining the species by means of the institutions of marriage, the family, and education; yet the same institutions require the prolonged delay of the satisfaction of the sexual urges (until adulthood, well after puberty), and thus violence is done to the physical and psychic well-being of most individuals.[90] The progress of scientific knowledge discloses a "disproportion between science and the life of man"; the infinite task of science is beyond the power of any individual to complete, and the few insights that even the most comprehensive minds achieve are only a small part of the totality of possible knowledge. Human mortality stands in the way of the satisfaction of the deepest longing of the lover of knowledge and becomes the source of a complaint against existence that is utterly unknown to a subrational being.[91] Social inequalities are an evil grounded in reason, for through mere convention certain individuals are empowered to enjoy unnecessary pleasures while others are required to struggle to satisfy even the most necessary desires. In all three areas, reason institutes a disproportion between its manner of satisfying a primary good (even where this is natural) and certain natural and given conditions of human life. And in each case, it is not nature itself which is rightly blamed for the problem.

The debt Kant acknowledges to Rousseau for this account of the basic human tensions is, as one should already realize by now, not for the latter's celebration of mere "nature," prior to the institutions of reason and culture. Whereas nature is indeed not to blame for the human problems, the solutions to these problems have to be the work of human freedom; with respect to such solutions "nature" can only stand for an ideal that is utterly unknown to the prerational condition of human or nonhuman nature. Thus the "entire aim" of Rousseau is this: he seeks to "close the circle" of human history by bringing the social order into accord with the idea of nature; his effort is to bring culture to a new level by combining the advantages of culture and nature in a "union of extremes."[92] "Nature" itself can surely not effect this union; humanity must be re-created or given a second nature in the realm of culture.[93] This Kantian intepretation of Rousseau's endeavor embraces, chronologically and philosophically, the account of reason in the *Critiques* and provides the latter with its underlying problematic of culture and its relation to the human good.[94] But we return to the point that fundamentally divides Kant and Rousseau: the former's hope or expectation of a universal solution to the human problems on the plane of reason requires him to look at history as the realm in which "hidden forces" can bring about a reconciliation of the species and the individual.[95] The recovery of "nature" by the individual of highest culture (the philosopher) is still for Rousseau an occurrence of the greatest rarity in human history.

Thus the very difficulties in human reason that Rousseau uncovered have to be turned against themselves, on a universal scale, to achieve the consummation of culture anticipated by Kant. The disproportion between the character of reason and the existence of the human individual can be removed only through a legislative transformation of both that is originally not "intended" by either. The individual as such is not teleologically directed, by nature, to a fulfillment in reason. But he must acquire, somehow, a telos of a rational sort. The species, on the other hand, can pursue its cultural advance only through reason; yet it tends to employ reason for ends that are imperfectly conceived and often self-contradictory. The true telos is not properly viewed, or viewed at all, by either individual or species, until history unfolds the dialectical consequences of the failure to have that telos.

The historical development of reason that must transpire, and that is already transpiring, is thus grounded in the very problem it must resolve: the lack of proper relation between the individual organic being and the universality of reason which is indifferent to the existence of such a being. Nature, while not directly responsible for the problem (since reason, not instinct, expands all human faculties), has provided conditions: nature is stepmotherly in not providing individual human beings with all the instinctual means to care for themselves. In this regard nature constitutes human beings completely differently from the other animal species.[96] Individual private ends of survival and gratification can be attained only with the help of the species and, furthermore, only through the constructions of reason that take the place of instinctual accommodation existing in other "social" animals. This is the point behind the assertion that man is the only being needing education. The individual, merely to survive, needs training in basic skills and arts that only the species affords.[97]

Yet the acquisition of such rational instruments, serving merely natural ends, deepens the dependence of the individual on the species and compels him to take on tasks and purposes alien to his original goals. The spontaneity of human reason is the ground of the most enslaving and troublesome dependencies. Natural conditions offer only the first impulse toward their creation. Human dependence is so problematic because it is not dependence on an unchanging natural order, but largely a self-inflicted dependence on the artificial and technical order of human reason. The spontaneity of reason must effect a new order reducing harmful dependence; the individual wins back autonomy, but abandons, to some extent, his primary orientation by mere inclination. The teleological problem is resolved in this way: moral reason supplies the telos that is otherwise lacking for "culture," in which the technical and instrumental use of reason has been altogether out of relation to the inescapable "individuality" of human existence. The problem most basic to reason is then a historical problem, because the original divergence between the ends of individual and species is what makes history possible; the final end of reason, accordingly, is not solely an end of individuals but one for the whole species to realize within history.[98] This final end, however, is the unification of the divergent ends or the attainment of accord between rational freedom and individual happiness.[99]

The structure of human reason entails the divergence within "empirical history" of individual and species in their ends, and the continuing conflict between their ends is "the greatest hindrance to the progress of the human species in its vocation."[100] Thus the rectification of this conflict is the essence of reason's self-correction and fundamental to the achievement of the rational ideal. Until that rectification occurs, every human being is actually a member of two realms of ends and at odds with himself. One could say that until then "rational animal" does not designate a single species, or does not exist. Modern philosophy and its culture have discovered that reason is autonomous of the soul, or that reason does not belong essentially to the individual as organic whole. The unity of man was dissolved in the Cartesian uncovering of the new universal instrument, the *mathesis universalis* with its foundation in the Archimedean autonomy of human consciousness. But the problem of the wholeness and unity of man has asserted itself with dreadful force in the epoch of Enlightenment: the universal instrument of reason confounds itself and collides with both happiness and the progressive mastery of nature. The realm of purposes, left empty by the discrediting of postulated natural inclinations and passions, has to be filled by freedom and its ideal constructs.

Now the question arises whether that ideal, which includes the satisfaction of the natural inclinations in some accord with moral freedom, can be at all approached in the realm of empirical history. Reason has to construct, it seems, its own version of an "appropriate" satisfaction. The "violence" performed on the inclinations by progressive reason has to be moderated or undone; that violence is partly due at least to a faulty view of happiness. For while reason advances, the natural inclinations have remained crude and raw; the individual's conception of happiness has not kept pace with reason.[101] The fault for this situtaion thus does not lie in the natural inclinations themselves, but in the culture which should refine and ennoble them. Reason on a technical level works marvels in the advancement of talents, sciences, and "luxury," but fails to moralize and refine the concept of satisfaction. The idea of happiness remains "immature" and in tutelage to a primitive view of natural inclination. The individual is in great measure himself to blame if he is at odds with the species' rational advance; he conceives his personal satisfaction in a way that opposes his interest to the universal interest.

Therefore the conflict of individual happiness and the rational species can be seen as belonging to an "age of transition from natural want, through luxury, to the institutions of reason"; this is an age in which technical reason exacerbates desire because reason has not yet enlightened and refined desire itself; it is the period of "greatest conflict" between individual well-being, still conceived in an "animalistic" way, and rational humanity; from this conflict "all vices arise."[102] Moral obligation, taken in a very wide fashion, thus includes the effort to refine the concept of happiness; the "origin of evil" is purely human and man is accountable for it; for when humanity left the condition of greatest simplicity and "gave itself over to devising schemes" with the imagination, it embarked on the restless and debilitating quest for a chimerical happiness which is the true source of the "conflict."[103] Thus Kant offers numerous criticisms of the faulty concepts of happiness, for the moral law "places restricting conditions on the boundless longing for happiness."[104] The formula of "happiness in proportion to moral worth" expresses that restriction. When the heads of state seek to promote the happiness of their kingdoms and their personal glory by belligerent foreign policies, they evince a faulty and culpable view of happiness; for only in the condition of universal peace can "those capacities that make our species worthy of respect be properly developed."[105] And more generally, humanity itself is to blame if it does not leave behind the very ancient but "destructive prejudice" that nature and hence happiness as the satisfaction of nature remain always the same; against this we must hold that "we do not yet know what nature is."[106]

Kant accordingly offers no "dogmatic" account of a highest good and concept of happiness in conflict with a liberal view of the individual's right to define his end of happiness for himself. The very indeterminacy of the meaning of nature will not permit it. On the other hand, the individual is given a new obligation and one that points to the beginning of the illiberalism of later modern idealism; the individual should seek only to be happy "insofar as he is the author of happiness and this happiness is grounded in principles of the universal good."[107] The formal requirement of a happiness pursued in harmony with the universal good (or sought only in accordance with maxims that pass the test of universalizability) is identical with the formal requirement of free authorship of happiness. The idea of happiness should not slavishly follow the authority of mere nature. On the contrary, "nature" must be understood, even in the realm of the inclinations, to obey the authority of legislative reason.

Such suggestions, rather mutedly stated to be sure, point to how a "system" of culture, uniting freedom and nature, may have to be conceived. The final system of culture must rest on a plan that dictates the mode of pursuing happiness, if not its content. For "our culture is without plan, animated only by luxury (as in the sciences, pursued in haphazard fashion), and it is not determined by the end of the universal good"; accordingly "to the very present moment the civil order has depended more on accident and the will of the stronger than on reason and freedom."[108] A culture organized on a moral plan requires that happiness be grounded in rational self-activity and not in passive enjoyment. For humanity should produce all its perfections out of itself.[109] The "vocation of man is the development of all talents, and of happiness and good character upon the basis of the highest art," that is, it is the approach to the condition in which "perfect art has become nature."[110] "Perfect culture" is defined as a "system of happiness and the perfection of human freedom."[111] This ideal still eludes humanity because it "has not yet set up a new purposive order, according to a system"; nature and culture are thus still at odds, and "happiness has not arrived with progress"; the question that faces man is "how the system of happiness will be established wherein perfect art becomes nature"; this is the system Rousseau proposes, of a culture that "would no longer do violence to nature, but fully perfect nature"; for "the unity of happiness and morality arises from the process of civilizing and moralizing." [112]

Kant's various hypothetical schemes and "ideas" for the course of human history revolve around this central point: nature in man is to be remade in the image of moral "art," or according to the archetype of perfected humanity present in universal reason. It is clear that nature in man, by itself, does not tend toward this goal. The dialectic of passion and of instrumental reason is to push humanity unwittingly and unwillingly to the goal that will save it. [113] Ultimately, this dialectic will force on humanity the recognition that only within its own reason can it find the outline of the comprehensive "system" that brings emancipatory freedom into accord with a purposive and sanctioning "whole."

Epilogue

In this volume I argue that the problems of reason from which the critical philosophy arises are centrally problems in the end of reason. More specifically, the modern account of reason, as a methodical instrument subordinated to the ends of passion and emancipated from a metaphysical order, generates various perplexities that threaten belief in the theoretical and practical competence of reason. The difficulties first become clearly apparent to Kant in the practical realm: the passionate individualism that seeks emancipation from dogmatic authority is endangered by its own rational instrument of emancipation. The growth of reason in the modern culture of freedom seems to increase human dependence and to enslave the will to artificial desires. Modern freedom seems, unwittingly, to undermine itself. To escape this consequence the accounts of reason and freedom have to be revised; in particular, the human rational powers have to be ordered in the light of a new account of their end.[1]

The critique of metaphysics has a practical aim, for it is above all a critique of speculative doctrines of "ends"—of dogmatic teleologies that bring reason into conflict with itself. All such doctrines erroneously suppose that a natural object or goal, one existing independent of human spontaneity, is able to supply a final telos for the same spontaneity. The resolution of the dialectic ensuing from such doctrines is the "transcendental" approach in metaphysics. This approach is the elaboration of the a priori and necessarily presupposed conditions of all rational activities, on whose basis reason is enabled to come into a final self-consistent unity. On the plane of the moral will, reason subordinates itself freely to the conditions of universality that per se rule out its subordination to natural inclination. On the plane of speculative inquiry, it subordinates its theoretical use of the unavoidable metaphysical concepts of objectivity to a finite (phenomenal) sphere of cognition, thereby removing the conflict between the moral (noumenal) use of these concepts and our finite mode of cognition. Theoretical inquiry can thus proceed confidently with unification of natural phenomena under laws (employing mathematics as the "master of nature"), without fear of dialectic. Moral reason can at the same time postulate and advance toward its ideal goal of the totality of freedom realized in the world, which goal is the satisfactory correlate of the dialectical speculative ideas of totality.

Thus it is the determination of a noncontradictory end or completion of reason's interests which compels Kant (and, he claims, all humanity eventually) to adopt the transcendental approach. The whole problematic of a new teleology grounded on freedom has an important source in the lack of teleology in the authoritative Newtonian account of nature, but that is only one source. In the various pre-Kantian efforts to define a moral end in passion or sentiment, the explicit claim was to have found a method in the science of human nature that was neutral to first causes and consistent with Newtonian principles. Yet Rousseau showed Kant that those efforts could not prevent the self-undermining or "alienating" dialectic of instrumental reason. Human nature points to no determinate end, of inclination, passion, or sentiment, and furthermore reason in the service of mere nature has malignant consequences. Most dramatically, the problem emerges in the relation of the individual to society or the species as the individual seeks satisfaction of the passions. The individual is dependent on the species for his satisfaction; neither he nor the species has a determinate natural end, however. The individual is dependent on a "whole" whose unity and telos is doubtful and which in all past culture has rested on an accidental and merely technical foundation. In sum, the individual member of the species finds no true completion in this "whole" of which he is naturally part.

The elaboration of this point, and its implications, by Rousseau and Kant is fundamentally consistent with the spirit and intent of modern philosophy. For the new modern emphasis on individual liberties and rights is premised on a similar insight into the lack of accord or harmony between the individual and society or the species as spurious unities postulated to be natural "wholes" by earlier philosophy.[2] The quest of these great critics of the earlier Enlightenment is for a more secure and noncontradictory version of that individuality—one that is cognizant of the dangers of "culture" posed by a hitherto unknown dynamic of reason. Individuality can protect itself against a self-subverting dialectic only if it is grounded in an autonomy that legislates over the passions and that carefully regulates the merely instrumental employment of reason.

Yet it is not only for preserving individuality and its emancipatory striving that Kant initiates the transcendental approach. That approach is also intended to provide a justification of moral sacrifice (and the nobility associated with it) and a satisfaction of the metaphysical urge to grasp the whole. Transcendental philosophy issues in a "system" that fulfills and reconciles these apparently diverse ends, showing their true unity. The foundation of this unity is disclosed in the self-consistent principles of universal reason, that is, the common reason. That reason insists on the supremacy of its own legislation and will brook no superseding of its authority by any dogma, power, or institution representing a merely "particular" interest of tradition, privilege, or worst, blatant tyranny. The true wholeness of reason is achieved on its most universal and common plane, wherein the self-assertion of freedom is most reliable and incorruptible.

It is arguable that all later versions of transcendental reflection are also grounded in a "horizon" defined by a universal common reason, where that horizon may be termed "life-world," the "temporality of existence," or the "interpretative horizon" of the historical consciousness. At this point it may be useful to consider briefly how the transcendental tradition emerging from Kant has exacerbated certain weaknesses in Kantian thought, while it has also neglected some of its strengths. The forms of transcendental philosophy that achieved prominence after Hegel reveal the great change in the situation of philosophy wrought by Hegel's "mediation" of the Kantian dualities. The rejection of all speculative metaphysics in the Neo-Kantian reaction against Hegel and Schelling reasserted the dualisms of nature or theoretical science and freedom or moral and historical science, without the guiding teleological problematic present in the original Kant. The doctrines of the highest good and of the ultimate end could appear to be only superfluous, at best, to the genuine transcendental concerns of giving foundations to the sciences. The emaciation of Kant into the theorist of the sciences of "fact" and of "value" meant that much of the original intent of critical philosophy was ignored or lost.[3] The subsequent developments of transcendental thinking in Husserl and Heidegger, which are much concerned with a critique of the distinction between the realms of fact and value in Neo-Kantian philosophy, did not, for all their profundity, regain the ground that was lost.

To recover the original transcendental problematic one must grasp how Kant conceives transcendental argumentation as a regress from certain given features of the human condition that are indeed dualistic but not in the form of absolute dichotomies. Man is both free and dependent, individual and social, transcending inclination and bound by it, and characterized by spontaneous and receptive powers. The peculiar relation between the terms of these dualities gives rise, in both the speculative and practical realms, to the necessity for law in the ordering of the human powers. That is, because the spontaneous powers transcend a strict determination by the dependency (receptivity) of man upon nature, but never transcend it wholly, the human powers can come into conflict with themselves. Thus on the practical level, the arbitrary way in which man can choose to go about satisfying the inclinations does not at all assure him of an appropriate satisfaction; the arbitrary will naturally tends to come into conflict with itself and other wills. The human will cannot *create* the natural conditions that limit its quest for satisfaction. Similarly speculative reason can come into conflict with itself through a failure to relate the spontaneous (a priori) concepts to the realm of dependent intuition in an appropriate way; reason's spontaneity does not include a creative power to determine the whole object of cognition through concepts alone.[4] Had it such a power, reason would not experience self-contradiction in any form.

In its different versions Kant's transcendental mode of arguing is intended to protect reason against its own tendencies to arbitrariness or against its own inherent impulses toward tyranny. Such tendencies or impulses are the presupposition for the necessity of the self-ordering and self-limiting legislation of reason. Transcendental legislation thus has meaning only in relation to a given form of human reason or will that manifests certain recalcitrant (but not fixed) attachments to a narrow and merely instrumental perspective favoring "one's own," or the "particular," against the unifying perspective of the universal. That particularism is identical with reason's subordination to "mere nature." Thus a certain persisting imperfection in the human situation lies behind the necessity for law; it also points to the natural basis of philosophy as the effort to comprehend and come to terms with that situation. Yet the universal perspective that comprehends and legislates is not itself "natural" but is attainable only through a mastery or overcoming of nature. Such mastery, however, can never be so total or complete as to remove all the natural particularism of reason—except in the "ideal." Paradoxically, the ideal of totality for which reason strives is thinkable or meaningful only on the basis of the original dualism that would be overcome in the "limit case" of the ideal's attainment.

All the same, Kant starts from certain features of the human situation that are natural, apparently permanent, characterized by contradiction and imperfection, and profoundly related to man's political mode of existence. The pervasive Kantian concern with "law" assumes such features; "law" rests upon natural conditions although its own principle is freedom. Whereas the "ideal" would seem to mean the total realization of freedom (and the total subordination of nature to it), Kant never permits us to think beyond the horizon of "law." To think beyond it in any way opens the gates to dialectic and "fanaticism." The ideal, in order to function as the principle of a highest systematic legislation, has to remain infinitely remote and elusive in order to maintain its salutary foundation in law.

The need for law indicates certain abiding and natural features of the human situation and makes possible the ascent of common reason to a philosophic perspective. All earlier philosophy would have recognized and understood these aspects of Kant's starting points. What is novel in Kant, and what later philosophy takes farther, is the assumption that the common reason contains within itself a foundation for an autonomous systematizing legislation, or that common reason, by dint of "freedom," is per se both unified and implicitly philosophic. On this assumption, the natural, contradictory, and political character of human life begins to lose its solidity and to appear evanescent. Thus later transcendental thought does not begin from the experiences and phenomena that Kant still saw with some clarity. The tensions between human freedom or spontaneity and the natural conditions of such freedom dissolve within the standpoint of the pure consciousness of phenomenological reflection or are swallowed up in the homogenizing "ontological" horizon of hermeneutical thought, wherein Being is only a problem of interpretation.

Therefore the questions posed by the watershed of the Kantian revolution crucially include this question: Do we best understand the nature of "reason" and its "end" by starting from human contradictions that cannot be "resolved" in any final way, without destroying the texture of human life itself? This question might also lead us to wonder if philosophy is not better understood as the comprehension, rather than as the "resolution," of the basic problems of human existence. With this wonder we at the same time cast doubt on the claim of Kant, and his successors, that philosophy must answer for the totality of human welfare.

Notes

Preface

1. Alexis de Tocqueville, *The Old Regime and the French Revolution*, trans. S. Gilbert (Garden City, N.Y.: Doubleday, 1955), 139–40.

2. Edmund Husserl, *The Crisis of European Sciences and Transcendental Phenomenology: An Introduction to Phenomenological Philosophy*, trans. D. Carr (Evanston, Ill.: Northwestern University Press 1970), 10–16. Husserl's thought is the last great attempt to defeat, by means of "foundational" inquiry, the skeptical argument that philosophical reason is incapable of grounding faith in rational freedom.

Introduction

1. *KrV* Bxxiv–xxxv and A795–830/B823–58.

2. I am referring to Heine's famous aperçu. For Kant's statement, "I have therefore found it necessary to deny *knowledge*, in order to make room for *faith*," see *KrV* Bxxx. See G. J. Warnock, "The Primacy of Practical Reason," in P. F. Strawson, ed., *Studies in the Philosophy of Thought and Action* (London: Oxford University Press, 1968), for a clear statement of the limited interpretation and a disparaging assessment of *primacy*.

3. *Ak* XIX, R 6612. All translations are mine unless otherwise noted. In this study I rely, with some reservations, on the dating of the *Reflexionen* by Erich Adickes, who describes the *Nachlass* materials and his dating criteria in *Ak* XIV, xviii–liv. For a discussion of the problems in dating Kant's *Reflexionen*, with some criticisms of Adickes, see N. Hinske, "Die Datierung der Reflexion 3716 und die generellen Datierungsprobleme des Kantischen Nachlasses," *KS* 68/3 (1977): 321–40.

4. *Bem*, in *Ak* XX, 1–192. For discussion of the title, the date, and the nature of the materials found in these *Reflexionen*, see chap. 2, sec. 2 below, and the further references cited in the notes to the text of that chapter.

5. *Bem*, in *Ak* XX, 44.8–16. An introductory, and very restricted, discussion of this reflection and others showing Rousseauian influences is found in Ernst Cassirer, *Rousseau, Kant and Goethe*, trans. J. Gutmann, P. O. Kristeller, and J. H. Randall, Jr. (New York: Harper and Row, 1963). See chapter 3 for a full discussion of the philosophical content of these *Relexionen*.

6. Several European scholars, however, have argued for a more pervasive Rousseauian influence, especially J. Schmucker, D. Henrich, and H. de Vleeschauwer. Schmucker authored what has been until now the only extensive discussion of the *Remarks* in print (see *UEK*). It is fair to say that none of the significant discussions of Rousseau's importance for Kant has adequately treated the question of the Rousseauian sources of Kant's account of reason. Various scholarly views are discussed in more detail in chap. 2, sec. 2. Henrich writes in *SV*, 183–84: "Jean-Jacques Rousseau was the

author who most influenced Kant, through his ideas but also through the emotional and imaginative side of his thought." For Henrich's and de Vleeschauwer's suggestions of a profound systematic role for Rousseauian ideas within Kant's philosophy, see below, n. 26 to chap. 2. The present study expands on such suggestions and shows that one must go beyond the usual view that Rousseau's impact on Kant, apart from a few ideas taken from the *Social Contract*, is transient or merely a matter of emotional provocation. L. W. Beck suggests a larger significance in *CPrR*, 1–8, and writes of a "Rousseauistic revolution" in Kant's thought, in *EGP*, 489–96. But in the latter passage Beck defends the fairly conventional thesis that "the more important philosophical impact" is made by the *Social Contract* among Rousseau's writings. He also asserts that this impact is not visible until the *Foundations of the Metaphysics of Morals*. Were this so, it would exclude the breadth of influence on Kant that begins as early as 1764, in the *Remarks*, and which originates most of all in Rousseau's *Emile*. Klaus Reich notes (see *RK*, 6) the revolutionary character of *Emile*'s effect upon Kant, on the basis of a limited acquaintance with a portion of the *Remarks*; the full text was not available until 1942 (see n. 4 above). But Reich confines the importance of *Emile* (and Rousseau generally) for Kant to "moral anthropology"; Rousseau shakes Kant's allegiance to Shaftesbury's "religion of culture" and to its moral and cultural optimism. Rousseau shows Kant that culture cannot be the ground of human dignity (*RK*, 8–11, 26–27). Reich believes Rousseau to be another theorist of "sentiment" and thinks that the pure morality of unconditioned imperatives shows few traces of Rousseau; the latter's important discovery that the evils of culture are man's work, and not nature's, has no impact on the principles of practical philosophy, in Reich's view (*RK*, 6–7, 12–19). In such arguments Reich fails to see that the problem of *reason*, as it emerges in the questioning of cultural optimism (Enlightenment), is integral to the laying of the foundations of moral reason. Reich only briefly notes (very accurately) that Kant understands "culture" to be instrumental to the moralizing of the human race (p. 24). This point, however, is not related by Reich to Kant's reception of Rousseau, but to a rehabilitation of Shaftebury's cultural optimism, in response to Rousseau's account of the evils of culture (pp. 19–26). Insightful suggestions concerning philosophical affinities and common concerns of Rousseau and Kant have been made in two recent additions to the Kant literature: W. A. Galston, *Kant and the Problem of History* (Chicago: University of Chicago Press, 1975), and S. M. Shell, *The Rights of Reason: A Study of Kant's Philosophy and Politics* (Toronto: University of Toronto Press, 1980).

7. See the discussion in chap. 2, sec. 2, for the merits of the *Remarks to the Observations*, in particular, and for concurring views of other scholars (Henrich and Schmucker) on these merits.

8. See especially *KrV* A840/B868 and *KpV*, in *Ak* V, 107–110, and the discussion in chap. 4.

9. See chap. 4, sec. 4, for a fuller discussion of the propaedeutical role of theoretical inquiry and its moral end. For the statements of *KrV* on the theoretical propaedeutic, see A11–12/B25–26 and A841/B869. One of Kant's earliest references to this subject is in a letter to Moses Mendelssohn of April 8, 1766; see *KPC*, 54–57. See also the author's essay, "On Kant's Socratism," in *PIK*, 87–105.

10. See especially chaps. 4 and 5 throughout.

11. The following passages help to make this point.

For there can be no *will* without an end in view, although we must abstract from this end whenever the question of straightforward legal compulsion of our deeds arises, in which case the law alone becomes its determinant. But not every end is moral (that of personal happiness, for example, is not); the end must be an unself-

ish one. And the necessity of an ultimate end posited by pure reason and comprehending the totality of all ends within a single principle (i.e., a world in which the
highest possible good can be realised with our collaboration) is a necessity experienced by the unselfish will as it *rises beyond* mere obedience to formal laws and
creates as its object the highest good. The idea of the totality of all ends is a peculiar kind of determinant for the will. For it basically implies that *if* we stand in a
moral relationship to things in the world around us, we must everywhere obey the
moral law; and to this is added the further duty of working with all our powers to
ensure that the state of affairs described (i.e., a world conforming to the highest
moral ends) will actually exist. (*KPW*, 65; *UG*, in *Ak* VIII, 279– 80)

> But although for its own sake morality needs no representation of an end which
> must precede the determining of the will, it is quite possible that it is necessarily
> related to such an end, taken not as the ground but as the [sum of] inevitable con-
> sequences of maxims adopted as conformable to that end. For in the absence of all
> reference to an end no determination of the will can take place in man, since such
> determination can be followed by no effect whatever. (*Rw*, 4; *Re*, in *Ak* VI, 4)

Note also the definition of "maxim of reason" as "the inner principle of choice among
various ends" (*L*, in *Ak* IX, 24), pointing to an intrinsic connection between reason and
end. See further the definition of practical reason as "the highest faculty determining
the final end [*Endzweck*] of the faculty of desire" (*KU*, in *Ak* V, 197). Purposiveness is
essential to a "finite" rational being having desire.

P. Riley, in his important study, *Kant's Political Philosophy* (Totowa, N.J.: Rowman
and Littlefield, 1983), has properly given teleology its central position in Kant's moral
and political philosophy and indicated its centrality to the whole of critical philosophy.
By distinguishing between moral *incentives* (characterizing a pure moral will) and moral
ends (that arise necessarily on the basis of pure morality), Riley has shown how politics
(and "culture" more generally) is of first importance morally through furthering moral
ends, even if it cannot affect moral incentives (at least directly). Furthermore Riley
shows that the moral law itself has a primary teleological formulation (as the duty to
respect rational agents as "ends in themselves," which implies the project, for all moral
beings, of furthering humanity as a "kingdom of ends").

12. In chapter 5 I offer a resolution wherein I shall also discuss the approaches to
this issue adopted by some of the principal writers on it. See the writings listed in n. 4
to chap. 5.

13. Y. Yovel, in *KPH*, has written what is to date the richest and most interesting
account of the highest good in Kant, as the "totalizing concept of the sum of rational
ends," with a discussion of its role within the whole of reason. He notes that the
priority of the highest good within philosophy "introduces the primacy of pure practical reason into the definition of philosophy as wisdom" (*KPH*, 232, n. 12). He makes
insightful connections between that priority and the Kantian notions of system, architectonic, and the realization of the idea of totality in history. The explications of "history" and "highest good" are indissolubly linked in Kant, because the latter concept
represents the unity of freedom and nature as a goal to be achieved in the realm of
history, which Yovel calls the realm of "objectified moral praxis" (p. 79). Finally, Yovel
observes the close relation in Kant between "metaphysics and moral history," noting
that "moral practice was the domain [for Kant] in which those metaphysical interests
of the mind that could not be satisfied in the field of knowledge were to be re-
channelled and find a valid critical expression" (p. ix). Ultimate worth accrues to man
and the natural world through moral practice and not through a highest self-sufficient
divine or metaphysical first principle, apprehended by the theoretical intellect.

Yovel has thus advanced well beyond the purely formal treatment of the highest good. Nonetheless, Yovel's account lacks a crucial dimension: missing are the precritical origins of the relation of the highest good or the end of reason to history and culture in the encounter with Rousseau and in the critique of earlier modern (as well as ancient) accounts of the end of reason. If that dimension is missing, so is the basis for a full understanding of how the new doctrines are intended by Kant to solve the essential problems in "reason" bequeathed to him by past philosophy.

14. In several essays, Dieter Henrich has shown how the Rousseauism of Kant's account of the moral in terms of the spontaneity of the self-legislative will is present in Kant's thinking as early as 1764. For this see the essays by Henrich, HK and UKfE. Henrich also demonstrates how only in the later 1780s does Kant altogether abandon the effort to deduce the moral law (and the pure motivation of the moral will) from nonmoral rational spontaneity. For this see the essays "Ethik der Autonomie" in *SV*, 6–56, and BsE. That effort, still present in the *Foundations of the Metaphysics of Morals*, is replaced by the ungroundable fact of moral autonomy in the second *Critique*. See also n. 21 to chap. 2.

15. See chap. 5, sec. 1, and the critiques of Düsing and Gueroult presented there, for their neglect of the primary motive for introducing the highest good in the "Canon" of the *Critique of Pure Reason*.

Chapter One

1. Kant's most familiar statements about the revolutionary character of his thought refer to the revolution in metaphysics instituted by his critique of reason. The Kantian revolution is conceived in analogy to the great revolutions in the history of mathematics and natural science (Greek geometry, Copernicus and Galileo; see *KrV* Bx–xxiv in several places and A853/B881), although Kant never actually uses the phrase "Copernican revolution," contrary to almost universal belief; see I. B. Cohen, "Kant's Alleged Copernican Revolution," in *Revolutions in Science* (Cambridge: Harvard University Press, 1984), 237–53. Kant, as is well known, avoids associating his intellectual revolution with political revolution, but it is obvious that he associates it with a very large scale and gradual "reform" or "evolution" toward new ways of thinking in all spheres of public and private life; see *Ak* VIII, 36 and 269, and P. Burg, *Kant und die Französische Revolution* (Berlin: Duncker und Humblot, 1974). When Kant's contemporaries and immediate successors speak of a Kantian or "transcendental" or "idealist" revolution, it is surely with practical, as well as theoretical, dimensions in mind. Kant's philosophy is not the first philosophy to propose a total revolution in human affairs as its intended consequence, but it may be the first to do so with such openness; see Descartes, *Discours de la méthode*, esp. pt. 2. For the connection later thinkers make between Kant's thought and "revolution," see Hegel's letter to Duboc, July 30, 1822 (cited by K. Schmitz in *PIK*, 229); W. Dilthey, *Leben Schleiermachers*, in *DGS* XIII.1, xxxviii and 183–207; F. Schlegel, fragment of a dialogue on Freemasonry, in *Gotthold Ephraim Lessing. Ernst und Falk. Mit den Fortsetzungen Johann Gottfried Herders und Friedrich Schlegels*, ed. I Contiades (Frankfurt a.M.: Insel Verlag, 1968), 79–80. According to Schlegel, the Kantian idealist revolution is of greater import than the French Revolution, "taking place in the inner depths of the human spirit"; it is better understood as "the self-discovery of humanity" than as just another system or school of philosophy.

2. *Lo*, 28; *L*, in *Ak* IX, 24. See also *KrV* A839/B867–68: "Philosophy is the science of the relation of all knowledge to the essential ends of human reason (*teleologia rationis humanae*)," and the *Reflexionen* discussed in chap. 4. sec. 4. Translations of the *Critique*

of Pure Reason are from the Norman Kemp Smith translation (New York: St. Martin's Press, 1965).

3. See the passages from *L* and *KrV* cited in n. 2 above. For the sources of the language of philosophic architectonic in Kant's period, see G. Wolters, *Basis und Deduktion: Studien zur Entstehung und Bedeutung der Theorie der axiomatischen Methode bei J. H. Lambert (1728–1777)* (Berlin: Walter de Gruyter, 1980), 19–20.

4. The account of the philosopher's highest activity as a form of legislation does not originate with Kant; it is found in Machiavelli and persists in the modern period through Nietzsche. Descartes, like Kant, draws close analogies between philosophic founding, legislation, and architecture; see *Discours de la méthode*, pt. 2. These analogies point out that the modern form of philosophizing is an ordering of human rationality toward an end prescribed by a legislative will. Not theoretical receptivity to a given natural order but the artificial constraint of methodical procedure is the form cognition must take if the mind is to acquire knowledge useful to the ends of such willing. The human standpoint of the need for "mastery" determines the order of significant knowledge. Nature in itself, as given and prior to methodical reduction and reshaping, shows no regard for such human needs. In Kant's time, Rousseau is a principal representative of the account of the philosopher as supreme legislator. In the German academic tradition, Reimarus speaks of reason as an autonomous power that obeys "laws" that it prescribes to itself; see N. Hinske, "Reimarus zwischen Wolff und Kant," in *LZA*, 9–32. Reimarus's view is to be distinguished, however, from Kant's view that the autonomous laws of reason prescribe the order of natural law to the phenomena of sensibility.

5. This conception of Kant's enterprise has recently been very ably proposed in W. J. Booth, *Interpreting the World: Kant's Philosophy of History and Politics* (Toronto: University of Toronto Press, 1986).

6. For an account of the modern foundations and the theoretical rejection of first causes that is instrumental to establishing the practical goal of such foundations, see R. Kennington, "Descartes and the Mastery of Nature," in S. F. Spicker, ed., *Organism, Medicine, and Metaphysics* (Dordrecht: Reidel, 1978), 201–23.

7. For the definition of *Enlightenment* see Kant, *Beantwortung der Frage: Was ist Aufklärung?*, in *Ak* VIII, 33–42. For the theoretical dictum "reason has insight only into that which it produces after a plan of its own, and it must not allow itself to be kept, as it were, in nature's leading-strings," see *KrV* Bxiii.

8. *KrV* Bii: "*Sed utilitatis et amplitudinis humanae fundamenta moliri.*" For an account of the relation of Bacon to Kant, see Solomon Maimon, *Baco und Kant*, in Maimon, *Gesammelte Werke*, II, ed. V. Verra (Hildesheim, 1965), 499–522. For the subordination of theory to practical ends in the German Enlightenment, see W. Schneider "Praktische Logik" (on the Thomasian school) and W. H. Arndt, "Die Vernunftlehre von Reimarus in Verhältnis zur Rationalismus und Aufklärung," in *LZA*. Perhaps because the Enlightenment project remained controversial on the European continent, while it found a relatively stable and enduring home in the Anglo-American world, scholars on the Continent have retained the awareness that modern philosophy since Bacon and Descartes has been fundamentally concerned with a "mastery of nature" for human benefit. Thus *PRE*, 42–65 and 191–95 (on British empiricism as concerned with the causal control of phenomena for human ends); L. Landgrebe, "The Phenomenological Concept of Experience," *Philosophy and Phenomenological Research* 34/1 (1973): 1–13: "Science in the modern era understood its task in the terms Descartes assigned it: with science man should become the '*maître et possesseur de la nature*'"(p. 2); T. Seebohm, "The End of Philosophy: Three Historical Aphorisms," in H. J. Silverman and D. Ihde, eds., *Hermeneutics and Deconstruction* (Albany: SUNY Press, 1985), 11–23, esp. n. 3, where he attacks the "modern [i.e., contemporary] myth" that theory and practice

were separated in earlier philosophy: "That Descartes postponed the treatment of ethics does not exclude that ethics is the final goal. Already the title of Spinoza's main work: *Ethica ordine geometrico demonstrata* indicates the goal again. No word has to be lost about the 'final cause' of Thomas Hobbes' thought in this respect."

9. Scholars have noted that at midcentury, around 1755, there are signs of awareness of a "crisis" concerning the foundations of modern thought in a number of thinkers. L. P. Wessell writes of a "cognitive crisis of the Enlightenment"; see his *G. E. Lessing's Theology. A Reinterpretation* (The Hague, 1977), and Kuehn's *SCS*, pp. 36–51. In Germany this crisis closely corresponds to the introduction of the writings of Hume and Rousseau: simultaneously, the intellectual world was exposed to a skeptical critique of the theoretical underpinning of modern scientific emancipation and to a shattering indictment of its moral telos. Together these writers proposed a formidable challenge to modern theoretical analysis and modern natural law. See also L. Krieger, "Kant and the Crisis of Natural Law," *JHI* 26/2 (1965): 191–210.

10. For the distrust of the natural tendency of the human mind, see *KrV* A5/B9 and *ED*, in *Ak* VIII, 333–36. Cf. Francis Bacon, *The Advancement of Learning*, ed. G. W. Kitchin (London: Dent, 1915), 132–34, *Novum Organum*, bk. 1, XXXVIII–LXVIII, and Descartes, *Principles of Philosophy*, pt. 1, LXX–LXXV. For the discovery of foundational principles through the inspection of consciousness, see the account of its origins in the early Descartes by P. R. Kraus, "From Universal Mathematics to Universal Method: Descartes' 'Turn' in Rule IV of the *Regulae*," *JHP* 21/2 (1983): 159–74.

11. The discussion of the *Prize-Essay* of 1764 in chap. 4, sec. 5, below, establishes Kant's "precritical" agreement with the main thrust of modern "epistemology."

12. See Descartes, the sixth of the *Meditations*, for the account of how the employment of methodical reason, and its attendant doubt of the natural theoretical tendency of man to trust images in perceptions, must presuppose guidance by another "teaching of nature": that the pleasant is to be pursued and the painful avoided. Thus methodical "doubt" of the body cannot be maintained to the point of denying the fundamental and "ordinary" bodily experiences which alone can give a certain motive and telos to reason as instrument of mastery.

13. See *Meditationes de cognitione, veritate et ideis*, in G. W. Leibniz, *Philosophische Schriften*, ed. C. I. Gerhardt (Berlin, 1875–90), IV, 422–26. Note Kant's criticism of Leibniz at *KrV* A270–71/B326–27 (and incidentally, the criticism of Locke as well). Heidegger in *MFL*, 37–69, proposes that the Leibnizian ideal of cognition is a modern interpretation of the *intuitus* of the divine intellect in Thomistic scholasticism, and that it belongs to the fundamental intent of Kant's critique of reason to show the impossibility of this ideal as an ideal for human cognition. Essentially Leibniz would correct Cartesian accounts of knowledge by arguing that insight into real possibility of substances is accessible to the human mind only in the form of an intuited totality of attributes that is not only "clear and distinct" but "adequate," i.e., expressing the infinite series of grounds, or *requisita*, that are necessary and sufficient for the being of the individual substance. Leibniz repeatedly states that the infinite analysis needed to uncover that totality is not completable by human minds; he nonetheless regards the ideal of that totality as the correct metaphysical formulation of knowledge of the real possibility of humanly knowable substances, a view Kant will surely reject. Already in the *Prize-Essay*, as we shall see, Kant begins the criticism of the "rationalist" position that metaphysical concepts of grounds admit in principle of total intuitive clarity. The Leibnizian contrast between "intuitive" and "symbolic" cognition, central to Heidegger's discussion, is basic to the terms of Kant's argument. See chap. 4, sec. 5, below.

14. Kant's notions on the distinction between "form" as the element in knowledge contributed by the spontaneity of reason and "mattter" as the receptive element

shaped by form may have been stimulated by reading Leibniz's *Nouveaux essais,* which was first published in 1765. That distinction is elaborated for the first time by Kant, in a published work, in 1770. (See below, chap. 4, sec. 5.) Thus on the crucial issue of reason's spontaneity, there may be a confluence of suggestions from the works of Rousseau and Leibniz. But Rousseau's contribution, since it relates to the moral autonomy of reason, freedom, and the self-subverting aspects of freedom, more fundamentally shapes the whole systematic problem of reason's end. See G. Tonelli, "Leibniz on Innate Ideas and the Early Reactions to the Publication of the *Nouveaux Essais* (1765)," *JHP* 12/4 (1974): 437–54. Shaftesbury must also be considered as an inspiration to many German writers for a more spontaneous, dynamical, and "creative" sense of reason, through his notion of genius. See *PRE,* 157–202, and F. Meinecke, *Die Entstehung des Historismus, Werke,* IV, ed. C. Hinrichs (Munich: R. Oldenbourg Verlag, 1959), 13–27.

15. See the opening lines of the first edition preface to the *Critique of Pure Reason* (*KrV* Avii–viii). This dialectic is intrinsic to human reason and is inseparable from the teleological tendency of human reason to seek wholeness. Accordingly, there should be a sense, Kant believes, in which this dialectic points toward a satisfactory consummation of reason's striving. See *KrV* A669–704/B697–732.

16. Kant expresses this fundamental point in terms of the consequences of "transcendental realism," i.e., the assumption of the knowability of things in themselves, at *KrV* A543/B571: "Were we to yield to the illusion of transcendental realism, neither nature nor freedom would remain." H. Allison has developed an account of the critique of theoretical reason in which the avoidance of the error of transcendental realism is the primary motive of the critical elaboration of the "epistemic conditions" that cannot be abrogated by a finite or "discursive" mind. See H. Allison, *Kant's Transcendental Idealism: An Interpretation and Defense* (New Haven: Yale University Press, 1984). D. Henrich has pointed more directly to the fundamental practical significance of the critical enterprise. The primary function of transcendental argument is not to show how knowledge is possible. "Although it however actually has this function, nevertheless its genuine function is the disclosure of a world in which self-conscious life is possible" (*SV,* 186).

17. Modern analysis and synthesis are inseparable from the "way of ideas" or, as it was called by Reid, the "ideal theory" of knowledge, common to "empiricists" and "rationalists" of the modern period. Experience is reduced to, and grounded in, intuitable certainties ("ideas") that may or may not be receivable through the senses. But in either case it is their immediate certainty to consciousness that guarantees their veracity. Yet they occupy an intermediate position between the knower and the object that raises questions about how well or how much they can determine the nature of independent objects, or substances, in the world. Already in the early 1760s Kant maintains a critical distance from some aspects of this modern approach, as we shall see below (chap. 4, sec. 5). While he does not abandon what is often called the "representational" approach to knowledge, he notes that in addition to immediate certainties (ideas or representations), knowledge has as "judging" a logical or discursive element, or, one could say, a certain "intentionality" for an object beyond the immediately given. Leibniz and Wolff had required a place for such intentionality in knowledge, at least insofar as the analysis of the attributes of a substance must take one beyond immediately clear and distinct attributes, toward an "adequate" cognition of the totality of "grounds." Kant agrees with them that metaphysics cannot dispense with a "discursive" element in its quest for understanding the grounds of the possibility of things. But in opposition to German rationalism, Kant will argue that the intuitive and discursive elements are wholly different in kind from each other. That points to Kant's making a decisive break with the whole of modern "analysis."

In the view of H.-J. Engfer, the continuity of the German Enlightenment before Kant, with the earlier modern philosophers, is located precisely in the adherence to an understanding of the principal method of philosophy as "analysis." See *PA*, esp. 29. Engfer is much interested in Kant's critique of any philosophical method that would employ mathematical analysis and synthesis as model, and he notes that philosophical discussion of the analytic method generally disappears in Germany after Kant. N. Hinske also notes Kant's rejection of the "analysis of the Enlightenment," in *Kant als Herausforderung an die Gegenwart* (Munich: Karl Alber, 1980), 34. See also G. Tonelli, "Analysis and Synthesis in XVIIIth Century Philosophy prior to Kant," *Archiv für Begriffsgeschichte* 20 (1976): 178–213.

The confidence of the nineteenth century that it had superseded Enlightenment went together with a rejection of "the method of analysis" in all the sciences. See H. Taine, *The Ancient Regime*, trans. J. Durand (New York: Henry Holt, 1876), 181–83. As Taine states, both religious revival and German metaphysics were factors in this change. Kant's criticism of analytic-synthetic procedures is discussed below, chap. 4, sec. 5.

18. *KrV* A61/B86: "General logic, when thus treated as an organon, is called *dialectic*" (Kant's emphasis). For Kant's descriptions of the various kinds (general and transcendental) and functions (canonical in the correct uses, dialectical in the erroneous uses) of logic, see *KrV* A53/B77, A60–61/B84–86, and *L*, in *Ak* IX, 13–14 and 20. The *Critique* argues that metaphysics is not a science of discovery and cannot avail itself of either logic or mathematics as an organon for the extension of knowledge into the supersensible objects of metaphysics. Thus it cannot employ intuitive constructions, as does mathematics, to enlarge our knowledge. The fundamental metaphysical concepts (substance, object, thing, cause, etc.) are not constructible or intuitable; see *KrV* A844/B872, A847/B875 n., and A713–38/B741–66. This restriction on method applies as much to the transcendental inquiry into the conditions of inquiry as it does to "transcendent" and uncritical inquiry. Logic also cannot be used by metaphysics for purposes of discovery; it can offer only a formal extension of knowledge. Yet it is more akin than mathematics to metaphysics in its "discursive" procedure. General or formal logic in fact provides the basis for articulating the categories, or the pure concepts, of metaphysics. This close relation to metaphysics, however, is what can lead the latter astray, since it is tempting to think that logic by itself may be able to determine the "totalities" of interest to metaphysics. Mathematics also charms the metaphysician as a possible source of metaphysical knowledge, for within its own realm (intuitive and phenomenal knowledge) mathematics is "master of nature" (A725/B753). To sum up these points: logic and mathematics attract the metaphysician with their apparent promise of offering self-evident *archai* to first philosophy. But unfortunately metaphysics cannot have such *archai* (axioms, definitions, postulates as first premises), and thus this allure is the source of an illusion (A727–38/B755–66). Logic and mathematics provide metaphysics with primary elements of the whole context of possible knowledge, but their own concepts and procedures are unable to disclose that whole context (which is the concern of the critical propaedeutic). See *Ak* XVIII, *R* 4935.

19. *KrV* A409/B463: Reason, as the faculty seeking a determination of the totality of conditions, "makes this demand [for totality] in accordance with the principle that if *the conditioned is given, the entire sum of conditions, and consequently the absolutely unconditioned (through which alone the condition has been possible) is also given*" (Kant's emphasis). Thus the ground of the theoretical conception of an absolutely determined whole (needing no further determination) is a logical feature of our reason whereby reason assumes a completed series of conditions (or higher premises) for a given condition (or consequence). This logical feature cannot account for the urge to totality itself. It only

accounts for the fact that human reason always must attempt, abortively in Kant's view, to determine the ideas of totality by means that are inappropriate to them: the ground and consequence reasoning of a discursive and finite mind. Ideas of totality could be known not merely as formal or regulative schemata, but as intuitively apprehended concrete objects, only by an "archetypal" or transfinite intellect. For only in such a mind would the spontaneity that produces logical form or concepts also thereby produce a totality of intuition or content for its concepts. But a totality of intuitions must necessarily elude minds such as our own.

20. *KrV* A12/B25: "I entitle *transcendental* all knowledge which is occupied not so much with objects as with the mode of our knowledge of objects in so far as this mode of knowledge is to be possible *a priori*." The first concern of the transcendental inquiry is "to investigate the possibility of concepts *a priori*" (A65–66/B90–91), which is to say, to determine the source, and therewith the scope of valid application, of the concepts that have a pure use. These are the metaphysical concepts such as cause, substance, and thing, which, Kant notes, have in modern metaphysics been called the subject of "ontology." This latter science has claimed to supply synthetic a priori knowledge of things in general, but its central concepts serve only to provide the conditions for the use of our understanding in experience. Its proud claims must be abandoned (A247/B303). What is left of ontology is only the transcendental account of the discursive source and application of such concepts: "Ontology is nothing other than a transcendental logic" (*Ak* XVII, *R* 4152). Kant's primary concern with the status of the pure concepts sheds much light on the otherwise perplexing fact that his "transcendental deduction" presupposes the objectivity of experience. For Kant's concern is not to prove the fact of that objectivity, but to employ it as the starting point for demonstrating the function and limits of the pure concepts. On this see KTD. Also for the nature of Kant's regressive argument see DC, and see chap. 4, sec. 5, below.

21. See especially *KrV* B131 and B134n.

22. For this view of the deduction, see the author's "Kant on the Primacy and the Limits of Logic," *Graduate Faculty Philosophy Journal* 11/2 (1986): 147–62. See *KrV* B144–45 and A271/B327.

23. *KrV* B166–68.

24. The primary question of the critique of theoretical cognition is "whether metaphysics as a science is possible," as Kant repeatedly asserts. See *KrV* Bxiv–xv, Bxxii, and B18–24. The other questions of "possibility" (about mathematics and the pure science of nature) are subordinated to this one; the answers to these questions are needed as aspects of an inquiry into the primary question. Heidegger speaks of "the misguided search for an epistemology in Kant" among Neo-Kantians and notes that the real problem of the "objective reality of the categories" is to "understand the essence of the categories" as "real determinations of objects (as appearances) without having to be empirical properties (of appearances)" (*MFL*, 65). See n.112 to chap. 4, below.

25. Note the criticism of philosophical appeal to human nature implicit at *KrV* A316–17/B373–74. Kant's principle for the definition of the end of reason, a new concept of freedom, is incompatible with the assertion that nature determines a more or less permanent condition for the human species. Kant's critique of the principles of Scottish common sense philosophy is of a piece with the general turn away from human nature as the source of first principles, whether practical or speculative. Common sense or common reason is reliable in its practical form, but in that form it rests on, or is identical with, the pure moral will. The "naturalism" of the theoretical principles of the common sense philosophers is wholly unacceptable to Kant, since the natural tendencies of the mind in speculation, prior to "criticism," are "dialectical." See *SCS*,

167–207. It may come as a shock to many readers of Kant to learn that Rousseau is not principally another "naturalist" for Kant, but rather *the* thinker who most profoundly points to the deficiency of all naturalism.

26. For Kant's account of the moral origin of metaphysics, see *KrV* A852–53/ B880–81: in the "theodicy" problem of rectifying the disproportion between moral worth and happiness in this life, i.e., the problem of the confirmation of a moral cosmos. I show in chapter 4 how this is central to the new moral idealism created by Kant. Also, I show how the primacy of this issue in metaphysics is connected with the post-Rousseauian criticism in Kant of pursuit of theoretical knowledge for its own sake, decried by Kant as "philodoxy"; see, for example, *L*, in *Ak* IX, 24. The origination of the metaphysical urge for totality in moral necessities accounts for the otherwise strange-sounding language in Kant, about the ineluctability of metaphysical thought for every human reasoner.

27. *KrV* B23. This view of the basic perplexities should be contrasted with Aristotle's in *Metaphysics* 995a24– b4 and 993a30–b12.

28. The critique of the natural tendencies of the mind, so basic to modern philosophy, is explicitly compared to Hobbes's account of the legal order as the remedy to the injustice and violence of the state of nature, at *KrV* A751–2/B779–80: "In the absence of this critique, reason is, as it were, in the state of nature." See *Ak* XVIII, R 5112: "Metaphysics is like the police of our reason with respect to the public security of morals and religion." The earlier modern philosophers thought that natural passion or sentiment could guide "method" to bring about correction of the worst ills of the natural mind. As we shall see, Kant turns instead to autonomous moral reason, implicit in every reasoner, as the agent for such guidance.

29. Kant's view of himself as Socratic is discussed in detail in chap. 4, sec. 4. My intent here is not to characterize ancient Socratic dialectic as "contemplative," but to point to the fact that its practical endeavors are not subordinated to, or governed by, an assumed telos found in the opinions of common reason (as in Kant's conception of philosophy). Those opinions form the necessary starting point of philosophy, offering it dialectical "hypotheses" from which to ascend to the highest principles; they cannot in any way define the goal or end point.

30. This should explain why the tempting analogy between Socrates's arguments against sophistry and Kant's arguments against the instrumental Enlightenment is misconceived. Indeed Socrates sees that there is a profound kinship between sophistry and common "opinion" in the city; in the end, these two will always be allies against the true philosopher. Socrates has no hopes of enlightening the mass of men and of converting them into defenders of philosophy. It is a drastic simplification of the human problem, from Socrates' point of view, to regard sophistic intellectuals as the primary source of the evils afflicting us; they are a symptom rather than the cause. Kant is closer to committing this error of simplification with his trust in the soundness of common reason and his effort to locate in it the reliable corrective to false philosophy, and even the telos of true philosophy.

31. *KrV* Bxxxiv.

32. *KrV* Ax.

33. For the vicious progress of (1) speculations about the whole within the Schools, (2) academic skepticism about reason's theoretical competence in metaphysics, eventually passing beyond the Schools and into the public, and (3) popular outbreaks of fanaticism and other extreme dogmatisms, all hostile to the free and self-critical use of reason, see *W*, in *Ak* VIII, 138n. and 143.

34. See the remarkable passage at *Ak* XVIII, R 6215, pp. 504–5, for the threat posed to the legal order by the current situation in philosophy. Speculative or religious doc-

trines that overthrow the rule of reason also destroy the rule of law, which rests on the moral form of free rationality: it is only as a rational being that man is aware of the moral duty to leave the natural state of lawlessness and to submit to the constraints of civil life. There is a very intimate connection between Kant's doctrine of legality as the sole basis for justice in civil life and the importance of the dissemination of "critical" philosophical thought for a healthy civic order. See A. Altmann, "Prinzipien politischer Theorie bei Mendelssohn und Kant," in *Die Trostvolle Aufklärung: Studien zur Metaphysik und politischen Theorie Moses Mendelssohn* (Stuttgart-Bad Canstatt: Frommann-Holzboog, 1982), 192–216.

35. *KrV* Bxxxiv: "it is therefore the *duty* of the Schools, by means of a thorough investigation of the rights of speculative reason, once and for all to prevent the scandal which, sooner or later, is sure to break out among the masses" (my emphasis); and *KrV*, B xxxi.

36. *Ak* XVIII, *R* 4936.

37. *KrV* Aix–xii and Kant's letter to J. H. Lambert of December 31, 1765, in *KPC*, 49. See *SCS*, 38–40, where Kuehn discusses Kant's reference to "the current crisis of learning" in this letter.

38. *KpV*, in *Ak* V, 107.

39. *Bem*, in *Ak* XX, 48.1–7.

40. See Kant's letter to Mendelssohn of April 8, 1766, in *KPC*, 55.

41. This is a central theme of the discussion in chapter 3 of the reflections of 1764–65.

42. See *G*, in *Ak* IV, 387–92 and 403–5. See *SCS*, 191: "Kant, like all enlightenment philosophers, consciously attempted to defend and justify common sense. His critical philosophy was not meant to supersede common sense, but to strengthen it." Also see Kuehn's remarks that critical investigation of common sense and of reason is necessary because they contradict each other (p. 203), and that "in Kant's critical philosophy the struggle (dialectic) between common reason and philosophy emerged as an important formative influence. And Kant's thought, like that of most of his contemporaries, may be considered a sustained attempt to balance the aspirations of common sense and critical reason" (p. 246). One might also say that Kant's view of the relation of his criticism of metaphysics to common reason implies that as philosopher he lives at an extraordinarily propitious or "absolute" moment. The Kantian critique comes neither too soon (for the dialectic has been fully exposed to the thinking public) nor too late (for the dialectic has not yet undermined all confidence in reason). I owe this last observation to Nathan Tarcov.

43. Thus Lord Shaftesbury, Berkeley, Buffier, Hume, Reid, and the Scottish common sense school, and in Germany Thomasius, Crusius, and many later figures. An excellent discussion of the importance of the Scottish common sense philosophers for Germany is *SCS, passim*. Writing of the period of 1755–80 in Germany, Kuehn asserts (p. 44) that "to establish the principles of common sense and morality more clearly and to defend them against exaggerated speculations of certain philosophers . . . may be said to have been *the* task of all the philosophers of the period." The various attempts to secure common sense typically had the form of a "rational empiricism" that took elements from British empiricism and German rationalism.

Berkeley may seem an unlikely figure to characterize as defender of common sense, but his attack on materialism is meant to be a defense of the commonsense view that the ordinary perceptual experience of things—and not the abstract concepts of the "modern way of explaining things"—discloses the reality of the sensible world. His idealism is meant to be the remedy to skepticism generated by Cartesian-Newtonian principles. The alliance he tries to forge between a startling new idealism and common sense shares many features with the efforts of Hume and Kant. Much of what we call "epistemology" was originally designed as such a defense of the human experience of human affairs against the encroachments of metaphysics; it therefore belongs to a conception of human reason according to which "the end of speculation be practice." See Berkeley, "Preface" to *Three Dialogues between Hylas and Philonous*.

44. See *SCS*, 195–207, for a discussion of the the the difference between practical and theoretical common sense, with respect to reliability. Practical (moral) common sense is basically only in need of philosophical clarification; theoretical common sense is far more dialectical. Yet "criticism" in both cases is a necessity in order to "justify" the sounder tendencies in each kind of common sense.

45. The fragments bearing the title "Über Optimismus" (ca. 1754) are in *Ak* XVII, R 3703–7, pp. 229–39. A discussion of these is found in UKfE. Some interesting literature was produced by other leading thinkers, notably by Lessing and Mendelssohn, for the same prize question. See *EGP*, 314–19; A. Harnack, *Geschichte der Königlich Preussischen Akademie der Wissenschaften zu Berlin* (Berlin: Reichsdruckerei, 1900), I, 403–9; A. Altmann, *Moses Mendelssohns Frühschriften zur Metaphysik* (Tübingen: J. C. B. Mohr, 1969), 184–208; and an introductory essay by L. Strauss, *Moses Mendelssohn: Gesammelte Schriften*, ed. F. Bamberger and L. Strauss (Berlin: Akademie Verlag, 1929; reprinted 1972), II, xv–xx.

46. See *Allgemeine Geschichte und Theorie des Himmels*, in *Ak* I, 215–68, esp. 306–23 and 349–68. Also see the concluding section of the essay on the Great Lisbon Earthquake of 1755, in *Ak* I, 455–61.

47. Kant discerns that attacks on reason are increasingly a feature of modern culture. See *KrV* A669/B697: "The mob of sophists, however, raises against reason the usual cry of absurdities and contradictions, and though unable to penetrate to its innermost designs, they nonetheless inveigh against its prescriptions." The failure of theoretical reason to justify the moral order may give rise to a "wish to dispense with reason altogether, and to submit ourselves to the mechanism" (*MS*, in *Ak* VI, 355).

48. The project of this delimitation is central already to writings of the 1760s, after the *Remarks*. The first form of this program is discussed in chap. 4, sec. 4.

49. See *CPrR*, 118, and *KpV*, in *Ak* V, 3, for the concept of freedom as "the keystone of the whole architecture of the system of reason and even of theoretical reason," so that a demonstration of the impossibility of freedom "would endanger reason's essence and plunge it into an abyss of skepticism." Because Rousseau for Kant is the chief thinker establishing the nature and importance of freedom, Kant places him in an altogether different class from other critics of the Enlightenment. Thus compare his statements on Rousseau at *MA*, in *Ak* VIII, 116–118, with those on F. H. Jacobi at *W*, in *Ak* VIII, 133–34.

50. The noble and the sacred can be understood in remarkably different ways, as befits a category that does not at all obviously belong to the rational and the universal. But unlike those who turn to the ancient city, or medieval Christianity, or the plurality of modern national traditions for their account of the noble or sacred, Kant attempts to ground it on universal reason. For some of the principal themes of Romantic-Idealist thought, and their relation to Kant, a valuable discussion is A. O. Lovejoy, "The Meaning of Romanticism for the Historian of Ideas," *JHI*, 2/3 (1941): 257–78. See also the essays of Isaiah Berlin in *Against the Current: Essays in the History of Ideas* (New York: Viking, 1980), esp. "The Counter-Enlightenment," 1–24, and "Hume and the Sources of German Anti-Rationalism," 162–87. The various protests against modern thought and life were all supported by the reading of Rousseau and were, in many cases, directed against the denial of freedom in the soul-destroying "mechanism" of such doctrines as d'Holbach's. Thus see Goethe's account of his youthful dissatisfaction with such doctrines in the 1770s, in *Dichtung und Wahrheit*, bk. 11.

51. For an account of the early modern rapprochement or "contract" between philosophy and society, which is the essence of modern Enlightenment, see R. Kennington, "René Descartes," in J. Cropsey and L. Strauss, eds., *History of Political Philosophy*, 3d ed. (Chicago: University of Chicago Press, 1987), pp. 421–39.

52. *Discours sur les sciences et les arts*, 1750, written in response to a question proposed by the Academy of Dijon, "whether the restoration of the Sciences and Arts has contributed to the purification of morals" (*OC*, III, 1–30). For a discussion of this *First Discourse*, see V. Gourevitch, "Rousseau on the Arts and Sciences," *Journal of Philosophy* 69 (1972): 737–54. See also L. Strauss, "On the Intention of Rousseau," in M. Cranston and R. S. Peters, eds., *Hobbes and Rousseau: A Collection of Essays* (Garden City, N.Y.: Doubleday, 1972), 254–90, and A. Bloom, *Politics and the Arts* (Ithaca: Cornell University Press, 1968), xi–xxxiv. Kant refers directly to the *Discourse* in his later writings (*MA*, in *Ak* VIII, 116); it was a work well known in Germany and discussed by leading thinkers such as Lessing and Mendelssohn. Rousseau's position was not wholly unacceptable to the thought and experience of the best minds of the age. Mendelssohn, while ultimately parting company with Rousseau, was open to the view that "certain truths which are useful to man as an individual can sometimes be harmful to him as a citizen." See *JGP*, 43.

Rousseau's impact on Germany was enormous, although it has not been adequately assessed. See L. Levy-Bruhl, "L'influence de Jean-Jacques Rousseau en Allemagne," in *Annales de l'école libre des sciences politiques*, (Paris, 1887), II, 325–58: "Through Jacobi, Kant, and Fichte, the thought of Rousseau entered, so to speak, into the very soul of Germany" (p. 356). Dilthey, when speaking of the remarkable "transformation of the sense of life" occurring in Germany in the period 1760–80, ascribes central importance to "Rousseau's new ideal of life" (*DGS*, XIII.1, 190).

53. See the argument of *Discours sur l'origine et les fondements de l'inégalité parmi les hommes* (the *Second Discourse*), in *OC*, III, 109–23, and further discussion below, chap. 2, secs. 2 and 3.

54. Thus in Rousseau's argument, the true corrective of Enlightenment will still be a form of enlightenment; the corrected Enlightenment will apply the modern principles of nature and human nature, but in a more radical way, to achieve new accounts of virtue and political order. Note Rousseau's high praise of Bacon, Descartes, and Newton —"these Preceptors of Mankind"—and his endorsement of the coincidence of political power with the wisdom of such men; *DS*, in *OC*, III, 28–30. Such a coincidence is required to cure the ills of a corrupted society; a society that had not been corrupted by the development of reason would have no need of science and surely would be preferable to the society that needs the rule of philosophers. But that is not our situation. Rousseau's condemnation of the arts and sciences is subtly qualified, and it is consistent with his own literary activity; see his *Preface de Narcisse*, in *OC*, II, 959–74.

55. See chap. 2, sec. 2, and chap. 3 as a whole for the support of this assertion.

56. But see the discussion that follows, and also chap. 3, sec. 2 below, for the large differences that separate Rousseau and Kant on the subjects of the will, freedom, and autonomy.

57. *Em*, 278–79, 303–4.

58. Such "trust" is always a somewhat precarious and and arbitrary matter in earlier modern thought. Thus love of glory and destructive amour-propre are surely as natural as fear of death or the instinct of self-preservation, yet only the latter are wholly dependable and accorded the status of being truly "rational." There is never mere reliance on given human nature in the early moderns; always present is some effort at instruction, transformation, and the use of the artificial constraints of "method." The highly problematic status of anything proposed as a natural telos in early modernity

leads not surprisingly to the eventual conquest of nature by the ideas of "culture" and "history." Rousseau's thought is the moment of transition: it combines the "weakness of reason" of early modernity with the dissolution of the authority of nature. For an especially vivid account of that weakness, see *RP*, 141– 52 (eighth Promenade).

59. According to Rousseau, man is born free but necessarily loses that freedom as a member of society; the political philosopher's concern with an "ideal" regime is with defining a condition of legitimate servitude. Political life by its nature cannot offer the prospect of total emancipation. See *CS*, in *OC*, III, 347–67. For the near-miraculaous character of the philosopher's attainment of relative peace of mind and autonomy, see *RP*, 35–42 (first Promenade).

60. Kant's rejection of any dissimulative rhetoric that distinguishes between philosophic and nonphilosophic readers is trenchantly announced at *KrV* A749/B777. See *Ak* XVIII, R 4898: the present age is one in which frank objection to theological views will actually further the reconciliation of reason and religion, and "we need no longer dissemble in metaphysics." Yet Kant also says that "while all that one says must be true, this does not mean that it is one's duty to speak out the whole truth in public." See *Ak* XII, 406 and Reiss's discussion, *KPW*, 2. K. Pölitz, the editor of the lectures on philosophical theology, notes in his introduction that Kant's published views on religion were modified to fit the changing policies of the Prussian court and that "those who understand the sage of Königsberg according to the spirit of his system will not be in doubt about which views are more in that spirit." See *Ak* XXVII. 2.2, 1514–16. In general Kant expects philosophy in its critical form to achieve an ultimate identity between the interests of knowledge and the interests of moral life, and prudence on the part of philosophy is a temporary necessity. That Rousseau employs a dissimulative rhetoric reflecting his thoughts on the permanent natural inequality of man and the irremediable foundation of social life in prejudice has been very forcefully argued by H. Meier, in his introduction to a critical edition of the second *Discours*. See *J.-J. Rousseau: Diskurs über die Ungleichheit. Kritische Ausgabe des integralen Textes* (Paderborn: Schöningh, 1984), xxi–lxxvii.

61. Kant asserts this in numerous passages. See *KpV*, in *Ak* V, 114; *I*, in *Ak* VIII, 18–19; *W*, in *Ak* VIII, 139; *ED*, in *Ak* VIII, 337.

62. *G*, in *Ak* IV, 395–96 and 399 (*CPrR*, 60): "men can make no definite and certain concept of the sum of all inclinations, which goes under the name of happiness." Also *KU*, in *Ak* V, 430: happiness is the "mere idea of a condition," which is not abstracted from human instincts, and which man tries to realize under empirical conditions, but to no avail. It is a misbegotten product of the imagination and the understanding, "projected" in diverse and arbitrary ways. No "definite universal and stable law" can arise from the pursuit of the "fluctuating concept" of happiness.

63. *G* ,in *Ak* IV, 393–401.

64. See *L*, in *Ak* IX, 23–26: philosophy is essentially the legislation of a systematic unity among all ends of a rational being, as "wisdom," and such legislation is impossible if reason is not autonomous.

65. *G*, in *Ak* IV, 429.

66. *KU*, in *Ak* V, 429–36, and *ED*, in *Ak* VIII, 330–31.

67. *G*, in *Ak* IV, 390. A remark on the relations between self-legislation, ends, and the moral law is in order here. To escape the dialectical and alienating consequences of natural teleology, human reason must be self-legislating; by itself, however, self-legislation will not secure autonomy. Self-legislation (which always has an "end" in view) must take place under a certain "form" to guarantee its autonomous character; that form is the principle of universalizability, which guarantees that the "end" of the will in a given "maxim" cannot enslave the will to a particular "interest" or inclination. It is clear however that this "form," the supreme moral law, is not itself something

"legislated" by reason. For were it legislated, reason would require a yet higher "form" to secure the nonarbitrariness of this legislation. The moral law is an ultimate "fact of reason." It would seem to be the case, then, that the moral law as the form of the willing of all ends is not itself an end and that all ends are arbitrarily adopted by a legislative will. Yet not all ends are such arbitrary objects of the will's legislation. The human rational capacity to subordinate itself to the "form" of legislation entitles that will itself to *be* an end. Both the supreme moral law and humanity as "end" are, in Kant's view, objectively "given" and not the results of legislation. Promoting the moral and natural perfection of humanity as the supreme end supplies a given objective principle for the architectonic ordering of all other ends; it determines for human rational agents a realm of ends that they "ought to will."

68. See *KrV* A840/B868 ("the idea of the philosopher's legislation"), and *KrV* A831/B859: "in regard to the essential ends of human nature the highest philosophy cannot advance further than is possible under the guidance which nature has bestowed even upon the most ordinary understanding." For the universality of the interest in metaphysics, see B21. For the identity between reason as legislative and reason as system forming, see *L*, in *Ak* IX, 24.

69. Kantian philosophy, as defense of the moral end of reason, is centrally a justification of postulated "ideas" that ground the sacred and noble. These "ideas," as constitutive of the moral end of reason, are not mere addenda to philosophy proper, but the essential supports of the possibility of reason in general. The young speculative idealists who took Kantian moral metaphysics as a starting point for their reflections in the 1790s did so by transforming "rational religion" in Kant, as based on the pure moral law. They sought to make a "new mythology," inspired by classical antiquity (an "aesthetic religion," uniting the realms of reason, poetic imagination, and the moralities of public and private life), into the ultimate telos and transcendental beginning for all philosophy. See the discussion of the so-called "oldest system-program of German idealism," which has been variously ascribed to Hegel, Schelling, and Hölderlin, in O. Pöggeler, *Die Frage nach der Kunst: Von Hegel zu Heidegger* (Munich: Karl Alber Verlag, 1984), 39–111 ("Die Neue Mythologie"). Also D. Henrich, "Historische Voraussetzungen von Hegels System," in *Hegel im Kontext* (Frankfurt a.M.: Suhrkamp, 1971), 41–72, and K. Düsing, "Die Rezeption der kantischen Postulatenlehre in den frühen philosophischen Entwürfen Schellings und Hegels," in R. Bubner, ed., *Hegel-Studien: Beiheft* IX (Bonn, 1973), 53–90. According to Pöggeler, what is new in this "new mythology" is its being created "in the service of ideas," where "idea" means above all "the destruction of dogmatic metaphysics by Kant's 'postulates'" (*Die Frage nach der Kunst*, 57).

70. This Kantian account of evil is discussed in chap. 5, sec. 3. As we shall see, Kant's famous account of "radical evil," which is usually alleged to point to Kant's fundamental break with modern rationalist optimism, attributes evil to the "intelligible deed" of man as rational; the notion of accountability here is altogether different from biblical original sin. Generally, all conceptions of history falling under the sway of German idealist conceptions of man and reason are characterized by this optimism. The core of this optimism is the assumption, or argument, that the moral order can ultimately be identified with actual historical institutions or with the course, or the goal, of history. See *GCH*, 80–81 (with special reference to Ranke).

71. Nietzsche expressly characterizes the philosophies of Hegel and Schopenhauer, as well as his own thought, as theodicy. See *The Will to Power*, trans. W. Kaufmann (New York: Random House, 1967), 223–24. Hegel understands his philosophical effort as essentially in the service of human well-being and intended to overcome the alienation of the human spirit. Thus K. Schmitz on Hegel: "Such is the measure to which philosophy must aspire; for if a philosophy cannot resolve the conflict and opposition

of thought and its other (being) than it cannot hope to resolve the conflicts endemic in
the actual life of society," in "Hegel on Kant," in *PIK*, 240. Consider also the statement
of Habermas: "What is perhaps specifically German is the philosophical concept of
alienation, both in the Hegelian-Marxist version and the early Romantic version taken
up by Nietzsche," in *Habermas and Modernity*, ed. R. Bernstein (Cambridge: MIT Press,
1985), 197. But seldom is this cluster of concerns in German philosophy taken back to
its primary source—Rousseau. An exception is the biographical study of Kant by the
Russian scholar A. Gulyga, *Immanuel Kant*, trans. into German by S. Bielfeldt (Frankfurt a. M.: Insel, 1981), 58–62: Rousseau moved Kant toward a general "critique of
modern civilization" through exposing "the contradictions of progress," thus initiating
"a revolution in all the ends of life" for Kant and his contemporaries. N. Rotenstreich
notes the similarity between Kant's notion of the self-inflicted tutelage of reason and
notions of the self-alienation of man in later thinkers (*JGP*, 45–46). S. M. Shell has
stressed the presence of themes of alienation (in connection with rights, selfhood, and
ownership) in her study of Kant's political philosophy, *The Rights of Reason* (see n. 6 to
the introduction, above). Relevant also is the claim of F. C. Beiser that Kant thought he
had "rescued reason from imminent self-destruction," but failed to do so to the satisfaction of the first generation of his readers, who then embarked on new speculative
defenses of reason that struck Kant as renewed "dogmatism"; *The Fate of Reason: German Philosophy from Kant to Fichte* (Cambridge: Harvard University Press, 1987), 6 and
passim.

   Whereas Kant, under Rousseau's tutelage, furthers the discussion of "culture" as a
central problem for modern moral-political life, he does so with the intent of preserving
the autonc · v u᷉ individuals from subservience to either the state or the "moral life" of
society. In c.᷉ .vords, Kant still seeks a "liberal" solution to the problems of liberalism: modern individualism's tendency to undermine itself through its own "culture"
of freedom must be rectified through historical processes that do not permit state or
society to impinge directly on the moral sphere or to determine a content for the idea
of happiness. But as we shall see below (chap. 5), the way in which happiness for Kant
is a problem that must be addressed by future reform of culture provides an opening
for later thinkers to discuss the role of politics and culture in less "liberal" terms. Kant's
manifold suggestions of "indirect" ways in which humanity's final end of perfected
autonomy with a proportionate happiness might be promoted within history clearly
failed to impress later philosophers of history as either coherent (given, among other
difficulties, Kant's gulf between legality and morality) or effective.

   72. For the beginnings and meaning of German *Bildung*, see Dilthey, "Die dichter-
ische und philosophische Bewegung in Deutschland, 1770–1800," in *DGS* V, 12–27.
Although much German philosophy is, as very often said, a "reaction" against "ratio-
nalistic" tendencies in earlier modern thought, its efforts to recover aspects of premodern or prephilosophic life always involve the "mediation" or reconstruction of such
aspects by philosophy. This is evident in the prominence of such categories as "individuality" and "creativity," not to mention the various forms of "irrationality" in German thought. The polemical arguments against "rationalism" reveal an intent that is
alien to the genuine problems of prephilosophic life. Such reconstructions, in other
words, are unduly impressed by the historicist assumption that ordinary life has no
enduring and natural features and that philosophy, having the power to overthrow the
bases of ordinary life, also has the power to "re-create" them.

   73. *KrV* A319/B376.

   74. See *KrV* Bxxxi. Kant's Socrates as critic of the sophists is also critic of speculation; he is a theoretical skeptic upholding the rights of moral reason. See *Ak* XXIV, 212,
par. 178, and G. Tonelli, "Kant und die antiken Skeptiker," in *SKpE*, 118, nn. 32 and

37. Kant's Socrates should also be compared, as an egalitarian, with Rousseau's Socrates; *DS*, in *OC*, III, 13–14.

75. An unambiguous statement of the practical reinterpretation of the metaphysical ideas is found in *ED*, in *Ak* VIII, 332–33n. The three *Critiques* argue for a restitution of the discredited speculative totalities in the form of practical postulates; that which is "transcendent" for speculative cognition becomes "immanent" for practical reason.

Chapter Two

1. Especially significant in this regard is Kant's frequent comparisons of his ideal of the highest good and ancient ideals thereof, chiefly the Epicurean and Stoic. Kant departs from his ancient predecessors by proposing an absolutely universal and egalitarian version of the ideal. See below, chap. 4, secs. 2 and 3.

2. Aristotle, *Nicomachean Ethics*, 1103a14–b26 (bk. 2, chap. 1). Among the major moderns there is a very remarkable effort by Locke to show how virtues appropriate to a modern liberal regime (moderation, industry, respect for the rights of others to the pursuit of happiness) can be formed by a kind of habituation, one that does not assume an autonomous rational power. The principle of moral education is an appeal to the passion of esteem or pride, as the desire to be *regarded* as rational, i.e., as free or able to rule oneself, and thus as able to master one's passions. The mastery of passion is thus effected by a ruling passion, not by autonomous reason. "Rationality" is perhaps nothing more, essentially, than this ruling passion. This moral education is clearly similar to that of *Emile*, with the important difference that Locke regards human sociality as both natural and desirable, since pride as the master passion is educable only through praise and blame. But the nonteleological moral psychologies of Locke and Rousseau, with their absence of any natural hierarchy in the structure of the human soul, are thoroughly modern. See the commentary and analysis of Locke's *Thoughts on Education* by N. Tarcov, *Locke's Education for Liberty* (Chicago, University of Chicago Press, 1984).

3. Surely Kant's emphasis on reason's teleological structure owes much to the diverse synthetic efforts of Leibniz and Wolff, to reconcile modern Cartesian and mechanistic accounts of nature with elements of Aristotelian and scholastic metaphysics. See C. A. Corr, "Christian Wolff and Leibniz, *JHI* 36/2 (1975): 241–62, for the divergent accounts of teleology in those two thinkers, and see *SPIK*, 1–92, for the relation of Kant to Wolff. See also C. Sherover, "Kant's Evaluation of His Relationship to Leibniz," in *PIK*, 201–28. From Kant's point of view, neither the Leibnizian renewal of Aristotle's *entelechies* in a new doctrine of substance nor Wolff's more strictly anthropocentric teleology offers a genuine reflection on the highest good as moral ideal. In Kant's estimation no previous metaphysics has provided an unambiguous foundation for human freedom. But a genuine doctrine of the highest good must be grounded in a clear assertion of human freedom. For Kant's critique of the highest good in Leibniz and Wolff, see UKfE, and for Kant's complaint that the highest good has been neglected by modern philosophy, see below, chap. 4, sec. 2, and n.18 in particular. Also *CPrR*, 173 and *KpV*, in *Ak* V, 64: "The moderns, among whom the concept of the highest good has fallen into disuse or at least seems to have become something secondary."

4. *KU*, in *Ak* V, 171–98 (Einleitung).

5. *Bem*, in *Ak* XX, 91–94 ("Von der Freiheit"). See the discussion below in chap. 3, sec. 2.

6. *UD*, in *Ak* II, 273–302, translated as *Enquiry concerning the Clarity of the Principles of Natural Theology and Ethics* in *SPW*, 3–35; published in 1764. The question of the Academy was, "Whether metaphysical truths generally, and in particular the funda-

mental principles of natural theology and morals, are not capable of proofs as distinct as those of geometry; and if they are not, what is the true nature of their certainty, to what degree can the certainty be developed, and is this degree sufficient for conviction [of their truth]?" See *EGP*, 441–43. A discussion of the importance of this work for the mature metaphysics of Kant is given below, chap. 4, sec. 5.

7. *SPW*, 34, and *UD*, in *Ak* II, 300. See *N*, in *Ak* II, 311, for a favorable reference to the efforts of Shaftesbury, Hutcheson, and Hume in the investigation of the first grounds of morality. See HK for an analysis of Kant's relation to Hutcheson, particularly as revealed in the *Prize-Essay*.

8. *UD*, in *Ak* II, 298–301. Moral sense in Hutcheson is indeed the source of a pleasure, but it is one that is specific to moral experience; there is no reduction of that experience to pleasures unqualifiedly selfish. The sense of the public good (*sensus communis*), closely allied to the moral sense, is "a determination to be pleased with the happiness of others and to be uneasy at their misery" (*SPW*, 155). Kant's *Beobachtung über das Gefühl des Schönen und Erhabenen*, in *Ak* II, 205–56, written about the time of the *Prize-Essay*, presents within the context of aesthetics an ethics whose principle is a disinterested love of the beautiful (qua "humanity") in human character. Kant's persistent concern with uncovering a link between moral nobility and the beautiful or sublime is of course related to the question he raised in his earliest philosophizing about the cosmic justification of moral life. Through Rousseau it becomes clear to Kant that such justification cannot be on the plane of disinterested aesthetic feeling, although the relation of such feeling to "freedom," the true ground of justification, remains of first interest to Kant.

9. J. Schmucker, in *UEK*, 252–56, has noted, in the *Essay*'s stress on disinterested and unconditioned (unanalyzable) moral feelings, an anticipation of the categorical imperative. Henrich's arguments in HK are along similar lines.

10. In Aristotelian accounts of the soul, the habituation of the appetitive or affective parts of the soul rests on such parts having a capacity to "listen" to reason, or, in other words, on such parts having a potency that is fulfilled in rational activity. By contrast modern views of the instrumentality of reason tend to divorce passion, or appetite, from reason; the affective part of the soul has no completion or fulfillment in the rational part. To deny the teleological structure of the soul (and thus to eliminate "soul" as the unity of the rational and affective) is basic to the modern effort of criticizing "dogmatism" or the philosophical supports of "fanaticism." For the human passions must not be subjected to any idea of a determinate completion or "highest good." Rousseau and Kant in a fashion restore the idea of the coeval nature of passion and reason; passion, being always formed by imagination and "ideas," cannot be anterior to reason. Yet they accomplish this restoration on the basis of a nonteleological psychology: the affective part of the soul has no completion in the rational; passion is acquired and malleable, and its "history" is indeterminate. In Kant's case, reason rules over passion without in any sense fulfilling ends to which the passions point; hence there are in his doctrine no "rational inclinations" of the Aristotelian sort. Although the refinement and civilizing of the appetites is an important part of Kant's account of how happiness can "appropriately" combine with virtue in the highest good, as the final end of culture, such civilizing is a matter of "disciplining" mere nature instead of completing a natural potential. The restoration of a decisive kinship between reason and passion, in the form of the intrinsic transformability of passion by reason without a telos that fulfills a natural potential, is basic to the new "historical" account of man. It is a primary source of all later views that the specific humanity of man should be understood as "culture." This is discussed in chap. 5, sec. 3, below.

11. Hume, who is a sort of moral sense theorist, frankly accords to reason only a

role instrumental to the passions, although the passions include benevolent feelings, or sympathy. Also in Hume's doctrine, virtue is wholly social, and its worth is measured in terms of its utility for the general welfare. Therefore the question does not arise for Hume whether social or moral virtue may need a justification that social life itself cannot provide. The resurgence of concern with the beautiful and the sacred as sources of such justification in other eighteenth-century authors indicates that Hume did not see a problem that others saw. Although one might call this awareness "ancient," it remains the case that the modern efforts to justify the moral life depart from ancient discussions, insofar as the modern thinkers suppose that the dimension of the sacred and the beautiful can be uncovered, or created, by strictly philosophical (as contrasted with poetic, mythical, and "exoteric") discourses.

12. *SPW*, 34, and *UD*, in *Ak* II, 300. For discussions of this passage, see *UEK*, 143, and HK throughout. See also BsE, 97, and *DKV*, 30–31. Schmucker and Ward both oppose the view of P. A. Schilpp that Kant was always a rationalist in ethics and never actually held a moral feeling doctrine.

13. This reconstruction is found in *UEK* (see especially pp. 252–55) and in Henrich, especially in HK.

14. For the full title and source, see n. 4 in the introduction, above.

15. *UEK*, 176–79. For the dating, history, and previous editions of the manuscripts, see G. Lehmann's introduction to the *Remarks*, in *Ak* XX, 471–75.

16. See the claim of Borowski, a student and early biographer of Kant, that Kant read all of Rousseau's published writings. F. Gross, ed., *Immanuel Kant: Sein Leben in Darstellungen von Zeitgenossen. Die Biographien von L. E. Borowski, R. B. Jachmann, und A. Ch. Wasianski* (Berlin: Deutsches Bibliothek, 1912), 79.

17. The direct references to *Emile* are at *Ak* XX, 9.14, 17.27–30, 29.4–16, 167.3–4, and 175.5–12. See *UEK*, 173: "Obviously we stand here before the most immediate and primordial engagement of Kant with the principal works of Rousseau, above all *Emile*." Schmucker's views are based on very detailed study of Lehmann's complete text and clearly should be preferred to P. A. Schilpp's underestimation of the importance of Rousseau and of these reflections for the origins of Kant's critical philosophy. Schilpp's judgments are based on an acquaintance with only the thirty pages of the *Remarks* printed in the Hartenstein edition of Kant. See *KPE*, 63–74.

18. *UEK*, 143.

19. Ibid.

20. Ibid., 174.

21. For the view that the main ideas of Kant's ethics are formulated by the middle 1760s, at least in embryo, see *UEK*, 256 and 261; HK, 66; UKfE, 404–8; and UKE, 252–63. Thus Henrich (UKE, 260): "Whoever has acquired knowledge of the marginalia of the *Observations* will not remain long in doubt as to whether the content of the first two sections of the *Foundations of the Metaphysics of Morals* could have been written already in the year 1765." Apart from the evidence supplied for this thesis by the *Remarks* itself, there is the significant announcement in Kant's correspondence in 1765 of the plan to write a "metaphysical foundation of practical philosophy"; *KPC*, 47–49, letter to Lambert of December 31, 1765. See *KPC*, 58–60, for "metaphysics of morals." The notion of a metaphysical morality or moral metaphysics is a novelty not found in any major philosopher before Kant, and it is directly related to Kant's discovery in 1764–65 of freedom as a metaphysical principle. There are already suggestions in the *Remarks* that freedom not only grounds morality but also accounts for the possibility of speculative reason, so that morality is the true foundation of metaphysics.

Scholars have shown, all the same, that Kant made important improvements in his moral philosophy between 1765 and 1784. Thus Düsing, in PHG, Gueroult, in VkrV, and Henrich, in BsE, argue convincingly that the fully elaborated doctrine of "respect for the moral law" as the sole moral motive is not yet presented in the 1781 edition of the first *Critique*. Düsing and Gueroult go too far, however, in concluding from this that Kantian moral principles are "heteronomous" until after 1781. See *Bem*, in *Ak* XX, 65.21–25 for the rejection of a theologically grounded morality, and *UEK*, 259–60, as well as below, chap. 4, sec. 3. See also n. 14 in the introduction, above.

22. The Herder notes (*Praktische Philosophie Herder*) are in *Ak* XXVII.1, 1–89, ed. G. Lehmann (1974). On the Herder notes, see UKE, 262 and *UEK*, 257–59. For the announcement of a new concept of freedom see above all *Bem*, in *Ak* XX, 145, 156 (Latin), 161.11 (Latin), 165.20, 31.10. Freedom is now the principle of both virtue and happiness. When Kant uses now the language of moral feeling, as in *Bem*, in *Ak* XX, 155, it is to express the notion of moral feeling as derived from the self-determining will.

23. HK, 56–57: "rational self-activity" and "self-relation" of the will are terms Henrich applies to *Bem*, in *Ak* XX, 144; HK, 65–66: "moral consciousness as grounded upon the self-agreement of the will," he applies to *Bem*, in *Ak* XX, 145. See also UKE, 257, and *UEK*, 257–59.

24. UKE, 257, for "immediate end," and HK, 56–57, commenting on *Bem*, in *Ak*, 144 and noting the shift from approval of goodness in others to approval of free powers in oneself.

25. UKE, 257: "It is under Rousseau's overwhelming influence that the formula of the categorical imperative emerges." K. Ward, while not grasping the full import of the *Remarks*, does note that it demonstrates "that Kant did often evince skepticism about moral feeling"; he asserts that "Kant is keenly aware of the inadequacy of the actual feelings of men to be the basis of a sound morality" (*DKV*, 32–33). Ward misses, or perhaps dismisses, Kant's claim in the *Remarks* that he finds in "freedom" a "fixed point" for morality beyond the phenomena of feeling.

26. Thus Henrich in BsE, 90, 111–13, has observed that one outcome of the Rousseauian revolution of 1765 is Kant's notion that moral philosophy is of higher dignity and systematically prior to theoretical philosophy. Kant comes to the view that the aim of philosophy above all other aims is to show the possibility of morality. Accordingly theoretical philosophy is negative and propaedeutical, preventing speculative errors that undermine morality. From the new standpoint Kant maintains that "the Socratic question of the *ti bioteon* can neither expect nor wish for a theoretical answer." The only form of "ontological hypothesis" that critical philosophy can tolerate is one that furthers moral insight. The demotion of the material world to a mere phenomenon is a necessary consequence of the primacy of justifying the reality of freedom, since that justification presupposes the limiting of deterministic-mechanistic causality to mere appearances. Henrich thus also writes, in *IO*, 13, that "after his Rousseauian turn Kant himself ascribed to transcendental philosophy only an instrumental role. Such philosophy is necessary in order to be able to defend the most essential interests of humanity, which taken together presuppose that the idea of freedom can be justified." Elsewhere Henrich notes that the theoretical and moral philosophies originate in similar problems (UKE, 260, commenting on *Ak* XXIII, 60), and he suggests some ways of thinking about all of critical philosophy as a transcendental justification of the worldview required by autonomy (*SV*, 183–88). Other scholars have mentioned that the critical defense of morality includes the reinterpretation of the basic themes of metaphysics (God, soul, and world) as ideas governing the practical projects of reason; thus PhG, 21, n. 76; KPH, ix (see n. 13 in the introduction above); H. de Vleeschauwer, "Wie ich jetzt die *Kritik der reinen Vernunft* entwicklungsgeschichtlich lese," *KS* 54 (1963): 351–68. The third of these stands out for the importance it gives Rousseau for the whole conception

of the "transcendental dialectic" of speculation and its resolution by a practical meta-physics. Schmucker, who has written the only detailed account of the *Remarks* and underlines the presence of Rousseau in Kant's moral philosophy, is not evidently inter-ested in the significance of Rousseau for the theoretical critique.

27. Note that the natural compassion found in the state of nature, according to the *Second Discourse* (which even in that state is not strong enough to override self-preservation in the case of a conflict between the claims of compassion and self-interest), plays no role in the foundation of civil society, nor in the citizen virtue described in the *Social Contract*.

28. As we shall see, Kant is responsive to this moral and political critique of com-passion in Rousseau, and it plays a role in the rejection of moral sense or philanthropic morality (see chap. 3, sec. 3). Yet Kant's cosmopolitan version of moral virtue is not easily made compatible with citizen virtue in Rousseau's sense. All the same, the sac-rifices required of genuine virtue play a role in Kant's recognition that philanthropic feeling is too fragile a basis for such virtue.

29. *CS* I, 8 (*OC*, III, 364–65) and the discussion in H. Gildin, *Rousseau's Social Con-tract: The Design of the Argument* (Chicago: University of Chicago Press, 1983), 10ff.

30. See *MA*, in *Ak* VIII, 116–18.

31. *DO*, in *OC* III, 142ff.

32. For this indefiniteness, see Machiavelli, *Discourses on Livy*, bk. 1, chap. 37, and bk. 2, Proemium; Bruno, *The Expulsion of the Triumphant Beast*, First Dialogue, pt. 1; and Hobbes, *Leviathan*, chap. 11, beginning.

33. See *DO*, in *OC* III, 143, for the reciprocal determination of human reason and desire. The paragraph beginning "Quoiqu'en disent les Moralistes" is arguably the key to the whole argument of the *Second Discourse*. While reason "perfects itself" only through the stimulation of the passions, the passions are in turn modified, and make "progress," through alterations in knowledge. One of the first and most important acquisitions in knowledge is the idea of death and its terrors; it separates human nature from mere animal nature. (See Kant, *MA*, in *Ak* VIII, 111–14.) The obstacles in the way of detached and comprehensive reflection on this mutual determination, suggested in the *Discourse*, are related to the themes of the "weakness of reason" and the philoso-pher's subjection to chance or "providence" in his efforts to attain clarity; see *RP*, and n. 58 and 59 to chap. 1. Considerations such as these are important to the emergence of "historicism" or to the argument that all understanding is conditioned by history.

34. The account in the *Discourse* of the relations between reason, self, and passion is closely followed by Kant. Thus *An*, in *Ak* VII, 266: "Passion always presupposes that the subject has maxims, according to which the inclinations have prescribed an end for him to follow. Thus passion is always bound up with the reason of the subject, and one can no more ascribe passions to mere animals than to purely rational beings." Also see p. 265: "Passion (*passio animi*) is an inclination that prevents reason from making a choice of inclinations through a comparison with the sum of inclinations." Passion is intrinsically rational in that it makes a claim on "totality" which prevents reason from regarding that totality detachedly. As such it is a self-contradiction within human reason.

35. *DO*, in *OC* III, 144ff.

36. Ibid., 146ff. See *SV*, 60–61. for the importance of Rousseau's analysis to later idealism, of the primordial connection between judgment (or concept) and the "I." Rousseau's uncovering of difficulties in any sensationalist account of the origin of speech and universals is similar to discussions of this problem by Maupertuis and Condillac; indeed Rousseau acknowledges a debt to the latter (*DO*, in *OC* III, 146). Maupertuis and Condillac tend to the opinion that universals, and therewith all sci-

ence, are free creations of the human mind for the ordering of the data of sensation. Condillac thus speaks of the invention of language as opening up a gulf between Art and Nature. Such views, however, did not lead these thinkers to espouse an "idealist" version of the spontaneity of reason, however close they were to it. See L. Gossman, "Berkeley, Hume, and Maupertuis," *French Studies* 14 (1960): 304–24, and H. Aarsleff on Condillac in *From Locke to Saussure: Essays on the Study of Language and Intellectual History* (Minneapolis: University of Minnesota Press, 1982), 146–224.

37. *MA*, in *Ak* VIII, 112.

38. See *An*, in *Ak* VII, 127, for the primordiality of the rational spontaneity of the "I": "That a human being can have the representation of the 'I' elevates it infinitely above every other living being on earth. Through its 'I,' a human is a person, and it is one and the same person by means of the unity of consciousness throughout all modifications it experiences." Spontaneity means fundamentally this capacity to maintain identity (and self-consistency), and it is basic to human dignity. For Kant's rejection of physiological or sensationalist accounts of the genesis of this capacity, see his reviews of Herder's *Ideen zur Philosophie der Geschichte der Menschheit*, in *Ak* VIII, 43–66.

39. See *RP* as a whole and the *Confessions*.

40. See the discussions of this point in Gildin, *Rousseau's Social Contract*.

41. Kant's criticism of theories of moral sense begins from doubts, as we have already noted, that were experienced before the *Remarks*. It appears that these doubts are connected with Kant's questioning of all doctrines that would base theoretical and practical philosophy on immediate and unprovable principles, such as those of Hutcheson and C. A. Crusius. Thus the exposure to Rousseau hastened and deepened a line of thinking that was developing a particular insight—that philosophy cannot argue from axioms or from subjective certainties alone. See UKE, 257–58 and D. Henrich, "Kant's Denken 1762/63: Über den Ursprung der Unterscheidung analytischer und synthetischer Urteile," in *SKpE*, 9–38. The terminus of this line of thinking is "transcendental" philosophy; see *Ak* XVIII, R 5036.

Chapter Three

1. Evidently Kant did not intend the *Remarks* for any eyes but his own, and it is indeed problematic for us to treat it as a "work." He did not expect later students of his thought to be concerned with its "origins," simply because he expected, or hoped, that his published arguments would by themselves be persuasive. The very fact of our investigation thus shows that we are inclined to think that the problems in the status of reason have not been solved by Kant's system, and that far from being satisfied with his solution, we feel a need to recover the original formulations of the problems that lie behind it. These have been to some extent hidden from view by the partial success of Kant's thought.

Concerning Kant's discovery of important aspects of the "dialectic" of reason around 1764–65, see N. Hinske, "Reimarus zwischen Wolff und Kant," in *LZA*, 30, who notes that a change took place in Kant's conception of the source of metaphysical error around then—from disregard of the rules of correct analysis (in the *Essay*) to an unconscious, spontaneous synthesis of reason. I propose that the *Remarks* contains the philosophical motives for that change. See also below, chap. 4, sec. 5.

2. The reference is to the page and line numbers in *Bem*, in *Ak* XX. Due to the quantity of citations from the *Remarks* in this chapter, I use this method of citing page and line in the text.

3. *DO*, in *OC* III, 124–26, 132–33.

4. See *Ak* XVII, R 3980.

5. This point is the same as one Kant makes in the ethics lectures and writings after 1764: the ancient prescriptions of human perfection fail to be universally applicable and effective; see discussion of this below, chap. 4, sec. 2. Kant's "idealism" thus has as one of its ingredients some of the "realism" of Machiavelli, Hobbes, and early modern thought. A distrust of the given nature of man is the background to the construction of the new "ideal," which has doubtful grounding in "nature." Thus Kant writes that the moral philosopher must first have knowledge of men as they *are* before he can assert how they *should be*. See *N*, in *Ak* II, 311: "In the doctrine of virtue I always ponder historically and philosophically what actually *happens*, before I point to that which *should happen*. In this way I would make clear the method one should use in the study of *men*" (Kant's emphases). Here, as in the case of Rousseau, the historical study of mankind is essential for removing the "accidental" from human nature. For in the new modern "realism," human nature is not understood as directed teleologically to certain perfections. The ages of greatest human virtue in the past were such owing to certain historical accidents, not to a human nature that will assert itself and flourish under favorable conditions. Premodern accounts of virtue made the error of identifying such peaks of humanity with human nature. The study of history corrects this error; it is a necessary propaedeutic to uncovering a truly universal human nature and thus to disclosing an ideal of excellence that is in principle approachable everywhere and always. Again it is to be observed that the new approach, which aims at conquering the accidental, owes its insight to historical accidents. The modern age shows us how little we can rely on forces tending to the good in nature and how rationality in man, departing from all natural regularity so manifestly in this age, compels us to turn to the only possible basis for the good—freedom. For a discussion of modern liberal thought as concerned with finding, in new notions of justice and the "self," "Archimedean points" independent of the contingencies of history and the ends and beliefs acquired in history, from which Archimedean points one can define a moral social order, see M. Sandel, *Liberalism and the Limits of Justice* (Cambridge: Cambridge University Press, 1982).

6. But the problem arises here that the idea of the next life is not natural to man (*Bem*, in *Ak* XX, 121.15–22.6) and that, more generally, religion may not be natural (104.13–24, 16.14–16, 112.10–15).

7. This idea of perfection should be compared with *An*, in *Ak* VII, 326–27.

8. This is because freedom must be understood, according to Rousseau, in opposition to the passions known to us from our ordinary experience, which are acquired and factitious, and which tend to deprive us of freedom.

9. For discussion of this Socratism, in which a certain quality of willing is the necessary condition for the proper conduct of theoretical inquiry, see below, chap. 4, sec. 4. See also, *L*, in *Ak* IX, 29 (Socrates comes closest of all men to the ideal of the wise man).

10. A full statement of these views on Providence is the later essay, *Über das Misslingen aller philosophischen Versuche in der Theodicee*, in *Ak* VIII, 253–72. See *MA*, in *Ak* VIII, 121–23.

11. *CS* I, 6, in *OC* III, 360–62.

12. *Em*, 585–95.

13. *CS* I, 7, in *OC* III, 362–64.

14. Schmucker, in *UEK*, 247–48, has observed some of the differences between the general will as political principle and Kant's moral self-legislation. It must be underlined that Rousseau's notion of a sovereign general will is only an account of a political institution ensuring justice for a particular society; this will is "general" but not "universal" or "cosmopolitan." Furthermore, its character is to be formed, in rather Platonic

(or Machiavellian) fashion, by great founders (such as Moses, Lycurgus, and Numa) who establish civil religions that instill habits of reverence for the foundations of the state; again, the general will is hardly a rational will. For Rousseau's criticisms of rational or universal moralities, see *Première version du contract social* (*OC* III, 281–346) and *Lettres écrites de la montagnes* (*OC* III, 683–897). Rousseau had a profound appreciation of those features of moral and political life that resist rational, not to say metaphysical, treatment.

The conflation or identification in German historicist thought of the metaphysical and the political has been discussed by Iggers, in *GCH*, 272 (in the conclusion of the 1968 edition), who notes that "the basic assumption of historicism was that . . . institutions, particularly the state, possessed a metaphysical reality." According to this metaphysics, the primacy of the "empirical private individual of natural-law theory with his concrete needs and desires" was replaced by an individual state, institution, or other "collective entity." Thus "historicism was not a very suitable theoretical foundation for political liberalism." Kant contributed to the development of such historicism, one can add, insofar as the empirical individual has become problematic in his thought and is in the process of being replaced by the "rational" individual, constituted by a moral will having a universal content or object. The manner in which morality has become metaphysical in Kant helps prepare the way for the later idealists' metaphysical treatment of politics. In this connection one might reflect on how the later modern metaphysics of the state as organism or of the "collective whole" in some other form (national, traditional, linguistic, proletarian, etc.) is ultimately indebted to the impoverishment of the individual soul that begins in early modern liberalism. Far from providing an answer to that impoverishment, it simply represents a more advanced stage of it.

15. See especially *G*, in *Ak* IV, 404, where the method of drawing the attention of common reason to its own principle, "without in the least teaching it anything new," is called Socratic.

16. *Bem*, in *Ak* XX, 29.4–6 and 29.13–14: "It is unnatural for one man to spend the greater part of his life teaching a child how to live. Jean-Jacques's sort of tutor is very artificial. . . . It were to be wished that Rousseau had shown how schools are to arise [from his *Emile*]."

17. Kant finds "strange and nonsensical opinions" in Rousseau, but at the same time he finds in him a combination of "a rare acuity of intellect, a noble flight of genius, and a sensitive soul of so high an order as is probably not to be encountered in any other author, of whatever age or nation." See *Bem*, in *Ak* XX, 30.4–7. For Kant's account of education in which habituation presents far fewer difficulties than in Rousseau's account, see *UP*, in *Ak* IX, 437–500, and *KpV*, in *Ak* V, 149–61.

18. Consider the connection between Locke's account of the origin of property (*Second Treatise of Government*, chap. 5, "Of Property," esp. sec. 27) and the Kantian moral dictum that every human being (i.e., rational will) has a right to be regarded as an "end" and should not be used as a "means." The Kantian dictum rests on the assumption that only a being that has a free will able to give itself purposes independent of inclination is entitled to be an "end." It follows that all other beings cannot be "ends," and they properly serve as "means" to the purposes of free beings. Nature as a whole has "value" only insofar as it furthers those purposes. See *KU*, in *Ak* V, 434–36 (sec. 84) and 442–43 (sec. 86). The corresponding thought in Locke is the view that nature's "almost worthless materials" acquire value through human labor (*Second Treatise*, secs. 42–43).

19. See *CS* I, 4, in *OC* III, 355–58, on voluntary slavery as a self-contradiction in willing. Self-esteem is largely absent in the natural state, but its first appearance is a human sense of superiority to other animals (*DO*, in *OC* III, 136). Perfectibility is neu-

tral to the distinction between freedom and mechanism, and implies no spontaneous power in Kant's sense (p. 142).

20. Note that the categorical imperative, or the principle of the universalizability of maxims, presupposes a coexisting plurality of wills that tend to come into conflict. No maxim could contradict itself if this were not so. Morality presupposes a world of beings that are mutually dependent, in other words (for there are no conflicts if there are no dependencies) it presupposes beings that have bodily needs (or something like them). Kant says at a number of points that "freedom" as we are able to understand it presupposes a "finite" or "sensible" mode of existence; see *KU*, in *Ak* V, 195–97 and *KrV* A534/B562. Similarly, the "I" cannot be known without external intuitions, since its mode of existence is "receptive" as well as "spontaneous" (*P*, in *Ak* IV, 336 –37). Even the noumenal "I" of moral agency is unthinkable except in relation to a desiring subject that has needs, for only thereby does it have the possibility of being moral.

In general, transcendental principles have application only within the context of finite conditions, i.e., for beings with a "dependent" mode of existence. This is related to the fact that all problems of theoretical cognition are subsumed under morality by Kant: (1) man has a dependent mode of theoretical cognition, and this dependency creates the situation in which reason has "needs" and "demands" that are unsatisfactorily met, due to either nature's fault or the fault of human reason; (2) this situation is not one that can be regarded as merely a fact to be accepted, for human reason has a "right" to satisfaction, since human reason is the unique source of "right"; (3) furthermore, human reason's frustrations are self-inflicted, and hence it has a "duty" to order itself so as to remove the cause of frustration. (Note that the transcendental arguments determine questions of "right" or *quid juris*: what is the "rightful" use of the categories, and what can reason "rightly" expect to know by means of them?)

21. See C. Orwin and T. Pangle, "The Philosophical Foundation of Human Rights," in M. F. Plattner, ed., *Human Rights in Our Time: Essays in Honor of Victor Baras*, (Boulder, Colo.: Westview, 1984), 1–22.

22. See *An*, in *Ak* VII, 268–75, for the central role that the passion for honor plays in Kant's moral psychology.

23. *DO*, in *OC* III, 152ff., for the natural man as neither virtuous nor (contra Hobbes) vicious.

24. See ibid., 157ff., for Rousseau's treatment of the unlimitedness of human sexual desire.

25. For discussion of the "unsociable sociability" that belongs to man as rational and that is basic to the stimulation of human talents in culture, see below, chap. 5, sec. 3.

26. Schmucker has effectively shown that Schilpp seriously errs in this matter. See *UEK*, 185ff.

27. See n. 22–25 to chap. 2, above.

28. On compassion, see *DO*, in *OC* III, 154–57, 125–26.

29. See *Em*, 62ff.

30. All of reason, including its highest satisfactions, is then subsumed under a moral view of the whole. Just as the "I" is constituted by the demand for self-rule and ownership of itself, reason's view of the whole is constituted by the demand that the whole reflect what is reason's "own" or that the whole support reason's self-rule. Hence happiness has to be apportioned according to the exigencies of virtue. Kant's view could hardly be farther from Aristotle's, according to whom happiness is the complete and self-sufficient good, and not needing justification. It is "beyond praise" and therefore beyond the range of moral judgment. This is not to deny that perfect happiness (in theoretical activity) to which this description properly applies is something different from the consideration of the just reward for moral excellence that be-

longs to the sphere of political deliberation. See *Nicomachean Ethics*, bk. 1, chaps. 5 and 12; bk. 8, chap. 1; bk. 10, chaps. 6–9. While perfect happiness for Rousseau is clearly not rational or theoretical in Aristotle's sense, his views on the moral status of perfect happiness remind one more of Aristotle than of Kant.

31. Thus the opening sentence of *Emile* (p. 5): "Everything is good as it leaves the hands of the Author of things; everything degenerates in the hands of man."

32. See *DO*, in *OC*, III, 131–32, 174–75.

33. "We take much more pleasure in some of our perfections when we are their cause, and especially when we are their free active cause. The greatest perfection is to subordinate everything to the free will. And the perfection of a free will as a cause of the possibility of something is much greater than all other causes of the good, even when the same reality can result from them" (*Bem*, in *Ak* XX, 144.17–45.3). As Kant writes later, the only actions that have moral worth, i.e., that deserve our respect, are the determinations of a good will. Such actions are morally valuable regardless of their consequences. The fortunate outcome of actions is something less perfect than a good will, because "it could be brought about by other causes and would not require the will of a rational being" (*CPrR*, 62 and *G*, in *Ak* IV, 401).

34. "The will is perfect insofar as it is in accord with laws of freedom, and is the greatest cause of the good. Moral feeling is the feeling of the perfection of such a will" (*Bem*, in *Ak* XX, 136.16–37.2). Moral feeling can also be understood therefore as the effect of the identification of the individual with the universal will: "The sweetness that we find in having regard for the well-being of others is an effect of the feeling of the universal will that would exist in the condition of freedom" (89.11–13). The universal will represents the ideal and original condition of freedom, insofar as it represents the perfect equality of all wills, and thus their free equality with themselves. See also *Ak* XIX, *R* 6598 (ca. 1769): "Moral feeling is not an underived feeling. It rests on a necessary inner law to contemplate and experience oneself from an external standpoint." That law is a necessity for the alienated will of social man, for otherwise his will has no assured way to "come back to itself." Again, the radical distance between Rousseau and Kant on the possible (and desirable) degree of rationality and universality attainable by a self-legislative will must not be forgotten; see n. 14, this chapter, above.

35. *KrV* A84–92/B116–24. See n. 20 above, second half.

36. Thus compare *Bem*, in *Ak* XX, 121.15–22.6 with 185.25–86.11: the awareness of mortality is not found in natural man, and would be of no use to him, whereas it is helpful for bringing social man to simplicity and tranquillity, through insight into the vanity of human strivings. What is bad for natural man can be good for corrupted man. This consideration applies especially to religion: natural man has no religion and is better off without it, but social man without religion is dangerous; see 57.1–9.

37. But common reason does not have adequate insight into the true theoretical principles. See *P*, in *Ak* IV, 259–60.

38. Thus Yovel, in *KPH*, 18–19, draws a contrast between "dogmatic" accounts of ends, rejected by Kant, and Kant's advocacy of "projected ends" that emerge when "the human subject explicates his own structure."

39. See *T*, in *Ak* II, 368–73, and discussion below, chap. 4, sec. 4, for Kant's first published account of this definition of metaphysics, appearing soon after the *Remarks*, in 1766.

Chapter Four

1. See *DS*, in *OC* III, 6.

2. *I*, in *Ak* VIII, 18, and see n. 25 to chap. 1.

3. For "nature" in its ideal sense as the perfection of human rational nature, see

I, in *Ak* VIII, 17–31. For state of nature as juridical, see *MS*, in *Ak* VI, 255–57, 305–8, where the meaning is the condition of absence of legal authority for the settling of disputes. Kant's translation of the ideal of natural equilibrium into the reason of every moral and rational agent makes it quite possible for him to revert to Hobbes's state of nature as the empirical condition of human beings prior to the emergence of civil society. The proximity of the *Remarks* to Hobbes was already noted above, in chap. 3, sec. 3.

4. See n. 20 to chap. 3.

5. See *KU*, in *Ak* V, 71–89.

6. When Kant in the letter to Garve of October 19, 1798, states that "the antinomy of reason . . . first aroused me from my dogmatic slumber and drove me to the critique of reason itself, in order to resolve the scandal of ostensible contradiction of reason with itself" (*KPC*, 252), he refers to all four pairs of theses and antitheses in the *Critique*, of which freedom and necessity is but one. Significantly he writes of "the antinomy" using the singular expression for the whole dialectic of reason.

7. Note the definition of culture at *KU*, in *Ak* V, 431: "Culture is the production of the aptitude of a rational being for arbitrary ends in general, and thus according to freedom." This definition is almost identical with the definition of reason at *I*, in *Ak* VIII, 18: "Reason in a creature is a faculty of widening the rules and purposes of the use of all its powers far beyond natural instinct; it acknowledges no limits to its projects" (trans. in *OH*, 13). See also the statement on culture at *UP*, in *Ak* IX, 449 ("A human being must be cultivated," etc.). Note that culture and reason are defined in terms of "ends," and specifically with respect to their "arbitrary" character. Whereas Kant speaks of culture mostly in nonmoral terms, as the realm of the cultivation of skill, prudence, technical and legal reason, he does not exclude the possibility of its acquiring a moral form; indeed his notions of the final goal of the human species require that he speak of culture in a moral way. See Kant's remark that "culture according to true principles, educating one to become both a human being and a citizen, has perhaps not yet begun and is certainly not completed" (*MA*, in *Ak* VIII, 116). Taken in this most comprehensive way, "culture" is equivalent to the whole range of possibilities open to human reason.

8. These points are expressed later by Kant in *KpV*, in *Ak* V, 110: "Virtue (as worthiness to be happy) is the supreme condition of whatever appears to be desirable and thus of our pursuit of happiness. . . . But these truths do not imply that it is the entire and perfect good as the object of the faculty of desire of rational finite beings. In order to be this, happiness is also required, and indeed not merely in the partial eyes of a person who makes himself his end but even in the judgment of an impartial reason, which in general regards persons in the world as ends-in-themselves. For to be in need of happiness and also worthy of it and yet not to partake of it could not be in accordance with the complete volition of an omnipotent rational being, if we assume such only for the sake of argument" (trans. in *CPrR*, 215). The ideal of the unity of freedom and nature in effect corresponds to the standpoint of regarding the world as remade by an omnipotent being, in accordance with moral demands that arise from finite beings. See *Re*, in *Ak* VI, 5–6.

9. Thus the human rational powers cannot reach their point of perfection except over many, perhaps endless, generations. Individual perfection is not attainable apart from species perfection (the equality of reason with itself entails the equality of the whole species). See *I*, in *Ak* VIII, 18–19.

10. Thus *UG*, in *Ak* VIII, 307–13: The answer to the question "Is the human race as a whole lovable, or is it an object to be regarded with distaste?" depends on the answer to another question: "Does man possess natural capacities which would indicate that the human race will always progress and improve, so that the evils of the past and present will vanish in a future good?" (trans. in *KPW*, 87, slightly modified).

11. *MS*, in *Ak* VI, 488–91.

12. The most illuminating of the early *Reflexionen* discussing "idea" and "ideal" are scattered through two groups from *Ak* XIX: *R* 6577–97 (from 1764–68) and *R* 6598–6611 (from about 1769). Most citations of reflections in the following section will be from these groups.

13. Scholars have pointed to important literary connections between Kant's use of these terms and Rousseau. Thus Henrich, in UKfE, esp. pp. 430–31, writes: "Kant owes to Rousseau the correct understanding of the word which he will use in the future to denote the projection of a maximum: the Platonic word 'idea' " (p. 431). Kant indicates this provenance in *VpR*, in *Ak* XXVIII.2.2, 994: "Rousseau's Emile and the education to be given him is a true idea of reason." The passage elaborates the meaning of "idea": it is a "universal rule *in abstracto*" representing a perfection never attainable by sensible beings, although we must use this rule to measure the excellence of sensible particulars, and even represent to ourselves the realization of the rule by an individual. This last representation is an "ideal": "An ideal is an individual case I bring under this rule." Kant thus points to the fact that Rousseau's literary presentation of an individual's perfect education is an "ideal" formed according to an abstract "idea." It is then not clear whether the idea can be practically realized: "Rousseau himself admits in his *Emile* that a whole lifetime (or the better part of it) would be required to give one single individual the education he requires." Also see *KrV* A567–71/B595–99 for the distinction between idea and ideal, and *Ak* XIX, *R* 6611.

The Rousseauian ideal in *Emile* is closely related to the ideal regime of the *Republic*, discussed at *KrV* A316–17/B372–74. Ideals and ideas are not simply fictions, but requirements of reason: they are necessary guiding conceptions for human reason, representing universal conditions under which the perfect development of human faculties is thinkable. Thus correctly understood, ideas and ideals refer only to the human faculties, not realities apart from the faculties. In Kant's view, Plato used the term *idea* sometimes correctly and sometimes not: correctly when applying it to the moral realm and incorrectly when referring it to archetypes of things in themselves, and thus as possible object of cognition; see *KrV* A314/B371n. Yet Kant's thought is much closer in any case to Rousseau than to Plato. For the sense of idea in Kant is that of a concept of perfection grounded only in freedom and the autonomous will, and not in any natural telos. We have seen from the *Remarks* how Rousseau for Kant is the most radical and profoundest critic of all earlier notions of nature and teleology. Plato however (in Kant's view) assumes that the cosmos provides the mind with a self-subsistent telos: "The mystical ideal of intellectual intuition of Plato" is criticized at *Ak* XIX, *R* 6611; the same reflection has a very Rousseauian conclusion. Finally, there is an important source of Kant's "ideal" in Hobbes, discussed below in n. 37.

14. A very interesting use of *idealisch* occurs at *Bem*, in *Ak* XX, 123.17–18.

15. For the "idea" as something of human rational devising, see *I*, in *Ak* VIII, 29–31.

16. *Bem*, in *Ak* XX, 9.14. A detailed relating of Rousseau to ancient moralists is found in *Ak* XVI, *R* 1644 (ca. 1769). Rousseau is sometimes paired with Cynic philosophers, as at *EV*, 9, where Rousseau is called "the refined Diogenes." There is a most interesting pairing of Socrates and Rousseau at *Ak* XV, *R* 193, where both are called "negative theorists." See also *Ak* XXIV.1, 330; *Ak* XIX, *R* 6611, cited in n. 13 above; and the references in *UEK*, cited in n. 17 below. Kant's placing of *Emile* and the *Republic* of Plato together in the category of examples of the "ideal," mentioned in n. 13 above, has a significance that is underlined at *Ak* XV, *R* 921, where Rousseau and Plato are cited. They are described as two thinkers who in "enthusiastic" fashion try to employ ideas beyond the limits of experience. The remark is not wholly critical in spirit, for Kant also says that he can learn much from such "enthusiastic geniuses."

17. See *UEK*, 307–14. Schmucker refers to various *Reflexionen* and also to the linking of Rousseau and Antisthenes in the *Remarks* at 17.23–30. Schmucker's judgment runs counter to one that was common before his work—that Kant's interest in ancient philosophy was spurred by his reading of the second edition (1767–68) of J. Brucker's *Historia critica philosophiae*. No doubt much that Kant knew about ancient philosophy came from that source; it is doubtful that it was the basis of his interest. Kant's reflections on "idea," as we have seen, are never in a purely ancient or Platonic vein. The importance of Brucker is stressed by those who are more impressed by Kant's "Platonism"; thus *KM*, 161–64; similarly H. Heimsoeth, "Kant und Plato," *KS* 56 (1965): 349–72. The term *idea* was used in eighteenth-century aesthetic discussions (thus by Winckelmann), and its appearance is connected with the revival of classical art. This may be important for Kant, as may be discerned at *Bem*, in *Ak* XX, 123.17–18, although the point being made about beauty here is rather Rousseauian. For the aesthetic use of "idea" in Kant see G. Tonelli, "Kant's Early Theory of Genius (1770–79)," *JHP* 4 (1966): 109–31; for other discussions of "idea," especially in aesthetics, in the eighteenth century see the same author's article "Ideal in Philosophy from the Renaissance to 1780," in P. Wiener, *Dictionary of the History of Ideas* (New York: Scribners, 1973), II, 549–52.

18. *Ak* XIX, *R* 6624: the moderns seek only the principle of moral judgment; Wolff's concept of perfection is abstract and formal; see also the beginning of *R* 6880, the remarks by Düsing in PhG, 12, and n. 3 to chap. 2 above.

19. *Ak* XIX, *R* 6874: The Epicureans and Stoics rightly emphasize that the human good is dependent on action and thus "artificial"; also *R* 6624: happiness according to the Epicureans is "self-produced" and not the result of chance. See the praise of the Stoics and Epicureans at *KpV*, in *Ak* V, 115–16, and Düsing, PhG, 9. See also *EV*, 7: the ancients saw that happiness springs from freedom of the will.

20. See *KpV*, in *Ak* V, 126: "The Greek schools were certainly correct in establishing the principle of morals by itself, independently of the postulate of God's existence and merely from the relation of reason to the will" (trans. from *CPrR*, 229, slightly altered). Plato is not accorded such praise, and his ideal is criticized as theological and mystical; see *Ak* XIX, *R* 6584, and n. 13 above. Plato confuses the terminus ad quem and the terminus a quo, which is to say, he confuses the product of morality (an idea of the divine) with the ground of morality (the rational will).

21. *Ak* XIX, *R* 6584, p. 95.11–12.

22. *Ak* XIX, *R* 6584: "*Summum bonum*. The maximum of happiness in the minimum of needs and simplicity" applies in a general way to these ancient ideals, with the appropriate qualifications for each school. In other reflections Kant interestingly connects "maximum" with "idea"—thus *R* 6596, where the notion of a maximum reflects reason's need to "find an extreme in every quantity" and is thus related to the need for "ideas." (Note also the statement about justice: "Just action is a maximum of the free will, when it is mutually respected.") Also *R* 6611: an idea "contains the greatest perfection from some point of view." The language of maxima and minima is related to the "state of nature" as a limit case or ideal of maximum freedom. Thus the Rousseauian version of "idea" is the starting point for the account of the ancient ideals as "maxima."

23. Kant shows little regard for, and not even much knowledge of, Aristotle's account of the soul, and he suggests that Aristotle is a kind of sensualist; see *Ak* XVII, *R* 4451. Surely Aristotle offers a much subtler and less codified version of the relation of reason to appetite than those of the later schools—one that is too subtle for Kant's purposes. If those later schools (which have a rather propagandistic character) lend themselves somewhat to Kant's analysis in terms of the extremes (maximum and minimum), Aristotle's account of virtue as a mean certainly does not.

24. See *DM*, para. 7, in *Ak* II, 395: Wolff has made the error of reducing the funda-

mental heterogeneity of intellect and sense to a merely logical distinction, and thus has "completely abolished, to the great detriment of philosophy, that noble institution of antiquity, the discussion of the character of phenomena and noumena" (trans. in *SPW*, 58). The writings and reflections of the 1760s show that Kant returned to this noble distinction by way of practical philosophy and its teleological function before he elaborated it within theoretical philosophy. As we shall see, the first such elaboration (in the *Dissertation* of 1770, quoted above) is guided by the practical telos. For other criticism of Leibniz and Wolff for having neglected the distinction, see *L*, in *Ak* IX, 36, and *KrV* A44/B61–62 and A270–71/B326–27.

25. See especially *Ak* XIX, *R* 6584, pp. 95.31–32 and p. 96.1–9.

26. As has been pointed out in notes above, Plato is in Kant's view even guiltier of such dogmatism than the later ancient schools. The notion of perfection as the nonempirical "extreme" gets partial support from Kant's reading of Plato, but our examination should prove that its meaning is decidedly unancient in most respects.

27. *Ak* XIX, *R* 6607, pp. 106–7. See also *R* 6584, the end: the Stoic wise man is "a correct ideal, but foolish as a genuine prescription for human conduct." And also the footnote at *KpV*, in *Ak* V, 127–28, which has a criticism of the Stoic "heroism of the sage," for its overestimation of the capacities of human nature.

28. *Ak* XIX, *R* 6607. See also *Ak* XVIII, *R* 4971: Epicurean virtue admirably promotes a "constant and joyful heart," but it is vitiated by the falseness of its moral principle. At *DM*, in *Ak* II, 396, Shaftesbury and his school are called qualified adherents of Epicurus. See also Düsing, in *PhG*, 10.

29. *Ak* XIX, *R* 6607.

30. Ibid., *R* 6584, the end.

31. Ibid., *R* 6607, the end.

32. See n. 5 to chap. 3, above.

33. Kant stated this point more directly at a later date. See *Re*, in *Ak* VI, 57–59: "Yet those valiant men [the Stoics] mistook their enemy: for he is not to be sought in the merely undisciplined natural inclinations which present themselves so openly to everyone's consciousness; rather is he, as it were, an invisible foe who screens himself behind reason and is therefore all the more dangerous" (trans. in *Rw*, 50).

34. *Ak* XIX, *R* 6579.

35. See Plato, *Meno* and *Gorgias*, and Aristotle, *Nicomachean Ethics*, 1099a31–1100a10, 1155a1–31, 1169b3–1170b19. Yet later antiquity offers certain thoughts far more congenial to Kant. Thus Seneca, *Moral Epistles*, XC: "The gods have given the knowledge of philosophy to none, but the faculty of acquiring it they have given to all. For if they had made philosophy also a general good, and if we were gifted with understanding at our birth, wisdom would have lost her best attribute—that she is not one of the gifts of fortune"; Seneca, *Ad Lucilium epistulae morales*, trans. R. M. Gummere (Cambridge and London: Harvard and Heinemann, 1920), I, 395. Kant's marked sympathy for the later ancient schools has some similarity to the preference of the early humanists for the Latin moral and rhetorical writers over Plato and Aristotle as moral teachers. Thus Petrarch declares that Aristotle teaches what virtue is, but does not "inflame" the soul with love of virtue. The concern with efficacy of moral teaching is expressed in the dictum *Satius est autem bonum velle quam verum nosse* (It is better or more sufficient to will the good than to know the truth). See C. Trinkaus, *The Poet as Philosopher: Petrarch and the Formation of Renaissance Consciousness* (New Haven: Yale University Press, 1979), 107–9. Yet this cannot be the last word on Kant's relation to antiquity. The new form of idealism Kant creates requires a reinterpretation of the architectonic and metaphysical interests of reason—one that results in a new "Platonism"; see nn. 13 above and 40 below, to this chapter. Kant's assessment of Plato and Aristotle is most fully stated in the late essay (1796) *Von einem neuerdings erhobenen vornehmen Ton in der Philosophie*, in *Ak* VIII, 387–406.

36. *Ak* XIX, *R* 6593, pp. 98–100.

37. Thus the ancients did not discern that the true *end* of moral reason is reason's determination of unity with itself; not seeing that, they were mistaken about the *conditions* for achieving that end. *Ak* XIX, *R* 6583 shows how the problem of the end arises from reason and culture, not from an enduring human nature: the sciences and arts are sources of new needs that weaken the human will and render it more subject to domination. "Every new need is a fetter that binds man to the laws, even when the laws are arbitrary." Because of the rational origin of the human problem, the answer to it involves more "art" than the ancients supposed. See *Ak* XIX, *R* 6611, p. 110, the paragraph on "the highest good."

In connection with art's primacy, the mention of of Hobbes in *R* 6593 is worth noting. His state of nature is called an "ideal" of the "external relations of the natural or primitive man." Kant sees that Hobbes is the forerunner of his attempt and Rousseau's to construct an ideal order that jettisons assumptions of natural tendencies of human nature to the good. Hobbes's notion of an ideal order of external relations is, as it were, transposed into the realm of individual virtue. Already the doctrine of Hobbes means the abandonment of natural law and its replacement by merely willed and positive law. The Hobbesian state that conquers the evils of the natural state prepares the way for such a statement of Kant as this: "Just as freedom contains the first grounds of all that begins, so is it also the only thing with self-sufficient goodness" (*Ak* XIX, *R* 6598). See also *R* 6605 for the connection between "perfection," "freedom," and the will's "not being subordinated to any foreign cause."

38. *EV*, 7–13 and *KpV*, in *Ak* V, 107–32.

39. Thus see *Ak* XIX, *R* 6584 (the Cynical ideal as a "system of simplicity"), and *R* 6606 (the "Epicurean system").

40. *T*, in *Ak* II, 315–73 and *DM*, in *Ak* II, 385–419. Unmistakably the idea of a moral system has assumed a teleological role for all uses of reason in the first edition (1781) of the *Critique of Pure Reason*. And there, as we shall see, the Platonic Idea, when purged of all "mystical" and "dogmatic" elements, and reinterpreted in terms of the most modern idea of reason as lawgiver, can be employed as the "architectonic principle for ordering the world according to ends" (*KrV* A318/B375). The central place for an ultimate telos in Kant's thinking certainly also leads one to recall Aristotle, *Nicomachean Ethics*, bk. 1, chap. 1, and *Metaphysics*, 994b.

41. See for example *Ak* XIX, *R* 6605: "The first rule of external good action is not to be in accord with the happiness of others, but to be in accord with their wills. Likewise, the perfection of a subject does not rest on its being happy, but rather on the fact that its condition is determined by freedom. Thus also the universally valid form of perfection can come into being only if actions stand under universal laws of freedom." The valid notion of perfection has to abstract from strivings for happiness (which are indeterminate) but has to take into account the mutual dependence of rational beings and hence the need for law.

42. *EL*, 6; *EV*, 7–8.

43. These statements are consistent with *KrV* A569–70/B597–98 where ideals are characterized as archetypes—not patterns of things in themselves, but patterns that are indispensable to the guidance of reason.

44. See n. 33 to chap. 3, above. See also *I* (third thesis), in *Ak* VIII, 19; *G*, in *Ak* IV, 396 ("reason . . . is capable of a contentment only of its own kind"); *Ak* XIX, *R* 7202, 7204, and 7311, which develop in various ways the theses that "happiness must rest upon an a priori ground that reason approves" and that "the noblest problem of morality" is to show how "morality could bring forth happiness through freedom, if morality were exercized by everyone."

45. *EL*, 252–53 ("The Ultimate Destiny of the Human Race"); *EV*, 317–19. The whole passage deserves consideration. It discusses the highest and final end of all uses

of reason, which is characterized thus: "The highest possible perfection of human nature—this is the kingdom of God on earth" (trans. in *EL*, 253).

46. *EL*, 10; *EV*, 13; see *KpV*, in *Ak* V, 126–29, especially the note at 127–28.

47. In the "Proem" to the ethics lectures, Kant insists on the need for effective
principles in moral philosophy: "We are forever hearing sermons about what ought to
be done from people who do not stop to consider whether what they preach can be
done" (*EL*, 1–5; *EV*, 1–6).

48. *EL*, 10; *EV*, 13.

49. At various times Kant links Christianity and Platonism for the defects they
share. Thus they are both criticized as "enthusiastic, fanatical, and mystical" at *Ak* XIX,
R 6611. They both would ground morality in union with a supreme reality, as deity or
as principle of intelligibility. As we have noted, Kant nevertheless thinks something
can be learned from "enthusiastic" doctrines (see n. 16 above). Kant regards the infinite futurity present in the Christian ideal as being in partial agreement with his account of the consequences that follow from the distinction between freedom and mere
nature: the conquest of the latter by the former is an infinite project, as Kant notes in
the last words of the ethics lectures. Scholars generally overstate the positive side of
Kant's treatment of Christianity. See *PhG*, 12ff.

50. Moses Mendelssohn was offended by the tone of the essay, which he found
frivolous and equivocal, and reported his displeasure in a letter not extant to Kant.
Kant found it necessary to defend his character and purpose in a reply to Mendelssohn
(the letter of April 8, 1766, in *KPC*, 54–57), wherein he asserts his conviction that
metaphysics is properly dedicated to "the true and lasting welfare of the human race."
In Kant's defense it can be said that the essay quite plainly asserts the practical and
moral end of theoretical inquiry. However its argument renders questionable the capacity of reason to criticize nonrational and "enthusiastic" conceptions of human destiny, and seemingly it is content to see speculative metaphysics collapse into skeptical
and Humean shambles. Through this essay one might have come to the conclusion
that Kant was joining the most radical critics of Enlightenment. But that Kant is not a
defender of any orthodox (or "fanatical") faith is indicated by the essay's conclusion.
More discussion of the *Dreams'* theoretical argument follows in sect. 5 of this chapter.

51. *T*, in *Ak* II, 368ff.

52. The hypothesis is at *T*, in *Ak* II, 333–37.

53. The German equivalent of "phenomenon" (*Erscheinung*) is used at *T*, in *Ak* II,
334–35, to characterize moral feeling as the phenomenal effect in us of the supersensible will. The contrast of phenomenon and noumenon is thus provided here with one
of its prime bases, although the Greek terms are not yet in use. Schmucker, in *UEK*,
252, 258–59, notes that this is the first appearance of the distinction in Kant's writings
and that its primary basis is moral. Ward, in *DKV*, 37–40, also observes that in the
Dreams, moral feeling is derived as mere "appearance" from "the formal principles of
reason interpreted as laws of action." Unlike Schmucker, he does not remark on the
importance of Rousseau and the new account of freedom for this step.

54. Again Kant characterizes moral feeling as a derived phenomenon; it is not an
ultimate principle. As the *Remarks* established, its ultimate ground is the free will. A
few years after the *Dreams* Kant also begins to use the term "pathological" for the entire
realm of feeling and sensibility, to distinguish practical motives taken from that realm
from the pure practical motives based on the free will. See *Ak* XIX, *R* 6601.

55. Kant briefly notes the similarity between this moral need to harmonize with the
universal will and the drive to bring one's judgment into accord with the judgment of
others. This latter drive expresses a need for aproval from other rational beings, i.e.,
amour-propre. Kant observes that this drive or passion appears to be a means by which
nature promotes unity and harmony among human beings. It is very much related to

moral feeling in that it rests on esteem for oneself and others as rational and free. As Kant will write in much more detail later, this amour-propre stimulates the development of rational faculties, promotes the refinement and discipline of inclinations, and through the conquest of mere "animality" in man, prepares for the domination of the moral motive. (See chap. 5, sec. 3, below.) The comparison of moral feeling and amour-propre in the *Dreams* and other writings underlines the fact that Kantian morality is a form of mastery of nature based on human rational self-esteem. Also, that this esteem compels a harmonizing with a universal will points to the circumstance that only in concert with others can the individual attain the full development of reason on which he esteems himself.

56. *T*, in *AK* II, 335–36.

57. Schmucker, in *UEK*, 260, accurately remarks that Kant in this passage suggests two possible ways to resolve the discrepancy between virtue and happiness—through "a law of nature" and through an "extraordinary divine will"—and that the second is for Kant philosophically the more problematic solution.

58. In his letter to Mendelssohn that defends the essay (see n. 50 above), Kant makes one of his most famous remarks about the reserve of his public utterances; see n. 60 to chap. 1.

59. Such investigations are the substance of the *Critique of Judgment*, but they are proposed at *KrV* A815–16/B843–44, in the idea of the whole as a systematic unity of ends.

60. *T*, in *Ak* II, 373: "There never has lived a righteous soul which could endure the thought that all comes to an end with death, and whose noble soul could avoid elevating itself to the hope of a future condition."

61. Those past ambitions all assume that there is an already existing harmony, or even identity, between human rational freedom and the given order of nature. But the only possible harmony is an "ideal" one. It is attainable only through the internal self-restriction and self-legislation of the human faculties—not through a correspondence of the human faculties to an external order or model.

62. *T*, in *Ak* II, 369. See also *Ak* XVIII, *R* 5112 (from the later 1770s): The mathematician, the aesthete (*der schöne Geist*), and the natural philosopher wrongly have contempt for metaphysics, since they too experience "from within" a need to raise metaphysical questions. "And since they as human beings cannot find their final end in the satisfaction of the purposes of this life, they cannot avoid asking: wherefore am I, wherefore is the whole?"

63. *T*, in *Ak* II, 372.

64. Ibid., 369: "Ultimately science arrives at the definition of its limits, as established by the nature of human reason."

65. Ibid., 368–69: "Reason that is matured through experience, and that has become wisdom, speaks with the voice of Socrates, who amidst the market's wares says serenely: 'How many things there are that I do not need.'" See *Bem*, in *Ak* XX, 77.6–12.

66. See *Ak* XV, *R* 193: "Wherever error is both seductive and dangerous, negative forms and criteria of knowledge are more important than positive knowledge, and the negative supplies the true object of our science." Both Socrates and Rousseau are mentioned as "negative theorists." See *KrV* Bxxiv, Bxxxi, B25, A795/B823.

67. *T*, in *Ak* II, 368.; *Bem*, in *Ak* XX, 181.1–4.

68. Some of the earliest uses of the phrase "critique of pure reason" are in *Ak* XVII, *R* 3964 and *R* 4455 (dating from 1769–72); also see *R* 3716. Even earlier is the important use of the term "critique" in *N*, in *Ak* II, 310–11.

69. *Ak* XVII, *R* 3918, 4467, and 4471; *Ak* XVIII, *R* 4970.

70. The principal reflections to which this discussion will refer are in *Ak* XVII–XVIII, the volumes of the metaphysics *Nachlass*. The chief groups are *R* 3716–17 (about

1765), *R* 3913–4480 (1769–72) in *Ak* XVII; *R* 4847–5127 (1776–78) in *Ak* XVIII. Adickes's very early dating of *R* 3716–17, (1762–64), which he defends in *Ak* XVII, 257–58, is persuasively disputed by Henrich in *SKpE*, 11, and by Hinske, "Die Datierung der Reflexion 3716," *KS* 68/3, cited in n. 3 to the introduction, above.

71. For philosophy as legislation, see *Ak* XVII, *R* 4467, 4468; *Ak* XVIII, *R* 4902, 4925, 4970, and 5112.

72. See *L*, in *Ak* IX, 26: "Philosophy is the only science that can provide an inner satisfaction, for it closes, as it were, the scientific circle, and only through it do the sciences receive order and coherence" (trans. in *Lo*, 30).

73. *Ak* XVII, *R* 3717: "Metaphysics is a useful science, not because it extends knowledge, but because it prevents errors. One learns what Socrates knew"; *R* 4457: "Criticism . . . serves to remove obstacles in the way of religion and virtue," and thereby secures a "wisdom that has more to do with dispensing than acquiring. Socrates." See also *R* 4284.

74. For the contrast of doctrinal or dogmatic practical science with zetetic, skeptical (or sometimes "cathartic") theoretical science, see *Ak* XVII, *R* 4445, 4455, 4457, 4465, and 4469; *Ak* XVIII, *R* 4865. It must be underlined that Kant's notion of a skeptical theoretical metaphysics is incompatible with skepticism for its own sake; thus see *Ak* XVIII, *R* 5037. The sole intent of the new skepticism is to bring about the securing of fundamental certainties. This is also the sole intent of Descartes's "doubt," which is from the start motivated by the desire for practical certainty (or mastery).

75. For morality or practice as organon, see *Ak* XVII, *R* 4445, 4453, 4457, and 4461; for theoretical criticism as propaedeutic see *R* 4457, 4459, and 4465; see also n. 9 to the introduction above, and especially the cited letter of Kant to Mendelssohn.

76. For theoretical science as corrective, disciplinary, or canonical, see *Ak* XVII, *R* 4453, 4455, 4459, and 4468; *Ak* XVIII, *R* 4865. There are times in the post-1781 writings when Kant settles upon the simple formula that practical philosophy legislates over freedom and theoretical philosophy legislates over nature. In such cases he is employing narrow understandings of both that do not really correspond to his own thought. Actually practical philosophy legislates over all uses of reason (moral and theoretical), with respect to ends. The crucial function of theoretical philosophy or theoretical critique is to legislate over reason so as to bring an end to its speculative dialectic. If it legislated over only nature (the phenomenal realm according to the laws of the understanding), theoretical philosophy would be the same as physics or natural philosophy. However, the theoretical propaedeutic is centrally concerned with the limits of the sciences of logic, mathematics, and natural philosophy, and with the validity of extending them (or methods derived from them) into the sphere of metaphysics. All philosophy is the self-legislation of reason, and theoretical philosophy is that portion of the legislation which circumscribes the field of the theoretical sciences in the light of the moral telos. Kant believes that he carries out a drastic change in the meaning of theory, in his best self-understanding, which departs from all earlier views of theoretical "analysis," since these maintained more continuity between first philosophy and natural philosophy than the "critique" allows. Sometimes Kant identifies without qualification "metaphysics" and "propaedeutic," such that the moral telos is yet higher than metaphysics (understood as the only possible form of theory); see *Ak* XVIII, *R* 4902, 4970.

77. *Ak* XVII, *R* 4241: God, freedom, and immortality "are the three concepts of reason that have an instrinsic importance, and they are systematically related; they give metaphysics as a whole its true seriousness"; see also *KrV* B395n. This reflection also asserts that "all rational knowledge has in the last analysis a relation to the practical." See further *Ak* XVII, *R* 4457 (for the necessity of metaphysics), 4459 (for the nobility of metaphysics): *Ak* XVIII, *R* 4865, and 5112; also *KrV* A800/B828.

78. *Ak* XVII, *R* 4459; see also *R* 4241 and 4461.

79. Ibid., *R* 3918: Metaphysics as "the science of the ends of our knowledge" does not have the function of "satisfying the desire for knowledge, but rather of determining the limits [of knowledge], which are partly positive, partly negative." Also *R* 4459: Metaphysical inquiry gets its true importance from providing the propaedeutic to wisdom, and neither from satisfying an "immediate desire for knowledge" nor from serving as an organon to other sciences (e.g., by securing foundations to natural science). *R* 4459 and 4467 characterize "wisdom" whose subject is the "worth" and "limits" of all forms of knowledge; *Ak* XVIII, *R* 4970 gives the name of "philodoxy" to the "culture and instruction of all talents," which is directed toward any ends and which does not consider the worth of the ends; see the criticism of the "mere theoretician" as "philodoxus" at *L*, in *Ak* IX, 24; also *KrV* Bxxxvii. Note the later statement at *MS*, in *AK* VI, 445, which distinguishes between "wisdom" that treats "ends," and the theoretical sciences (logic, mathematics, and speculative inquiry).

80. *Ak* XVII, *R* 4294, 4461, 4467, and 4471; *Ak* XVIII, *R* 4925, 4927, and 4970. In a later work, Kant makes the related distinction between two needs of reason—one unconditionally necessary (for the concept of a highest being to ground the highest good), and one only conditionally necessary (for a concept of a highest being to guide and regulate theoretical inquiry into the teleological order of nature); *W*, in *Ak* VIII, 139.

81. *Ak* XVII, *R* 4467; *Ak* XVIII, *R* 4925; cf. *KrV* A839/B867, and chap. 5, sec. 2, below.

82. *Ak* XVII, *R* 3716; also *R* 4284, 4459; *Ak* XVIII, *R* 4926; see *KrV* A831/B859.

83. *Ak* XVIII, *R* 4865.

84. *Ak* XVII, *R* 4284, 4291, 4464, and 4469; *Ak* XVIII, *R* 4865.

85. *Ak* XVII, *R* 4459 (on logical perfection); *Ak* XVIII, *R* 4926 (on the thinker's duty); *Ak* XVII, *R* 4291 (on morality's need of assistance from theory). On the philosopher's duty, see *KrV* A703/B731 and A726/B754.

86. *Ak* XVII, *R* 4445; *Ak* XVIII, *R* 5119 (on the harmful pretense to extend theoretical concepts into the realm of ends); *Ak* XVII, *R* 3918, 4284, 4458, 4464 (on the critical thinker's determination of the boundaries or "territory" of metaphysics); and *R* 4284 (on "the greatest benefit," which is practical, to come from metaphysics).

87. Especially *Ak* XVII, *R* 3948 and *Ak* XVIII, *R* 4865; also *Ak* XVII, *R* 4284, 4453, 4457, 4459, and 4464.

88. *Ak* XVII, *R* 4284: "Metaphysics . . . is the boundary-setting of the various sciences, and it confines man to his vocation"; *Ak* XVIII, *R* 4970: "Philosophy is the science of what is fitting in knowledge for man's vocation"; it decrees laws, the most important of which "limit reason's pretensions for the sake of humanity's end." See also *Ak* XVIII, *R* 5073: Critique is "preventive medicine" for a disease natural to reason, "to attach itself to other worlds and to escape from the circle of its proper concerns"; this is similar to the language at *Bem*, in *Ak* XX, 41.19–30.

89. *Ak* XVII, *R* 3716: Rational knowledge as "critique" is not a science of objects but a "science of the subject"; *T*, in *Ak* II, 369: Philosophy "judges its own procedure and has knowledge not only of objects, but knowledge of their relation to the human understanding."

90. *Ak* XVII, *R* 4468.

91. *Ak* XVIII, *R* 4849: "The end of metaphysics" is "to show the conditions of the absolute unity of reason, so that reason can be a perfect principle of practical unity, that is, of the harmonious combination of the sum of all ends." Reason is essentially "the faculty of the absolute unity of our forms of knowledge."

92. Thus *Ak* XVII, *R* 4464: In order to prevent reason from "confounding itself" and "destroying morals and religion," metaphysics is needed for the securing of "boundaries."

93. One cannot date precisely when Kant arrived at his antinomic or dialectical account of speculative reason. It is certain that the notion is well developed by 1769; we shall look at reflections from the *Nachlass* (*Ak* XVII, *R* 3913–93) from around that year clearly displaying this doctrine. Prior to that date there are a number of references to contradictions or antitheses between fundamental principles of reason, but these are not yet grounded in a conflict inherent in reason as a faculty. The various stages in Kant's approach to the antinomy doctrine are described in N. Hinske, "Kants Begriff der Antinomie und die Etappen seiner Ausarbeitung," *KS* 56 (1966): 485–96. Although Kant does not present a rational antinomy in the *Dissertation* of 1770, fundamental premises for an antinomy doctrine are elaborated there; the absence of the doctrine in that work could be the result of a decision not to publish such provocative (and as yet not wholly formed) views on the occasion for which the *Dissertation* was written—the required public defense of a thesis upon appointment as ordinarius to the university. See K. Reich's introduction to his edition of the *Dissertation*: *De mundi sensibilis atque intelligibilis forma et principiis* (Hamburg: Meiner, 1958). Kant himself points to the date 1769, in a later reflection, *Ak* XVIII, *R* 5037: "Originally I saw this doctrine as in a twilight. I attempted quite seriously to demonstrate propositions and their contradictories, not in order to establish a skeptical teaching, but because I had an intimation of how to uncover an illusion of the understanding and wherein it consists. The year 1769 gave me much light." See also H. Heimsoeth, "Vernunftantinomie und transzendentale Dialektik in der geschichtlichen Situation des kantischen Lebenswerkes," *KS* 51 (1959–60): 131–41.

94. See the references in n. 89 above. Also *Ak* XVII, *R* 4284: "Metaphysics is not science, and not learning, but merely the self-knowing understanding. Consequently it is a mere correction of sound understanding and reason." By saying that metaphysics is not a science, Kant seems to mean that it is unlike all other sciences in that its object is reason itself and its limits. He also describes it as "logical self-knowledge." See *R* 4468.

95. Ibid., *R* 3716, 255.10–12.

96. *UD*, in *Ak* II, 273–96; see n. 6 to chap. 2 above for the Academy's question on certainty in metaphysics, to which the *Essay* responds. A reflection roughly contemporary with the *Essay*, and probably a preparatory study for it, is entitled "On the Certainty and Uncertainty of Knowledge in General"; it offers an early version of the problem of bringing "knowledge into agreement with itself" (*Ak* XVII, *R* 3707). Thus when "objective certainty" is not available to us, error can be avoided, and certainty can still be had in the form of the "subjective certainty" that we lack objective certainty. The root of error in metaphysics is the "drive" to seek knowledge where none is available to us and thus not to remain content with the subjective knowledge of our ignorance. Kant significantly remarks that such error afflicts the "learned" more than the common man, who is "unconcerned with most of the things about which the learned are so zealous to have knowledge." This account of error would indicate Kant was receptive to Rousseau's tracing all evils back to a lack of accord between human desire and human powers, which discord especially is found among speculative men and in higher "culture" generally. See also the account of error and its avoidance in the fourth and fifth *Meditations* of Descartes.

97. *UD*, in *Ak* II, 275.

98. The *Essay*'s argument about the applicability of mathemetical methods in metaphysics is discussed by Engfer, in *PA*, 1–68. See also that author's essay, "Zur Bedeutung Wolffs fur die Methodendiskussion der deutschen Aufklärungsphilosophie: Analytische und synthetische Methode bei Wolff und beim vorkritischen Kant," in W. Schneiders, ed., *Christian Wolff, 1679–1754*, (Hamburg: Meiner, 1983), 48–65, and G. Tonelli, "Der Streit um die mathematische Methode in der Philosophie in der ersten

Hälfte des 18. Jahrhunderts und die Entstehung von Kants Schrift über die 'Deutlichkeit,' " *Archiv für Philosophie* 9 (1959): 37–66.

99. *UD*, in *Ak* II, 276–83, 290–92. In mathematics a single construction (such as a straight line) permits one to determine clearly the whole concept, or the universal; the universal can be exhibited *in concreto*. See *Ak* XVIII, *R* 5033: "It is easy to become aware of what is thought in arbitrarily formed concepts. Hence the evidence in mathematics." By contrast, metaphysical concepts are universals with very ambiguous realization in concrete instances, and thus there can be no a priori exhibition, with intuitive clarity, of the content of a metaphysical concept. The notion of a priori intuitability in a concrete instance, as applied here to mathematics, is later basic to Kant's account of space and time (the mathematicizable forms of experience) as a priori intuitions, and as distinct from the pure concepts of metaphysics—hence the unique problems that distinguish a transcendental logic of pure concepts from a transcendental aesthetic of pure intuitions.

100. *UD*, in *Ak* II, 283–86; see also the references to Newton, pp. 275 and 288. One must use the translation in *SPW* cautiously, especially on p. 17. Kant employs the same Newtonian method in the moral part of the *Essay*: the immediate certainties of moral feeling do not rest on any insight into their ultimate grounds (or the ultimate good of human beings). Clearly metaphysics of this Newtonian sort cannot supply knowledge of ultimate ends, but this is precisely why Kant does not remain satisfied with this approach to metaphysics. A theoretical metaphysics that offers no insight into ends cannot be the whole of metaphysics: there is a need for a new practical metaphysics which provides ends. Kant's adherence to Newtonianism in metaphysics should recall Hume's declaration of such adherence (*Enquiry concerning the Human Understanding*, sec. 1), but also should remind us of Kant's comparison of Rousseau to Newton: Rousseau's discovery of a law in the realm of ends is compatible with, while advancing beyond, the Newtonian account of nature. Newtonianism is deficient in metaphysics, if sufficient in natural philosophy.

101. Important examples of the discussion of this heterogeneity occur throughout the period 1765–1781; thus *N*, in *Ak* II, 303ff.; *DM*, in *Ak* II, 397–98; and *KrV* A713/ B741ff., A842/B872, and A847/B875n. This heterogeneity is fundamental to the argument emerging in the *Nachlass* reflections that the theoretical part of metaphysics is not a science of "extending" human knowledge, as is mathematics; see nn. 75 and 76 to this chapter.

102. See n. 89 above.

103. *T*, in *Ak* II, 370ff.

104. *Versuch den Begriff der negativen Grössen in die Weltweisheit einzuführen* (1763), in *Ak* II, 165–204. See G. Tonelli in U on the significance of this treatise.

105. G. Tonelli, with great erudition, argues that Hume is only one source among many that Kant might have drawn on in formulating such views; there are many such phenomenalistic and pragmatic accounts of metaphysics by the latter half of the century. See Tonelli, "Die Anfänge von Kants Kritik der Kausalbeziehung und ihre Voraussetzungen im 18. Jahrhundert," *KS* 57 (1966): 417–56, and idem, "Critiques of the Notion of Substance prior to Kant," *Tijdschrift voor Philosophie* 23/2 (1961): 285–301. Beck, in *EGP*, 445, notes that Kant was aware of Hume's arguments by the time of the *Dreams*, and yet that work does not show "any special tutelage to Hume." At least Kant does not yet seem bothered by Hume's primary question of the origin and justification of the causal concept. Yet M. Kuehn has documented how Hume's writings were central to German discussions of metaphysics after 1755 and has argued that Hume, rather than any other thinker, would have persuaded Kant to take the phenomenalist-instrumentalist view of causality in the 1760s. Kuehn makes a distinction between "Hume's principle" (of limiting all human knowledge to experience) and

"Hume's problem" (of the justification of metaphysical concepts); Kant surely accepted the former by 1766, but his famous "awakening from dogmatic slumber" through Hume's problem occurred sometime between 1769 and 1772. Kuehn's observations, which I find persuasive, are compatible with Tonelli's to the extent that Kuehn is claiming that what is really most distinctive about Hume's radical empiricism is his "problem." Thus it is right to say that Kant's greatest "debt" to Hume is not for the empiricist reduction of causality, which Kant could (but may not) have found in sources other than Hume by 1766. Kuehn misses that Kant's discovery of the significance of Hume's "problem" is preceded by the Rousseauian revolution and the new demand for a moral metaphysics. But he does observe the close connection between the problems of the antinomies and the Humean critique of causality; he proposes that Hume offered a source for both of the famous versions of the provocation for the "critical" awakening between 1769 and 1772—the antinomy of reason and the justification of causality. See M. Kuehn, "Kant's Conception of 'Hume's Problem,' " *JHP* 21 (1983): 175–93; also nn. 106 and 112 to this chapter, below. I cannot agree with Kuehn's view that the Kantian response to Hume's problem is solely a better justification than Hume gives of his own "principle" and that the "critique" is therefore "the continuation of an older enterprise" found in the *Dreams* essay. For Kant was moved by Hume's "problem" not simply because it forced him to think about Hume's "principle" in a different way; it was the Rousseauian effort to create a moral metaphysics, not just the issue of reason's theoretical limits, that made the "problem" so decisive.

106. Note Kant's statement at *P*, in *Ak* IV, 258n.: the principal danger of Hume's analysis is that by denying to reason any legitimate supersensible use of the causal concept, reason is "deprived of its most important prospects, which can alone supply to the will the highest aim for all its endeavors" (trans. in *Pr*, 6). See *KpV*, in *Ak* V, 54. The importance of Hume as a "negative" thinker, depriving theoretical reason of its pretensions by "showing that reason is not an organ of discovery," was noted by Hamann, Jacobi, and many others in Kant's time (see I. Berlin, sources in n. 50 to chap. 1 above). For Kant, however, Hume fails not only to ground the account of the limits of theory in an adequately rigorous and a priori "deduction"; he also fails to show that reason as practical is an organ of rational doctrines, though not of insights. The two failures are related, being grounded in the lack of all "spontaneity" in Hume's account of reason.

107. In *P*, in *Ak* IV, 258–59, Kant writes that Hume's opponents have tried to prove what Hume never doubted, namely, that the concept of cause is right, useful, and indispensable for the knowledge of nature. They do not address Hume's true concern, which is to inquire into the origin of the causal concept, to ascertain whether it allows of a use beyond experience. This is also the real problem for Kant after 1769 or so, who hopes to secure such a supersensible use for causality in order to satisfy the moral exigencies of reason, which constitute the core of metaphysics. Kant indicates that the security of the foundations of natural science was not the issue for him; see *P*, in *Ak* IV, 327. On this last point see G. Brittan on Kant's relation to Hume, in *Kant's Theory of Science* (Princeton: Princeton University Press, 1978), 122–31. Certainly Kant's way of posing the problem of the origins and scope of the causal concept is different from Hume's; see n. 112 below.

108. *Die falsche Spitzfindigkeit der vier syllogistischen Figuren erwiesen* (1762), in *Ak* II, 45–61.

109. Ibid., 57–61.

110. Kant's approach to judgment is similar to that of H. S. Reimarus, who also insists (in opposition to Wolff) that human judgment is always an act of "reflection," in which a singular representation is related to an object. Reimarus's thinking here, like Kant's, entails two other views—that judging is a self-conscious act and that logically

judgment is prior to concept. See H. W. Arndt, "Die *Vernunftlehre* von Reimarus im Verhältnis zum Rationalismus der Aufklärung," in *LZA*, esp. 61 and 63ff. Kuehn, in *SCS*, notes the similarity between the relation between representation and judgment in Kant, and between sensation and perception in Reid. He argues that Reid above all stimulated Kant to abandon the empiricist "simple ideas" account of judging and perceiving. But the *False Subtlety* essay (see n. 108 above) shows that Kant had his distinctive view of judgement by 1762; Reid's *Enquiry* was not published until 1764. Certainly the study of Reid could have strengthened a direction in Kant's thinking which had already begun by 1764. See *SCS*, 167–207.

111. See *KrV* B140–42, para. 19.

112. It could be said that, if Hume awakened Kant from a dogmatic slumber after 1766, it was only to have Kant raise a question that may not seem very Humean. Yet neither Hume nor Kant is primarily concerned with the justification of the beliefs of common sense about a knowable external world and its objects. Hume's inquiry concerns the ground and origin of metaphysical concepts. As Kant notes in the *Prolegomena*, it is this inquiry, not the justification of common experience, which is resumed by Kant. Thus Kant's "response to Hume" does not have as its primary aim the proof of the objectivity of ordinary judgments (which he does not doubt) nor the proof that such judgments have some extralogical necessity. Rather its principal aim is to delimit the necessary (a priori) use of the pure concepts, whose "purity" and validity as a ground of experience of objects are not in doubt, but whose scope is in question from a metaphysical standpoint. Kant's question differs from Hume's in that it is not about the ground of the causal concept (not assumed to be "objective" by Hume), but about the ground of the objectivity of that and other metaphysical concepts. And thus Kant's question, unlike Hume's, presupposes that some kind of objectivity is given with human reason. For the regressive nature of Kant's argument to the grounds of objectivity, see note 20 to chap. 1 and the references cited there. Kuehn, in *SCS*, 181–83, notes that the origin of the causal concept and the determination of the scope of valid application which depends on that origin are the real issues for Hume and Kant; thus "Transcendental Logic shows that none of the principles of the understanding, even if they are a priori, can be applied beyond sense experience" (p. 183). In this connection Kuehn questions the "traditional view" that Kant is concerned with "justification of knowledge claims in general," and thus with answering Hume in "a radical way" (pp. 204–5). He proposes that Kant more modestly "is intent upon justifying a very special type of knowledge claim, namely, those of the metaphysicians. Kant offers not a justification of knowledge, but a justification of metaphysics" (pp. 244–45). To draw the parallel in the case of Hume, one can say that he is not intent on the discrediting of all knowledge claims, but only those of metaphysicians. Both Hume's discrediting and Kant's combination of discrediting and justification take the form of an inquiry (based on different assumptions about judgment and its "objectivity") into the ground and origin of metaphysical judgments. See also n. 106 to this chapter, above.

113. See *Ak* XVIII, R 5037, cited in n. 93 above. The following studies of the insights of 1769 are very helpful, although their interpretations do not give as much weight to the role of the practical telos of reason as does mine: *EGP*, 438–63; U; *EKT*, 47–56; *KM*, 153–78. Also these intepreters have not seen the importance, for the problems of speculative reason, of the two notions of ground/object and their dialectical conflation.

114. *Ak* XVII, R 3717, 3974, 3976, and 3977, and *DM*, in *Ak* II, 398–406, for space and time as intuitive forms of experience, or of the realm of "appearances." Kant made important steps toward this account of space in his writing of 1768, *Concerning the Ultimate Foundation of the Differentiation of Regions in Space*, in *Ak* II, 377–83, and trans. in *SPW*, 36–43. Essential presuppositions of the a priori character of space are established there, namely, that space is an absolute whole underivable from relations be-

tween preexisting substances and exhibiting characteristics that are wholly inexplicable in terms of the ordinary "logical" relations that maintain between substances. The argument is directed against Leibniz's account of space.

See *DM*, in *Ak* II, 397–98 for mathematics as the true organon of intuitive cognition. Kant has at this point decidedly parted company with J. H. Lambert's project to formulate an organon of metaphysical knowledge. Although Kant earlier expressed some sympathy with Lambert's aims, he now proposes against them that the extension of human knowledge theoretically must be restricted to mathematical knowledge of mere appearances. See Lambert's letter to Kant, October 13, 1770, wherein Lambert makes plain their disagreement; *KPC*, 60–67.

115. Kant defines intuition as a power of discerning "immediately and singularly," without the mediation of universal concepts. It is not by definition passive or receptive apprehension; a creative intuitive apprehension of the singular is at least "problematically" conceivable. Human intuition happens to be of the receptive, i.e., sensible sort. See *DM*, in *Ak* II, 396–97, and *KrV* A19/B33, A68–69/B93–94. Kant's approach to intuition has certain premodern roots in the medieval definition of *intueri* as *cognitio singularis*, but of course the identification of the singular with space and time is quite modern. Crucial in the background to Kant is Leibniz's notion of the unique individual substance that ideally is intuitively cognizable: Leibniz restores "haecceity" on the basis of a modern rejection of generic universals. But the intuited singular for Leibniz is a true substance, a concrete whole. This is what Kant denies can ever be apprehended intuitively. We are left with homogeneous space and time themselves as the only intuited singular wholes.

116. See *Ak* XVII, *R* 3976, 3982, and *DM*, in *Ak* II, 392–94, for coordination and subordination; see also U.

117. Kant asserts that space and time have the advantage of evident "self-consistency" which metaphysical concepts lack due to the variability in their use, at *Ak* XVII, *R* 3942, 3977.

118. See *Ak* XVII, *R* 3946: Logic considers only the rules of the subordination of concepts, without regard for the specific "predicates of things" that are subordinated to one another; by contrast metaphysics treats specific predicates, the "first predicates of things," and is especially concerned with the origin of these in "the nature of human reason." See also *R* 3964.

119. For the nonconstructibility of metaphysical concepts, see *Ak* XVII, *R* 3940, 3948, 3978, and 4445; *Ak* XVIII, *R* 4920; and *KU*, in *Ak* V, 197n. see also the references in n. 87 above. For the impossibility of arriving at metaphysical concepts from the analysis of experience, see *Ak* XVII, *R* 3942, 3948, 3974, 3978, and *Ak* XVIII, *R* 4866.

120. *DM*, in *Ak* II, 387–92. See *Ak* XIX, *R* 6596 (1764–68): The human mind has an inclination to seek the maximum determination in continuous quantities (such as the spatial and temporal wholes).

121. *Ak* XVII, *R* 3922, 3928 (the principle of sufficient reason); *R* 3716, pp. 256 and 258 ("nothing can be posited absolutely").

122. Ibid., *R* 3717, p. 261; *R* 3973, 4165 (on the *ens necessarium* that cannot be thought).

123. Ibid., *R* 3969.

124. Ibid., *R* 3965, 4278.

125. See M. Thompson, "Singular Terms and Intuitions in Kant's Epistemology," *RM* 26 (1972–73): 314–43: there are no concepts of absolute singulars. See *Ak* XVII, *R* 4634: a judgment is a relation of two predicates; thus all concepts are predicates (which as such are universals) and even a subject-term is predicatively or mediately related to some object that is not uniquely designated by the subject-term. Thus one can never analyze a concept down to terms that are not further analyzable.

126. *DM*, in *Ak* II, 396–97, and the letter to M. Herz of February 21, 1772, in *KPC*, 70–76, especially p. 71: the *intellectus archetypi* "on whose intuition things themselves would be grounded."

127. On complete synthesis see *Ak* XVII, *R* 3717, p. 261; *R* 3974 and 3985. For the parallel *notio completa* in Leibniz, see the source in n. 13 to chap. 1. For Kant's critique of the possibility of arriving at a complete synthesis, see *Ak* XVIII, *R* 5710, and *SPIK*, 27–28.

128. *Ak* XVII, *R* 3928, p. 351; *R* 3948. Note also the assertion at *Ak* XX, 335: "The origin of critical philosophy is morality, with respect to the accountability for actions."

129. *Ak* XVII, *R* 3976 and 3988, p. 378.

130. Ibid., *R* 3974.

131. Ibid., *R* 3976. The inability of reason to bring this concept of "real ground" into play in the determination of the sensible is related to another limitation of reason: it cannot determine the real existence of anything from concepts alone (existence is not a predicate); see *Ak* XVII, *R* 3975, 3938, and *Ak* XVIII, *R* 5710.

132. *Ak* XVIII, *R* 6418: "All antinomies arise because one seeks the unconditioned in the sensible world."

133. *Ak* XVII, *R* 4372: "All judgments have a logical object."

134. Ibid., *R* 3959: ontology is falsely regarded as a "science of things in general"; *R* 3942: the categories necessary for our cognition are known by us to be thus necessary, but we are not entitled to claim that other kinds of minds think with them.

135. *KrV* A60–61.

136. *Ak* XVII, *R* 4152: "Ontology is nothing other than transcendental logic"; see *KrV* A57/B81–82.

137. Various aspects of the "transcendental deduction" of the legitimate and restricted employment of the pure concepts or categories are scattered through the *Nachlass* reflections of 1769 and after. Thus *Ak* XVII, *R* 4375, 4445: By their very nature (as discursive) the pure concepts relate to something "given"; *R* 3942, 3954, 3974, and 3978: accordingly the pure concepts are bound up with the representation of objects, and have theoretical validity only when being used for their representation; *R* 3938, 4375: the pure concepts cannot refer to a reality that exists wholly apart from our minds, and they serve only as conditions of our cognition; *AK* XVII, *R* 4276, 4473, and *Ak* XVIII, *R* 4851, 4877, and 4882: indeed the pure concepts can best be described as activities or functions of reason; *Ak* XVII, *R* 3936, 3942, and 3967: the understanding of pure concepts as "subjective" (and as not referring to things in themselves) permits a resolution of the conflict arising from the twofold "need" of reason. Further, *R* 4153, 4275: the fact that the pure concepts have validity only in relation to a sensible "given" (that they do not produce), and that they are only functions that underlie the determination of the sensible given as "objects," has the consequence that a deduction of their valid use starts from experience, wherein the categorial functions are exhibited through their "consequences." These functions cannot be known through an a priori intuition, as in mathematical constructions. Thus one can speak of an "epigenesis" of knowledge of the pure concepts, occurring on the basis of uncovering their employment in "the natural laws of reason." Thus *Ak* XVIII, *R* 5075: this mode of deduction is a *regressus* from experience. See *KrV* A736–37/B764–65: A philosophical principle (defining the function of a pure concept) "has the peculiar character that it makes possible the very experience which is its own ground of proof, and that in this experience it must always itself be presupposed."

138. *DM*, in *Ak* II, 387–89 (sec. 1), 395 (sec. 8), 410–11 (sec. 23); see also the letter to Lambert of September 2, 1770, in *KPC*, 58–60, on the "propaedeutic discipline" in the *Dissertation*.

139. *DM*, in *Ak* II, 411–12 (sec. 24).

140. Ibid., 410–11 (sec. 23), and 394–95 (sec. 7); see also *L*, in *Ak* IX, 23.

141. *DM*, in *Ak* II, 387–92 (secs. 1–2): Kant introduces the world as "whole" and the "simple" or ultimate constituent of the world as examples of such "ideas"; these ideas give rise to "problems of reason," for neither the whole nor the simple has a realization in human intuition. Nevertheless a "dogmatic" employment of ideas is valid in the noumenal or moral realm (pp. 395–96, sec. 9).

142. Ibid., 413 (sec. 25): Plato's ideas are the objects of intellectual intuition by a divine mind, but are wholly unknowable by our minds; p. 395 (sec. 7) for criticism of Wolff, and pp. 409–10 (sec. 22, scholium) for a related criticism of Malebranche. See also the letter to M. Herz of February 21, 1772 (especially *KPC*, 72–73), and n. 24 to this chapter, above.

143. *DM*, in *Ak* II, 394–95 (sec. 7).

144. Ibid., 395–96 (sec. 9). Quite oddly, the Kerferd translation omits the very important statement about freedom in the footnote to this section (*SPW*, 59). A closer rendering is: "We consider something theoretically to the extent that we attend only to those things that properly pertain to a being, but we consider it practically if we distinguish those attributes that ought to be present in it through freedom (*quae ipsi per libertatem inesse debebant*)."

145. *DM*, in *Ak* II, 395–96 (sec. 9).

146. *Ak* XVII, *R* 4242, 4243, and 4375.

147. *DM*, in *Ak* II, 396–97 (sec. 10); see p. 392 (sec. 3).

148. Ibid., 396–97 (sec. 10).

149. Ibid.: there is symbolic cognition of intellectual ideas, but no intuitive cognition. In terms of the *Dissertation*'s own account of possible human cognition, it is clear that such symbolic apprehension is not a theoretical grasping of any object *in concreto*.

150. Ibid., 395 (sec. 8).

151. See the reflections cited in n. 137 above.

152. *DM*, in *Ak* II, 393–94 (sec. 5) and 397 (sec. 11).

153. See the letter to Lambert of September 2, 1770, in *KPC*, 58–60, and to M. Herz of February 21, 1772, pp. 70–76.

154. The letter to Herz, cited in the note above, makes clear the uniqueness of the problem of the metaphysical concepts and that their objectivity has to be addressed now that the sources of the evidentiality and security of the theoretical sciences of mathematics and physics have been established. The problem of the "axioms of pure reason" is distinguished from that of the bases of the mathematical sciences; see *KPC*, 72. That a strong sense of "objectivity" must be assumed for Kant to pose his problem of pure reason is also evident from this letter: "I silently passed over [in the *Dissertation*] the further question of how a representation that refers to an object without being in any way affected by it is possible" (p. 72). Many commentators, supposing that Kant aims at proving objectivity for all our concepts, then claim that Kant assumes what he allegedly hopes to prove. (Another error of commentators is to think that Kant wants to establish what "objectivity" must be for *any* kind of mind, or that transcendental argument aims at showing indispensable conditions for experience of objects for any possible mind. Kant, however, begins with our conceptual and discursive mind, and its characteristic mode of objectivity, and explicitly notes that this is only one sort of possible mind and mode of experience; he does indeed begin with experience "under a certain description" and then investigates its conditions. His aim is not to show that this is the only possible kind of experience or that the conditions of our experience are the conditions of every possible sort of experience. It is to show that metaphysics has no right to claim a theoretical validity outside the context of its "conditioning" the kind of mind and experience we happen to have. This is decidedly a very "limited" purpose, which explicitly abjures the pretense of claiming that our mode of thinking and experiencing is the only possible mode; see *KrV* B145–46.)

155. Letter to J. Bernoulli of November 16, 1781, in *KPC*, 96–98. Kant notes that in the work of 1770 he had "ideas of a possible reform of this science [metaphysics]" which had not yet matured, and that the further working out of its program "created new and unforeseen difficulties" (p. 97).

Chapter Five

1. *KrV* A850/B878.
2. See the references in n. 7, chap. 4.
3. On propaedeutic, see *KrV* A11/B25ff. and A841/B869.
4. *KrV* A795–851/B823–79. For discussions of these chapters, see PhG, VKrV, and *KPH*; in addition, see J. Silber, "The Metaphysical Importance of the Highest Good as the Canon of Pure Reason in Kant's Philosophy," *Studies in Literature and Language* 1/2 (1959): 234–44, and L. W. Beck, *A Commentary on Kant's Critique of Pure Reason* (Chicago: University of Chicago Press, 1960), 8–10.
5. See especially PhG, 15–20, and VKrV, 436, 442–43.
6. *KrV* A803/B831.
7. Kant insists in the Canon upon the pure basis of morality, abjuring a "pathological" foundation and distinguishing between prudential and pure practical maxims. Already in the *Dissertation*, moral philosophy is a division of "pure philosophy" (*DM*, in *Ak* II, 396). In the Canon, the "practical" encompasses both kinds of maxims, being concerned with "everything that is possible through freedom" (*KrV* A800/B828). Surely it is the case that in its account of pure practical reason, the Canon offers few insights into its foundations; this omission is deliberate. Kant says that the *Critique* will not discuss those foundations; it is concerned only with theoretical philosophy, and at this time, Kant identifies this part of philosophy with its "transcendental" part (A805/B833). Yet Kant does not identify transcendental and pure philosophy; it is then an error to conclude that the exclusion of the ground of morality from transcendental philosophy entails its exclusion from pure philosophy (see A810/B829; Gueroult draws this false conclusion in VKrV, 436, validly, using the false premise of "identity"). Of course in the *Critique of Practical Reason*, transcendental inquiry is expanded to include the ground of moral reason. This step is necessary, for Kant sees that he must establish that there is no immediately available intuition or "datum" of freedom; the freedom of the will is known to us only indirectly, through the "fact of the moral law" and its power to oblige the will. In other words, Kant establishes more rigorously the separation of the ground of morality from any alleged extramoral or theoretical evidences of its bases. His addressing a "dialectic of practical reason" in the concept of the highest good is also part of this securing of practical reason. The Canon speaks of the human free capacity for disinterested determination of the will as a "datum" of experience; while Kant clearly means here a datum of a wholly nontheoretical sort, the real nature of this datum is not at all clarified. The question of the relation of the datum of freedom to the laws of the phenomenal realm is quite obscure (*KrV* A802–3/B830–31). Kant eventually takes the view that freedom is not a "datum" at all. Yet the Canon's statements on this datum of freedom do not imply that morality is based on feeling. Kant's assertions here that moral philosophy must consider the relation of its pure laws to the human faculty of feeling are compatible with the views of the later *Critique*, which investigates the special nature of "respect for the law" among the affective states. Kant remarks explicitly in the Canon that moral laws command absolutely, not hypothetically (A807/B835) and that "objective laws of freedom" in morality determine an "ought" that is wholly independent of the "is" (A802/B830). Again, the sparsity of comments on the moral foundations is not a deficiency of the Canon, if it does not seek to give such foundations. One has to place the Canon within the context of theoretical philosophy and its propaedeutical function.

8. *KrV* A796/B824. On this account of the Analytic's character, its subject matter is the employment of reason in metaphysical inquiry and the correction of past notions of that employment. The account of "ordinary experience," i.e., of the immanence of the categories of concern to metaphysics in ordinary experience, becomes thematic through that primary investigation. Accordingly, the Principles of Pure Understanding (A148/B187ff.) are best understood as principles determining that employment of the categories, with respect to the aims of metaphysics, and not merely as informing the reader of the epistemological conditions of his experience.

9. Ibid., A795–97/B823–25.

10. Ibid., A796/B824.

11. Ibid.; see A313–14/B370–71 for reason's necessary interest in ideas transcending the sensible world, and A743–44/B771–72 and A805/B833, for the "ends to which the whole endeavor of pure reason was really directed."

12. Ibid., A642/B670ff.

13. Ibid., A797–804/B825–32.

14. Ibid., A798–99/B826–27; see *KpV*, in *Ak* V, 54–55.

15. Thus *KrV* A532–58/B560–86: The resolution of the Third Antinomy of speculative reason, concerning the antithetical cosmological views of causality (freedom and determinism), establishes that a free (uncaused) first cause is thinkable, and nothing more. Freedom's real possibility must be demonstrated through some other "datum," such as the moral will, which lies outside the scope of the propaedeutical inquiry.

16. Ibid., A797/B825. One can relate this to Yovel's observation that reason is a "self-sufficient teleological system."

17. Ibid., A798/B326.

18. Ibid., A666/B694.

19. Ibid., A800/B828. See also the footnote at B395: "Metaphysics has as the proper objects of its inquiries three ideas only: *God, freedom,* and *immortality.* . . . . Any other matters with which this science may deal serve merely as a means of arriving at these ideas and of establishing their reality." This is a statement of the by now familiar point that all theoretical metaphysics is merely propaedeutical (and instrumental) to a moral telos.

20. For this notion of the systematic connection between the ideas, see *KrV* B395n. and also *Ak* XVII, R 4241.

21. *KrV* A804–6/B832–34.

22. Ibid., A805/B833 and A803/B831.

23. Ibid., A806/B834.

24. Ibid., A807/B835; see *Ak* XIX, R 7205: "Morality is the science which contains the a priori principles of the unity of all possible ends of rational beings."

25. *KrV* A808/B836.

26. Ibid., A807–8/B835–36.

27. Ibid., A807/B835. The emphasis is Kant's.

28. Yovel is one author who misses Kant's deeper intent and who treats the Canon as a very otherworldly statement on the highest good. Readings of Kant's highest good that do not place chief responsibility for its attainment in the human will or human history and that make use of the deus ex machina of attainment through the supersensible action of a deity are not in accord with Kant's conceptions of virtue, happiness, and the highest good, dating back to 1765.

29. Ibid., A809–10/B837–38.

30. This position has been well argued by R. Pippin, "On the Moral Foundations of Kant's *Rechtslehre*," in *PIK*, 107–42. It lies outside the immediate scope of Pippin's inquiry, however, to consider other possible sources of the importance of the pursuit of happiness to morality, which can be subsumed under problems of "culture." Thus it is of much concern to Kant that the rational progress of the species (which includes

its moral progress) not be detrimental to the species' chances for attaining happiness; reason would prove to be fatally flawed should it destroy the basis of happiness. There is also the consideration that the mode of the pursuit of happiness, if not the specific content of ideas of happiness, has favorable or unfavorable effects on the will and its capacity for moral self-determination. Both issues are taken up in this chapter, sec. 3; they clearly point to the fact that Kant does not relegate the solution to the problem of happiness to the next life, at least not wholly.

31. *KrV* A316-17/B372–74.

32. ibid., A809-10/B837–38, and A811/B839.

33. The manner in which Kant so closely links freedom and happiness in the Canon should not be understood, as it is by Düsing and others, as the sign of the Canon's "heteronomous" teaching. Kant writes here that it is a "reason free from all private purposes" that seeks to bring about the accord between virtue and happiness; he also explicitly rejects the view that "the prospect of happiness makes possible the moral disposition" (*KrV* A813/B841). Yet one must grant that Kant's "ideal" is far removed from both Christian and Stoic asceticism.

34. See especially *KrV* A803/B831.

35. Ibid., A814/B842ff.; see *W*, in *Ak* VIII, 137ff.

36. *KrV*, A819/B847. The purely moral function of the supreme being is underlined by this assertion: "We shall not look upon actions as obligatory because they are commands of God, but shall regard them as divine commands because we have an inward obligation to them" (A819/B847).

37. For the criticism of anthropomorphic conceptions of the supreme being, see *KrV* A689-702/B717–30.

38. Ibid., A697/B725.

39. Ibid., A814/B842.

40. Ibid., A816/B844.

41. Ibid., A815/B843.

42. Ibid., A816/B844.

43. Ibid., A816-17/B844–45. See also *Ak* XVIII, *R* 4904: freedom is the presupposition of all uses of reason; and *Critique of Judgment*, Introduction, sec. 9.

44. *KU*, in *Ak* V, 416–85 (the "Doctrine of Method" as a whole).

45. *KrV*, A832-51/B860–79.

46. Ibid., A852-56/B880–84.

47. Ibid., A832/B860.

48. Ibid., A832-33/B860–61; see Axx.

49. Ibid., A832/B860 and A838/B866.

50. Ibid., A833-34/B861–62.

51. Ibid., A840/B868n.; see *L*, in *Ak* IX, 23–26.

52. *KrV* A834/B862.

53. Ibid., A838-39/B866–67.

54. Ibid., A840/B868; see *KpV*, in *Ak* V, 108–9.

55. *KrV* A839/B867; also *L*, in *Ak* IX, 24, and *Ak* XVII, R 4467; *Ak* XVIII, R 4902.

56. *KrV* A839/B867 and A850/B878.

57. Ibid., A850/B878.

58. *Ak* XV, R 1524.

59. *KrV* A842/B871.

60. Ibid., A842/B871; see B21.

61. For the archetype of the philosopher present in all reason, see also *KrV* A568/B596ff.

62. *G*, in *Ak* IV, 403–4: the common reason evinces great subtlety of self-examination, Kant claims, in an effort to assure itself of the purity of its motive.

63. *KrV* A817/B845; also A830/B858n. and see *KU*, in *Ak* V, 439–40.

64. *KrV* A849/B877.

65. Ibid., A834–35/B862–63.

66. Ibid., A836–37/B864–65, A842/B870ff.

67. Ibid., A844/B872.

68. Ibid., A852/B880ff.

69. *Ak* XVIII, *R* 5072.

70. Ibid., *R* 4936.

71. Ibid., *R* 5035. The conditioning of philosophic progress by history is mentioned also at *KrV* Bxxxvi–xxxvii. Yovel's brief remarks on this subject, *KPH*, 238–39, do not relate this aspect of "history" in Kant to the final practical end of reason and of philosophy's "idea."

72. See n. 60, chap. 1, above.

73. In *VpR*, in *Ak* XXVIII.2.2, 135–40, there is a purely "cultural" treatment of the problem of evil and theodicy, which illuminates the whole discussion of philosophical theology. Yet the *Religion within the Limits of Reason* has its own very important indications of the cultural perspective. See especially the opening paragraphs of pt. 3, *Re*, in *Ak* V, 93–95: Human social existence and the reciprocal human dependence which it presupposes contain the "causes and circumstances" of the entry of evil into human life, which entry can be seen as man's own fault. For it is as a social being that man develops passion, i.e., the excess of desire beyond the powers of satisfaction, thereby placing the gravest obstacles in the way of the sovereignty of pure moral principles. Also extremely revealing is the paragraph in *ED*, in *Ak* VIII, 332 (in *OH*, 74–75): Man is himself the cause for his feeling existence as a burden; the cause lies in the fact that progress in the culture of talents, arts, and taste precedes moral progress, a situation dangerous to both morality and physical well-being. The disproportion, otherwise expressed, is that "needs increase much more vigorously than the means to satisfy them." In other words, the principal evils of human life have a cultural origin.

74. In addition to the discussion of the *Remarks* above, see *Ak* XVI, *R* 1644.

75. I make extensive use of reflections from *Ak* XV, especially *R* 1417–1501 (dating mostly from the 1770s) and 1521–24 (from the 1780s). These reflections state most of the themes and analyses of the better-known passages from essays and major critical writings of 1781 and after, treating the problems of history and culture. From these reflections one becomes more convinced that such passages do not treat matters that are merely peripheral to Kant's account of reason.

76. *Ak* XIX, *R* 6593.

77. Kant frequently stresses the value of the empirical evidence acquired from history, concerning the origin, nature, and goal of the rational faculties. There are even empirical signs of the moral progress made by the human species in the course of its history; see *ED*, in *Ak* VIII, 332.

78. *Ak* XV, *R* 1498, 779–80.

79. Ibid., *R* 1499, p. 782; see also *R* 1500, p. 785: man is an animal in need of a master.

80. Ibid., *R* 1499, p. 782.

81. Ibid., p. 784.

82. Ibid., *R* 1498, p. 779.

83. Ibid., *R* 1499, p. 782; see *R* 1500, p. 788: man discovers a source of honor in free activity.

84. Ibid., *R* 1499, p. 785.

85. Ibid., *R* 1500, p. 788; see *KU*, in *Ak* V, 429–36 and 442–45. Kant's employment of the trope, stemming from late antiquity (the elder Pliny, Quintilian, and Lactantius) and revived in the Renaissance (Erasmus and Bruno), of "nature as stepmother" to the human race, helps us see that Kant's reconstruction of the human beginnings has cer-

tain nonbiblical sources and intentions. For some history of the trope, see J. Kraye, "Moral Philosophy" in *The Cambridge History of Renaissance Philosophy*, eds. C. Schmitt and Q. Skinner (Cambridge: Cambridge University Press, 1988), and for Bruno on the benefits to man of nature's harshness, see P. Rossi, *Philosophy, Technology, and the Arts in the Early Modern Era* (New York: Harper and Row, 1970), pp. 79–80.

86. *Ak* XV, *R* 1499, p. 784.

87. Ibid., *R* 488; this is a relatively early reflection, from 1764–69, and its theme of spiritual disturbance is further discussed in the essay of 1764, *Versuch über die Krankheiten des Kopfes*, in *Ak* II, 257–71.

88. The point deserves reiteration—that moral freedom, which is for Kant the sole basis for such self-accord, is impossible to conceive outside the context of "receptivity" or of a mode of existence that is finite and sensible. Thus the idea of complete moral self-determination includes the idea of a "world" in which that completion is possible. Moral virtue is intrinsically the ground of a "worthiness" of living in such a world; it cannot be understood as worldless noumenality. A world that is entirely in accord with moral perfection cannot be characterized by irreconcilable hostility between freedom and nature. That is not to say that the "happiness" of which moral virtue is "worthy" is identical with a crude notion of total instinctual fulfillment.

89. *Ak* XV, *R* 1499, p. 783: In the human species' progress toward rational perfection, it is "the individual who loses" with respect to private satisfactions, yet "he wins as a part of the whole," which gains in moral perfection and dignity. See *I*, in *Ak* VIII, 18: "In the human species those natural capacities directed to the use of reason are fully developed only in the race, not in the individual."

90. *Ak* XV, *R* 1417, p. 617, and *R* 1499, pp. 782–83.

91. Ibid., *R* 1521, p. 889; see *R* 1499, p. 783: "The sciences do not belong to the vocation of individual humans, for they refine the species and ameliorate the evils that preponderate in the luxurious state." The progressive nature of science with its problematic relation to mortality is one important reason for Kant's rejecting the account of philosophy or knowledge as having a chiefly contemplative, rather than chiefly practical, end.

92. Ibid., *R* 1498, pp. 778–79, and *R* 1520, p. 890.

93. Ibid., *R* 1417.

94. Thus see the famous praise of Rousseau at *MA*, in *Ak* VIII, 115–18, of 1786.

95. See, for example, *I*, in *Ak* VIII, 22–23 (theses five and six).

96. "Every other animal than man attains its vocation" as an individual. See *Ak* XV, *R* 1524, p. 896; *R* 1521, p. 887; *R* 1499, p. 781.

97. *UP*, in *AK* IX, 441ff.

98. *Ak* XV, *R* 1454, p. 635: "For human beings the vocations of individual and species are naturally different," and thus "the history of humanity is different from the history of a single human being."

99. Ibid., *R* 1524, p. 896.

100. Ibid., *R* 1521, p. 888.

101. Ibid., *R* 1454, and also *MA*, in *Ak* VIII, 116–18.

102. *Ak* XV, *R* 1454.

103. Ibid., *R* 1521, p. 890; see the treatment of imagination in *MA*, in *Ak* VIII, 111ff.

104. *G*, in *Ak* V, 130.

105. *UG*, in *Ak* VIII, 307n.

106. *Ak* XV, *R* 1524, p. 896.

107. Ibid., pp. 896–97.

108. Ibid., p. 897.

109. Ibid., *R* 1498, p. 779.

110. Ibid., *R* 1449, pp. 635–36.

111. Ibid., *R* 1521, p. 891.

112. Ibid., *R* 1523, pp. 895–96.

113. The dialectic of the passions and of technical reason operates through the increasing destructiveness and costliness of wars, the consequent exhaustion of resources and popular disgust with bellicose policies, and the movement universally toward republican constitutions and a federation of states outlawing war. See *UG*, in *Ak* VIII, 307–13; *Zum ewigen Frieden*, in *Ak* VIII, 341–86; and *KU*, in *Ak* V, 429–34. It is wrong to suppose that this dialectic belongs only to a "natural history" leading to legal reform, which must be kept separate from "moral history" leading to the ethical commonwealth of morally perfect beings, as has been supposed by some writers; see *KPH*, 72–77. The dialectic of the passions is crucial to the moralizing and civilizing of the inclinations, which is indispensable to moral progress. In this connection, one should remark on the importance for Kant of aesthetic culture in the refining and civilizing of the inclinations, as a "preparation" for a true moral culture: the paths toward the moral improvement of humanity are many and various, embracing politics, religion, education, and culture generally. All these paths must be conceived "historically," that is, as the unfolding of a free rationality that gradually discovers how to emancipate itself from the dogmatic authority of mere nature, which in the end means from the authority of reason's own dogmatic conceptions of nature.

Epilogue

1. The way in which reason enslaves or perplexes, rather than liberates or enlightens, in the thought of Hume, Rousseau, and Kant discloses how a profound overturning of the Platonic account of the relation of reason to opinion has occurred in the eighteenth century. It is now metaphysics that is the true sophistry and the source of the beclouding illusions of the "cave"; the liberation from this cave is by means of a critique of reason's competence. The light to which mankind as a whole ascends is ordinary opinion or custom (Hume), untutored natural simplicity (Rousseau), or the dictates of common moral reason (Kant).

2. But ancient philosophy is aware of some of the spuriousness of these unities, and the philosophic life is seen as an engagement with truth that is always conducted with full consciousness that human life conceived purely politically is doubtfully natural. From the ancient perspective, however, the individual's independence cannot be understood in terms of universal rights and can be grounded only upon the exercise of rare moral and intellectual virtues.

3. The "collapse of idealist metaphysics" in the decades following Hegel's death included the collapse of the accounts of the end of reason in Kant and Hegel. See M. A. Gillespie, *Hegel, Heidegger, and the Ground of History* (Chicago: University of Chicago Press, 1984). Thereby the role of the philosophy of history in the Neo-Kantian revival is completely transformed such that "philosophy of history in the material sense, which discusses human history as a meaningful process, had given completely way to philosophy of history in a purely formal sense as the logic and epistemology of historical thought" (Iggers, in *GCH*, 125, citing Ernst Troeltsch).

4. At this point it is appropriate to touch upon salient differences between Kant's notion of a rational system and the later idealist systematics. Kant's regressive transcendental procedure, starting from ultimate ungroundable features of reason, simply uncovers the diverse but mutually conditioning principles that render possible a consistent and nondialectical employment of the original "facts" (of the logical power and of the moral will). Thus because Kant presupposes the logical faculty and its implicit categories and only "deduces" that such categories (of object in general) have a certain necessary and restricted employment in the determination of objects, later idealists

charge that Kant's deduction is "incomplete"; see DC. The regression to the transcendental context of possibility is only meant to show that the fundamental elements of cognition or willing cannot be employed outside that context and that the same context, when observed, protects those elements from distortion. But this is not an effort on Kant's part to deduce the whole ground of the reality of those elements, which is attempted in the deductions of later idealism. Kant's approach necessarily tolerates, even requires, a plurality of principles, since a finite mind can be "spontaneous" only in relation to independent sources of "receptivity." There is no attempt to derive this plurality from a single principle, such as the "I" of later idealists. Transcendental analysis therefore never becomes metaphysical synthesis; such analysis is never even entirely completed, as Kant asserts in the first *Critique*; instead there is a need for "constantly returning to the premises" (*KrV* A735/B763 and *Ak* XVIII, R 5036). As we have seen, the ultimate transcendental context is the one reconciling theoretical inquiry and moral reason, and this is the most comprehensive of Kant's "systematic" contexts regarding the end of reason. The two primary elements of this context are not deducible from each other, although they are complementary and mutually dependent; see *Ak* XVIII, R 6343, 6344, 6353 on the "ideality of space and time, and freedom" as the "two cardinal principles" of the system of reason. See Kant's letter to Fichte, August 7, 1799, for Kant's unqualified rejection of the Fichtean understanding of the transcendental, whereby the object of cognition is materially deduced from the productive-practical logic of self-consciousness; *KPC*, 253–54. We cannot consider here whatever changes of view might be found in the *Opus Postumum*. For the account of the transcendental procedure in Kant's moral philosophy, see *SV*, 6–56.

Index